Bible People

NELSON'S POCKET REFERENCE SERIES

Bible People

publishers since 1798

THOMAS NELSON PUBLISHERS
Nashville

Library of Congress Cataloging-in-Publication Data

Nelson's pocket reference Bible people.
     p. cm.
  ISBN 0-7852-4244-9
  1. Bible Biography Dictionaries. I. Thomas Nelson Publishers. II. Title: Pocket reference Bible people.
BS570.N45 1999
220.9′2—dc21
[B]
                                99–24254
                                  CIP

1 2 3 4 5 6 7 8 9 10 — 05 04 03 02 01 00 99

ABOUT THIS BOOK

Welcome to *Nelson's Pocket Reference Bible People,* a handy, compact-sized reference book that identifies people whose proper names occur in the Bible, excluding the deuterocanonical books.

The names are set out alphabetically as they are spelled in the King James Version, with variant spellings enclosed in brackets [ ]. The meaning of the name is then given in parentheses ( ). Under each entry, various individuals bearing this name are differentiated by boldface brackets, like this: [1]; [2]; and so on. Then follows a description of the character, with several Bible verses listed where the name occurs. (Not all verses could be given; so if the reader is considering a passage that is not cited in the section, he must choose the character that would most likely be identical with the person in his passage.)

Sometimes when discussing one person, the name of another person is mentioned. If that second person's name is followed by (also see), a separate entry for that name appears elsewhere in the book.

We have made no attempt to designate each person as a Palite, Harodite, Gileadite, and so on. Many of these designations refer to the ancestor of an individual; in other cases, they refer to the person's city, district, or distinctive clan.

It is often a guess as to which meaning is intended.

The meanings of the names are not infallibly accurate; they are simply interesting possibilities. These names are ancient and their history is obscure and uncertain.

Many people in Scripture bear the same name. In dozens of cases, we cannot determine whether an individual in one book is identical with someone having the same name in another book. In the ancient world, a person was often called by more than one name.

In the transmission of Scripture, copyists occasionally made errors. Surely Reuel was not also called Deuel, nor Jemuel called Nemuel, and so on. Yet which is original? Only in a few cases do we have any clues.

We find variant forms and contractions of names through the Bible. They probably presented little difficulty to an ancient reader. But this further complicates the identification problem for us.

The Hebrew genealogies are abbreviated at many points. At times it is difficult to distinguish a man from his ancestor. Consider also the problem of trying to match an abbreviated list with a fuller list. Either the names in the abbreviated list are independent of the longer list or they are already included in it. In other words, we may find the same person included in two lists or two different people in two lists.

In a few cases, our English versions use the same word to transliterate several similar Hebrew names. In these instances, we have recorded a separate entry for each Hebrew name (e.g., Iddo).

THE CHIEF PERSON
OF THE BIBLE

From the first page to the last, the Bible tells about God and His dealings with His creation—especially humanity. This book describes God to the extent that it is possible for finite human minds to comprehend. It also depicts God as the prime mover in the universe, yet One who has a plan and a purpose for each individual person. It has often been said that the Bible is "His story," the story of God's working to restore the kind of loving relationship with humanity that existed in the beginning, before people turned away into sin.

The Bible also presents God in three distinct expressions—God the Father, God the Son, and God the Holy Spirit. Christian tradition has long affirmed both the Oneness and the Threeness of God in the doctrine of the Trinity. In many respects each of the three can be viewed as a separate entity, yet they are inseparably part of the Godhead. Because of the preeminent place the members of the Trinity occupy in the Bible, any book on the people of the Bible needs to begin with a review of these three divine Persons.

God the Father

Before the first star began to sparkle, there was God. That fact opens the Bible: "In the beginning God created the heavens and the earth" (Gen. 1:1).

When the last star fades, and creation gives way to a celestial realm, God will be there—with His people. That fact closes the Bible in John's vision of the future: "People will worship God and will see him face to face. . . . The Lord God will be their light, and they will rule forever" (Rev. 22:3–5).

Between Genesis and Revelation is a sacred library written over more than a millennium. It is the story of God revealed in history, biography, law, prayer, song, proverb, prophecy, parable, letter, and vision. Through this story we begin to understand God, though only in part. For as Job asks, who can understand "the mysteries surrounding God All-Powerful? They are higher than the heavens and deeper than the grave" (Job 11:7–8).

Why God reveals Himself to humanity quickly becomes clear in Genesis. God created a good and idyllic world, and placed in it humans with whom He could fellowship. These humans chose to disobey Him. Because of this, and in ways we can't fully grasp, sin contaminated God's creation and severed His intimate relationship with humanity. Since that moment, God has been working to restore His creation and His relationship with humans.

God begins by teaching humanity about Himself through promises made and fulfilled in obedient people, like Noah, and through punishing evil people. Then through Abraham, God produces a race of people chosen to receive His special insights and laws, and to guide others in the ways of the Lord. He also sends prophets to remind these chosen people, the Jews, to obey Him.

Finally, God sends Jesus onto the planet and the Holy Spirit into the human heart to further reveal what He is like. The Bible doesn't explain how three distinct entities can be united as one. It simply states this as fact, then reports a wide array of astonishing miracles and testimonies to prove it. Who but God, for example, could silence a storm (Mark 4:39)?

From beginnning to end, the Bible paints a detailed and complex portrait of God. But all the descriptions are best expressed by John, a disciple of Jesus: "God is love" (1 John 4:8). Good news for humanity is that this love is offered to us, and when we accept it, it's ours forever.

Jesus

Jesus, the Son of God, is a central figure of the Bible—from beginning to end.

He was with God when the world was created, says the Gospel of John. He was the hope that the prophets anticipated in the Messiah—a deliverer sent from God to save humanity from sin and to bring peace on earth. And He is the fulfillment of that hope, as reported in the New Testament, especially the remarkable Gospels of Matthew, Mark, Luke, and John. His title, Christ, comes from the Hebrew word for messiah, translated into the Greek language of His day as *christos*.

Jesus' mother was the virgin Mary, engaged to Joseph, a carpenter from Nazareth. When Joseph learned his fiancée was pregnant, he planned to leave her. But an angel assured him that the child was from God.

On orders from the Roman emperor, the couple traveled to the hometown of their ancestors to be counted in a census; for Mary and Joseph this was Bethlehem, birthplace of King David. It was there, in a Bethlehem stable, that Jesus was born. Many Old Testament prophets predicted that the Messiah would come from David's family; Micah added that the birthplace would be Bethlehem (Mic. 5:2).

As a growing boy, Jesus worked with Joseph. When Jesus was twelve years old, He traveled with His family to the Jerusalem temple to celebrate Passover. There He astonished the scholars with His spiritual insights.

The Bible says nothing more about Jesus until He began His ministry at roughly thirty years of age. This was a ministry that spanned perhaps only three years, in the heart of a tiny Middle Eastern country. But this ministry has changed the values and lives of people throughout the ages and around the globe. Whether Jesus was healing illnesses, calming storms with a word, or teaching compassion, He gave humanity an intimate portrait of a God full of power and mercy.

Executed by crucifixion, Jesus also gave the world its greatest proof of both His deity and of life after death, for three days later He rose from the tomb. Over the next forty days He met many times with His followers, urging them to take His message to everyone. Then He ascended to heaven, but not before promising to return. The Bible concludes with the greatest hope of early Christians: "Lord Jesus, please come soon!" (Rev. 22:20).

The Holy Spirit

The Holy Spirit is one of three persons in what early Christians called the Trinity: God the Father, Son, and Holy Spirit. The Bible doesn't use the word "trinity," but it portrays all three divine persons as distinct yet equally God. For example, in Jesus' last words on earth He told

His followers to make disciples all over the world and to baptize converts "in the name of the Father, the Son, and the Holy Spirit" (Matt. 28:19).

The Spirit's role on earth has changed over history. When the universe was yet dark and lifeless, "the Spirit of God was moving over the water" (Gen. 1:2), involved in the miracle of Creation. (Old Testament writers usually called him the Spirit of God, though occasionally the Holy Spirit.) Throughout Old Testament times the Spirit empowers the heroes and leaders of Israel. When, for instance, the prophet Samuel anointed David as Israel's future king, "at that moment, the Spirit of the Lord took control of David and stayed with him from then on" (1 Sam. 16:13).

In those days, the Spirit's work was apparently limited to unique leaders and special occasions. But the prophet Joel, speaking on God's behalf, promised that a time was coming when "I will give my Spirit to everyone" (Joel 2:28). That moment arrived in a dramatic miracle on the day of Pentecost, a springtime Jewish celebration. Jesus had warned His disciples that He needed to leave, "but the Holy Spirit will come and help you, because the Father will send the Spirit to take my place. The Spirit will teach you everything and will remind you of what I said while I was with you" (John 14:25). Jesus further instructed the disciples to stay in Jerusalem until the Spirit arrived. As the disciples waited, "suddenly there was a noise from heaven like the sound of a mighty wind!" (Acts 2:2). The Spirit had come, filling each disciple with spiritual vitality that gave them courage to preach about Jesus and to perform miracles proving that their message came from God.

Thousands began converting to Christianity and receiving the Holy Spirit. "You are God's temple," the apostle Paul later explained to believers. "His Spirit lives in you" (1 Cor. 3:16). Christians guided by the Spirit, Paul added, will find themselves taking on the characteristics of godliness and rejecting sinful ways. "God's Spirit makes us loving, happy, peaceful, patient, kind, good, faithful, gentle, and self-controlled" (Gal. 5:22).

Aaron ("enlightened, rich, mountaineer"), the brother of Moses. He became the first high priest of Israel (Exod. 4:14, 30; 7:2, 19; 17:9–12; 29; Num. 12; 17).

Abagtha ("happy, prosperous"), one of the seven chamberlains of King Ahasuerus (Esth. 1:10).

Abda ("servant; worshiper"). [1] Father of Solomon's tribute officer, Adoniram (1 Kings 4:6). [2] A chief Levite after the Exile (Neh. 11:17). He is called Obadiah in 1 Chronicles 9:16.

Abdeel ("servant of God"), the father of Shelemiah, who was commanded to arrest Baruch and Jeremiah (Jer. 36:26).

Abdi ("servant of Jehovah"). [1] One whom David set over the song service (1 Chron. 6:44). [2] One who took a foreign wife during the Exile (Ezra 10:26). [3] A Levite contemporary with Hezekiah (2 Chron. 29:12).

Abdiel ("servant of Jehovah"), ancestor of a clan of Gad (1 Chron. 5:15).

Abdon ("service, servile"). [1] A judge of Israel for eight years (Judg. 12:13, 15). *See* Bedan. [2] A descendant of Benjamin who dwelt in Jerusalem (1 Chron. 8:23). [3] Firstborn son of Jehiel, mentioned in Chronicles (1 Chron. 8:30; 9:36). [4] One sent to Huldah to inquire of the meaning of the Law (2 Chron. 34:20).

He is called Achbor in 2 Kings 22:12. Possibly he is identical with [2].

Abed-nego ("servant of Nebo; servant of Ishtar"), name given to Azariah, one of the three friends of Daniel who were carried captive to Babylon. He was thrown into a fiery furnace (Dan. 1:7; 2:49; 3:12–30).

Abel ("a breath, vapor; shepherd"), second son of Adam and Eve, slain by his brother Cain (Gen. 4:1–10; Heb. 11:4; 12:24).

Abi, the mother of King Hezekiah (2 Kings 18:2). *Abi* is a contraction of *Abijah* ("Jehovah is father"), which she is called in 2 Chronicles 29:1. *See* Abi-albon; Abi-ezer.

Abia [Abiah, Abijah] ("Jehovah is father"). **[1]** A son of Samuel and wicked judge of Israel (1 Sam. 8:2; 1 Chron. 6:28). **[2]** The wife of Hezron (1 Chron. 2:24). **[3]** Son of Rehoboam and successor to the throne of Judah, an ancestor of Christ (1 Chron. 3:10; 2 Chron. 11:20—14:1; Matt. 1:7). He was also known as Abijam. **[4]** The seventh son of Becher the son of Benjamin (1 Chron. 7:8). **[5]** A descendant of Aaron appointed by David in connection with the priestly courses (1 Chron. 24:10; see Luke 1:5). **[6]** A son of Jeroboam I of Israel (1 Kings 14:1–8). **[7]** A priest of Nehemiah's time who sealed the covenant (Neh. 10:7). Possibly the same as the priest mentioned in Nehemiah 12:1, 4, 17. [8] *See* Abi.

Abi-Albon ("father of strength"), one of David's "valiant men" (2 Sam. 23:31). Also called Abiel (1 Chron. 11:32).

Abiasaph [Ebiasaph] ("my father has gathered"), a Levite whose descendants were doorkeepers of the Tabernacle (Exod. 6:24; 1 Chron. 6:23; 9:19).

Abiathar ("father of super-excellence or pre-eminence"), the only priest to escape Saul's massacre at Nob, he was a high priest in David's time. He was deposed by Solomon (1 Sam. 22:20–23; 1 Kings 2:27; 1 Chron. 15:11–12). First Samuel 21 says that Ahimelech [1] was the high priest when David ate the showbread, yet Mark 2:26 states this occurred in the days of Abiathar the high priest. There are several possible ways to resolve this problem: (a) An old rabbinic tradition says that the son of a high priest could also be designated a high priest; however, we cannot be sure how old this tradition is. (b) Abiathar may have been assisting his father as high priest and thus could be so designated. (c) Abiathar was more prominent in history than was his father

Ahimelech, so he is mentioned here instead of Ahimelech. If this is so (and it seems to be), then Abiathar is called the "high priest" before he actually assumed that office. Notice that Mark does *not* say that Abiathar was present when David ate the showbread; there is no need to suppose an error in this passage.

Abida [Abidah] ("father of knowledge"), a son of Midian listed in Genesis and Chronicles (Gen. 25:4; 1 Chron. 1:33).

Abidan ("father is judge; my father"), a prince of Benjamin (Num. 1:11; 2:22; 7:60, 65; 10:24).

Abiel ("God is father"). *See* Abi-albon, Ner.

Abi-Ezer [Abiezer] ("father of help"). [1] A descendant of Manasseh (Josh. 17:2; 1 Chron. 7:18). *See* Jeezer. [2] One of David's mighty men (2 Sam. 23:27; 1 Chron. 11:28; 27:12).

Abigail ("father [i.e., cause] of delight"). [1] A wife of Nabal and afterwards of David (1 Sam. 25:3, 14–44). [2] Mother of Amasa, whom Absalom made captain (2 Sam. 17:25; 1 Chron. 2:16–17).

Abihail ("father of might"). [1] A chief man of the descendants of Merari (Num. 3:35). [2] The wife of Abishur (1 Chron. 2:29). [3] Head of a family of Gad (1 Chron. 5:14). **[4]** A wife of Rehoboam (2 Chron. 11:18). **[5]** Father of Esther (Esther 2:15; 9:29).

Abihu ("he is my father"), a son of Aaron, destroyed with his brother for offering strange fire to God (Exod. 6:23; Lev. 10:1).

Abihud ("father of honor"), a son of Bela listed in Chronicles (1 Chron. 8:3).

Abijah ("the Lord is my father"). *See* Abia.

Abijam ("father of the sea [or west]"). *See* Abia [3].

Abimael ("my father is God"), a son of Joktan listed in Genesis and Chronicles (Gen. 10:26–28; 1 Chron. 1:20–22). The name may denote an Arabian tribe. Some scholars suggest a locality in Arabia is intended.

Abimelech ("father of the king"). **[1]** Many scholars believe the King(s) Abimelech(s) of Gerar in Genesis 20, 21, and 26 are not proper names but a royal title borne by the Philistine kings. The Psalm 34 title mentions Abimelech where Achish should occur. Since the story of Achish was well known, it seems improbable to regard this as a mistake, but rather a royal title of Achish, king of Gath. *See* Phichol. **[2]** A son of Gideon who tried to become king of Israel, and did reign for three years (Judg. 8:30—10:1). **[3]** *See* Ahimelech [2].

Abinadab ("father or source of liberality or willingness"). **[1]** A man of Judah in whose house the ark was placed (1 Sam. 7:1; 2 Sam. 6:3-4; 1 Chron. 13:7). **[2]** A brother of David (1 Sam. 16:8; 17:13; 1 Chron. 2:13). **[3]** Son of Saul slain by the Philistines (1 Sam. 31:2; 1 Chron. 8:33; 9:39; 10:2). **[4]** Father of one of Solomon's officers (1 Kings 4:11).

Abiner. *See* Abner.

Abinoam ("father of pleasantness"), father of Barak the general (Judg. 4:6, 12; 5:1, 12).

Abiram ("father of elevation"). **[1]** One who conspired against Moses and was destroyed (Num. 16:27; Psa. 106:17). **[2]** Firstborn son of Hiel who died when his father began to rebuild Jericho (1 Kings 16:34; see Josh. 6:26).

Abishag ("my father was a wanderer"), a beautiful woman chosen to nurse the aged David (1 Kings 1:3, 15; 2:17, 21–22). This woman may also be the heroine of the Song of Solomon, where she is simply called "the Shulamite."

Abishai ("my father is Jesse; source of wealth"), a son of David's sister, Zeruiah. He was one of

David's mighty men (1 Sam. 26:6–9; 2 Sam. 2:18; 10:10; 23:18).

Abishalom [Absalom] ("father of peace"), father of Maachah, the wife of Rehoboam (1 Kings 15:2, 10). He is called Absalom, another form of the name, in 2 Chronicles 11:20, 21, and Uriel in 2 Chronicles 13:2. *See* Absalom.

Abishua ("father of safety"). [1] A son of Phinehas, descendant of Aaron mentioned in Chronicles and Ezra (1 Chron. 6:4, 5, 50; Ezra 7:5). [2] A descendant of Benjamin listed in Chronicles (1 Chron. 8:4).

Abishur ("father of oxen"), a son of Shammai listed in Chronicles (1 Chron. 2:28–29).

Abital ("source of dew"), a wife of David (2 Sam. 3:4; 1 Chron. 3:3).

Abitub ("source of good"), a descendant of Benjamin listed in Chronicles (1 Chron. 8:11).

Abiud ("my father is majesty; father of honor"), a son of Zerubbabel and ancestor of Christ (Matt. 1:13).

Abner [Abiner] ("my father of light"), a shortened form of *Abiner;* the captain of the host under Saul and Ishbosheth (1 Sam. 14:50–51; 26:5, 7; 2 Sam. 2; 3).

Abraham ("father of multitudes"). When Abraham was 75 years old, childless, and married to an infertile woman, God asked him to leave his homeland and move to Canaan, now Israel. In return, God said He would make Abraham into "a great nation" (Gen. 12:2). Because Abraham obeyed, he became father of the Jewish people, and is revered by Jews, Christians, and Muslims as the epitome of faith.

God asked Abraham to sacrifice his only son, Isaac (Gen. 22:1–9).

Abraham, a descendant of Noah's son Shem, was born and raised near the Persian Gulf in the culturally advanced city of Ur. This was a town where most people worshiped idols, yet Abraham worshiped only the Lord and trusted him explicitly. Once, God tested Abraham's loyalty by asking him to sacrifice his son, Isaac, who had been born when Abraham was 100 years old. Deeply saddened but steadfastly loyal, Abraham built an altar, then raised his knife to kill Isaac. An angel stopped Abraham, saying, "Now I know that you truly obey God, because you were willing to offer him your only son" (Gen. 22:12). Early Christians saw this episode as a foreshadowing of God's sacrifice of Jesus.

Abraham's flocks and family grew large in Canaan. His great-grandsons, the children of Jacob, produced the extended families that became known as the twelve tribes of Israel.

Absalom ("father of peace"), a son of David who tried to usurp the throne from his father (2 Sam. 3:3; 13—19). *See* Abishalom.

Achaicus ("belonging to Achaia"), a Corinthian Christian who visited Paul at Philippi (1 Cor. 16:17).

Achan [Achar] ("trouble"), one who stole part of the spoil of Jericho and brought "trouble" on

Absalom's rebellion against David ended when he was hung in a tree and killed by Joab (2 Sam. 18:1–33, see page 9).

his people. He was killed for this (Josh. 7:1–24). In 1 Chronicles 2:7, he is called *Achar*.

Achaz, Greek form of Ahaz (also see).

Achbor ("a mouse"). **[1]** Father of a king of Edom (Gen. 36:38–39; 1 Chron. 1:49). **[2]** The father of the one sent to bring Urijah from Egypt (Jer. 26:22; 36:12). **[3]** *See* Abdon **[4]**.

Achim ("woes"), ancestor of Christ (Matt. 1:14).

Achish ("serpent-charmer"). **[1]** A king of Gath to whom David fled for safety (1 Sam. 21:27–

29). **[2]** Another king of Gath who bore the same name but reigned during Solomon's time (1 Kings 2:39–40). However, many believe the kings to be identical.

Achsa [Achsah] ("serpent-charmer"), a daughter of Caleb who married her uncle Othniel (Josh. 15:16–17; Judg. 1:12–13; 1 Chron. 2:49).

Adah ("pleasure; beauty"). **[1]** One of the two wives of Lamech (Gen. 4:19–20, 23). **[2]** One of the wives of Esau (Gen. 36:2, 4, 10, 12, 16). *See* Esau's Wives.

Adaiah ("pleasing to Jehovah; Jehovah has adorned"). **[1]** A son of Shimhi found in 1 Chronicles 8:12–21. **[2]** A Levite ancestor of Asaph (1 Chron. 6:41). Also called Iddo (1 Chron. 6:21). **[3]** Father of a captain who aided Jehoiada (2 Chron. 23:1). **[4]** Father of Jedidah, the mother of King Josiah (2 Kings 22:1). **[5]** One whose descendants resided in Jerusalem (Neh. 11:5). **[6]** One who married a foreign wife (Ezra 10:29). **[7]** Another who did the same (Ezra 10:39). **[8]** A Levite descendant from Aaron (1 Chron. 9:12; Neh. 11:12).

Adalia ("honor of Ized"), one of the sons of Haman slain by the Jews (Esther 9:8).

*God created Adam
as the first human being
(Gen. 1:26–31; 2:7).*

Adam ("of the ground; firm"), the first man. His
sin caused a curse to fall upon all the race
(Gen. 2–3; 1 Cor. 15:22, 45). He is listed in
the genealogy of Christ (Luke 3:38).

Adbeel ("languishing for God"), a son of Ishmael listed in Genesis and Chronicles (Gen.
25:13; 1 Chron. 1:29).

Addan. *See* Addon.

Addar ("height; honor"), a son of Bela listed in
Chronicles (1 Chron. 8:3). *See* Ard [2].

Addi ("my witness"), an ancestor of Christ (Luke 3:28).

Addon [Addan] ("strong"), a man who was unable to prove his Jewish ancestry when he returned from Exile (Neh. 7:61; Ezra 2:59).

Ader ("a flock"), a son of Beriah listed in Chronicles (1 Chron. 8:15).

Adiel ("ornament of God"). [1] A descendant of Simeon listed in Chronicles (1 Chron. 4:36). [2] A descendant of Aaron (1 Chron. 9:12). [3] Father of David's treasurer, Asmaveth (1 Chron. 27:25).

Adin ("ornament"). [1] Ancestor of returned captives (Ezra 2:15; Neh. 7:20). [2] One whose descendant returned with Ezra (Ezra 8:6). [3] A family who sealed the covenant (Neh. 10:14–16).

Adina ("ornament"), a captain of David's mighty men (1 Chron. 11:42).

Adino ("ornament"), a chief of David's mighty men (2 Sam. 23:8). Some identify him with Jashobeam [2]; others deny this.

Adlai ("lax; weary"), father of an overseer of David's herds (1 Chron. 27:29).

Admatha ("God-given"), one of the seven princes of Persia (Esther 1:14).

Adna ("pleasure"). **[1]** One who took a foreign wife (Ezra 10:30). **[2]** A priest listed in Nehemiah 12:12–15. *See also* Adnah.

Adnah ("pleasure"). **[1]** A captain who joined David at Ziklag (1 Chron. 12:20). **[2]** A chief captain of Jehoshaphat (2 Chron. 17:14). *See also* Adna.

Adoni-bezek ("lord of lightning [Bezek]"), a king of Bezek who was captured by Israel (Judg. 1:5–7).

Adonijah ("Jehovah is my lord"). **[1]** A son of David, executed by Solomon for trying to usurp the throne (2 Sam. 3:4; 1 Kings 1:2). **[2]** One sent by Jehoshaphat to teach the law (2 Chron. 17:8). **[3]** One who sealed the new covenant with God after the Exile (Neh. 10:14–16). **[4]** *See* Tob-adonijah.

Adonikam ("my lord has risen"), ancestor of returned captives (Ezra 2:13; 8:13; Neh. 7:18).

Adoniram. *See* Hadoram [3].

Adoni-zedek ("lord of justice or righteousness"), a king of Jerusalem defeated by Joshua (Josh. 10:1–27).

Adoram. *See* Adoniram; Hadoram [3].

Adrammelech ("honor of the king; Adar is a king"), a son of the Assyrian king Sennacherib who, with his brother, killed his father (2 Kings 19:37; Isa. 37:38).

Adriel ("honor of God; my help is God"), the man whom Merab married although she had been promised to David (1 Sam. 18:19; 2 Sam. 21:8).

Aeneas ("praise"), the paralytic of Lydda who was healed by Peter (Acts 9:33–34).

Agabus ("locust"), a prophet of Jerusalem who foretold suffering for Paul if he went to Jerusalem (Acts 11:28; 21:10).

Agag ("high; warlike"), a name or title of the kings of Amalek; it is probably not a proper name. However, if it is a proper name, it is used to refer to two persons: [1] A king mentioned by Balaam (Num. 24:7). [2] A king that Saul spared, but who was later executed by Samuel (1 Sam. 15).

Agar ("wandering"), the Greek form of Hagar (also see).

Agee ("fugitive"), father of one of David's mighty men (2 Sam. 23:11).

Agrippa. *See* Herod.

Agur ("gathered"), a sage who wrote Proverbs 30.

Ahab ("father's brother [uncle]"). [1] The seventh king of Israel. He was wicked and idolatrous and married a woman of the same character—Jezebel (1 Kings 16:28—22:40). [2] A false prophet killed by Nebuchadnezzar (Jer. 29:21–22).

Aharah ("brother's follower"). *See* Ahiram.

Aharhel ("after might; brother of Rachel"), a descendant of Judah (1 Chron. 4:8).

Ahasai ("my holder; protector"), a priest of the family of Immer (Neh. 11:13). *See* Jahzerah.

Ahasbai ("blooming; shining"), father of one of David's mighty men (2 Sam. 23:34).

Ahasuerus ("prince"). [1] The king of Persia whom Esther married. He is known as Xerxes to historians (Esther 1:1; 2:16; 10:3) [2] The father of Darius the Mede (Dan. 9:1). [3] Another name for Cambyses, king of Persia (Ezra 4:6).

Ahaz [Achaz] ("he holds"). [1] The eleventh king of Judah and an ancestor of Christ (1 Kings 15:38—16:20; Matt. 1:9). [2] A descendant of Benjamin (1 Chron. 8:35–36; 9:41–42).

Ahaziah [Azariah] ("Jehovah holds or sustains"). [1] The eighth king of Israel. He was weak and idolatrous (1 Kings 22:51; 2 Kings 1:18). [2] The sixth king of Judah; he reigned only one year (2 Kings 8:24–29; 9:16). He was also known as Jehoahaz (2 Chron. 21:17; 25:23).

His being called Azariah in 2 Chronicles 22:6 is an error; over fifteen Hebrew manuscripts and all recent versions read Ahaziah. *See* Jehoahaz.

Ahban ("brother of intelligence"), the son of Abishur of Judah (1 Chron. 2:29).

Aher ("one that is behind"), a descendant of Benjamin (1 Chron. 7:12). *See also* Ahiram.

Ahi ("my brother"). [1] Head of a family of Gad (1 Chron. 5:15). [2] A man of the tribe of Asher (1 Chron. 7:34).

Ahiah ("Jehovah is brother"). [1] A grandson of Phinehas (1 Sam. 14:3, 18). Some identify him with Ahimelech [2]. [2] One of Solomon's scribes (1 Kings 4:3). [3] A descendant of Benjamin (1 Chron. 8:7). *See also* Ahijah.

Ahiam ("a mother's brother"), one of David's mighty men (2 Sam. 23:33; 1 Chron. 11:35).

Ahian ("brother of day"), a descendant of Manasseh (1 Chron. 7:19).

Ahiezer ("helping brother"). [1] A prince of Dan who helped Moses take a census (Num. 1:12; 2:25; 7:66). [2] One who joined David at Ziklag (1 Chron. 12:3).

Ahihud ("brother of honor"). [1] A prince of Asher (Num. 34:27). [2] A member of the family of Ehud, descended from Benjamin (1 Chron. 8:7).

Ahijah ("Jehovah is brother; my brother is Jehovah"). **[1]** A prophet who prophesied the splitting away of the ten tribes (1 Kings 11:29–30; 14:2, 4–5). **[2]** Father of Baasha who conspired against Nadab (1 Kings 15:27, 33; 21:22). **[3]** A son of Je-rahmeel (1 Chron. 2:25). **[4]** One of David's mighty men (1 Chron. 11:36). **[5]** One who sealed the new covenant with God after the Exile (Neh. 10:26). **[6]** One set over the temple treasures (1 Chron. 26:20). *See also* Ahiah; Ahimelech.

Ahikam ("my brother has risen"), a member of the group sent to consult Huldah the prophetess (2 Kings 22:12, 14; 25:22; Jer. 26:24; 39:14).

Ahilud ("a brother born; child's brother"), father of a recorder appointed by David (2 Sam. 8:16; 20:24; 1 Kings 4:3, 12).

Ahimaaz ("powerful brother"). **[1]** Father of Ahinoam, wife of Saul (1 Sam. 14:50). **[2]** One of Solomon's officers (1 Kings 4:15). **[3]** Son of Zadok who remained loyal to David (2 Sam. 15:27, 36; 17:17, 20; 18:19–29).

Ahiman ("brother of man or fortune"). **[1]** A son of Anak who dwelt in Hebron (Num. 13:22;

Josh. 15:14; Judg. 1:10). [2] A porter in the temple (1 Chron. 9:17).

Ahimelech ("brother of the king; my brother is king"). [1] A Hittite friend of David (1 Sam. 26:6). [2] A priest, son of Abiathar and grandson of [3] (2 Sam. 8:17; 1 Chron. 24:6). Some think the readings in these passages have been transposed (i.e., they speak of Ahimelech the son of Abiathar instead of Abiathar the son of Ahimelech). But this seems unlikely, especially in 1 Chronicles 24. He is called Abimelech in 1 Chronicles 18:16. The Septuagint has Ahimelech here also. [3] One of the priests of Nob slain for helping David (1 Sam. 21:1–8; 22:9–20). *See also* Abimelech; Ahiah.

Ahimoth ("brother of death"), a descendant of Kohath (1 Chron. 6:25).

Ahinadab ("brother of liberality or willingness"), one of Solomon's royal merchants (1 Kings 4:14).

Ahinoam ("pleasant brother"). [1] Wife of King Saul (1 Sam. 14:50). [2] A woman of Jezreel who married David (1 Sam. 25:43; 27:3; 1 Chron. 3:1).

Ahio ("his brother"). [1] Son of Abinadab, in whose house the ark stayed for twenty years

(2 Sam. 6:3–4; 1 Chron. 13:7). **[2]** A descendant of Benjamin (1 Chron. 8:14). **[3]** A descendant of Saul (1 Chron. 8:31; 9:37).

Ahira ("brother of evil"), a chief of the tribe of Naphtali (Num. 1:15; 2:29; 7:78).

Ahiram ("exalted brother; my brother is exalted"), a descendant of Benjamin (Num. 26:38). He is called Ehi, possibly a contraction of Ahiram, in Genesis 46:21 and Aharah in 1 Chronicles 8:1. He is possibly the same as Aher (also see).

Ahisamach ("supporting brother"), one who helped build the tent of meeting (Exod. 31:6; 35:34; 38:23).

Ahishahar ("brother of the dawn"), one of the sons of Bilhan (1 Chron. 7:10).

Ahishar ("brother of song; my brother has sung"), an officer of Solomon (1 Kings 4:6).

Ahithophel ("brother of foolishness"), the real leader of Absalom's rebellion against David. When he saw that victory was impossible, he committed suicide (2 Sam. 15—17).

Ahitub ("a good brother; my brother is goodness"). **[1]** A son of Phinehas (1 Sam. 14:3; 22:9, 11–12, 20). **[2]** Father of Zadok the high priest (2 Sam. 8:17; 15:27; 1 Chron. 6:7–8). **[3]** A high priest of the same family who served during Nehemiah's time (1 Chron. 6:11; 9:11; Neh. 11:11).

Ahlai ("Jehovah is staying"). [1] A daughter of Sheshan listed in 1 Chronicles 2:31. [2] Father of one of David's mighty men (1 Chron. 11:41).

Ahoah ("a brother's reed; brotherly"), a son of Bela (1 Chron. 8:4).

Aholiab ("a father's tent"), one of the workers who erected the tabernacle (Exod. 31:6; 35:34; 36:1–2).

Aholibamah ("tent of the high place"). [1] A wife of Esau (Gen. 36:2, 5, 14, 18). [2] A duke of Edom (Gen. 36:41). *See also* Esau's Wives.

Ahumai ("heated by Jehovah"), a descendant of Judah (1 Chron. 4:2).

Ahuzam ("possession"), a son of Ashur, a descendant of Judah through Caleb (1 Chron. 4:16).

Ahuzzath ("holding fast"), a friend of Abimelech, king of Philistia (Gen. 26:26).

Aiah [Ajah] ("a vulture"). [1] A son of Zibeon (Gen. 36:24; 1 Chron. 1:40). [2] Father of Saul's concubine, Rizpah (2 Sam. 3:7; 21:8, 10–11).

Akan. *See* Jaakan.

Akkub ("lain in wait; pursuer"). [1] One descendant from David mentioned in Chronicles (1 Chron. 3:24). [2] A porter in the temple (1 Chron. 9:17; Neh. 11:19; 12:25). [3] Ancestor of a family of porters (Ezra 2:42; Neh. 7:45). [4] Ancestor of Nethinim who returned from the Exile (Ezra 2:45). [5] A priest who helped the people understand the Law (Neh. 8:7).

Alameth ("hidden"), a son of Becher (1 Chron. 7:8).

Alemeth ("hiding place"), a descendant of Jonathan (1 Chron. 8:36; 9:42).

Alexander ("helper of man"). [1] A son of the Simon who bore Christ's cross (Mark 15:21). [2] A kinsman of Annas and a leading man in Jerusalem (Acts 4:6). [3] A Christian with Paul when the Ephesians had a riot (Acts 19:33). Perhaps the same as [1]. [4] A convert who apostatized (1 Tim. 1:20). [5] A person who did much harm to Paul (2 Tim. 4:14). Perhaps the same as [4].

Aliah [Alvah] ("sublimity"), a duke of Edom (1 Chron. 1:51). He is called Alvah in Genesis 36:40.

Alian [Alvan] ("sublime"), a descendant of Seir (1 Chron. 1:40). He is called Alvan in Genesis 36:23.

Allon ("an oak"), a chief of Simeon (1 Chron. 4:37).

Almodad ("the agitator"), a son of Joktan (Gen. 10:26; 1 Chron. 1:20). Perhaps the name refers to an Arabian people that settled in South Arabia.

Alpheus ("leader; chief"). [1] The father of Levi (Matthew) (Mark 2:14). [2] The father of the apostle James (Matt. 10:3; Mark 3:18; Acts 1:13). Some identify him with Cleophas. *See* Cleophas.

Alvah. *See* Aliah.

Alvan. *See* Alian.

Amal ("laboring"), a descendant of Asher (1 Chron. 7:35).

Amalek ("warlike; dweller in the vale"), a son of Eliphaz and progenitor of the Amalekites (Gen. 36:12, 16; 1 Chron. 1:36; see Exod. 17:8-9).

Amariah ("Jehovah has said"). [1] Grandfather of Zadok the high priest (1 Chron. 6:7, 52; Ezra 7:3). [2] Son of Azariah, a high priest in Solomon's time (1 Chron. 6:11). [3] A descendant of Kohath (1 Chron. 23:19; 24:23). [4] A chief priest in the reign of Jehoshaphat (2 Chron. 19:11). [5] The one appointed to distribute the tithes (2 Chron. 31:15). [6] One who took a foreign wife during the Exile (Ezra 10:42). **[7]** One who sealed the new covenant with God after the Exile (Neh. 10:3; 12:2, 13). **[8]** One whose descendants dwelled in Jerusalem after the Exile (Neh. 11:4). **[9]** Ancestor of Zephaniah the prophet (Zeph. 1:1).

Amasa ("burden-bearer; people of Jesse"). **[1]** A nephew of David who became the commander of Absalom's army (2 Sam. 17:25; 19:13; 20:4–12). **[2]** One who opposed making slaves of captured Jews (2 Chron. 28:12).

Amasai ("burden-bearer"). **[1]** A man in the genealogy of Kohath (1 Chron. 6:25, 35; 2 Chron. 29:12). **[2]** A captain who joined David at Ziklag (1 Chron. 12:18). **[3]** A priest who assisted in bringing up the ark of the covenant to Obed-edom (1 Chron. 15:24).

Amashai ("carrying spoil"), a priest of the family of Immer (Neh. 11:13).

Amasiah ("Jehovah bears; Jehovah has strength"), a chief captain of Jehoshaphat (2 Chron. 17:16).

Amaziah ("Jehovah has strength"). **[1]** Son and successor of Joash to the throne of Judah. He was murdered at Lachish (2 Kings 12:21–14:20). **[2]** A man of the tribe of Simeon (1 Chron. 4:34). **[3]** A Levite descendant from

Merari (1 Chron. 6:45). [4] An idolatrous priest of Bethel (Amos 7:10, 12, 14).

Ami [Amon] ("master workman"), a servant of Solomon whose descendants returned from captivity (Ezra 2:57). In Nehemiah 7:59, he is called Amon.

Aminadeb ("people of liberality"), Greek form of Amminadab (also see).

Amittai ("truthful"), father of the prophet Jonah (2 Kings 14:25; Jon. 1:1).

Ammiel ("my people are strong; my kinsman is God"). [1] One of those who spied out the Promised Land (Num. 13:12). [2] father of Machir, David's friend (2 Sam. 9:4–5; 17:27). [3] *See* Eliam [1]. [4] A porter of the tabernacle in the time of David (1 Chron. 26:5).

Ammihud ("my people are honorable or glorious"). [1] Father of Elishama, the chief of Ephraim (Num. 1:10; 2:18; 7:48). [2] A Simeonite whose son helped to divide the Promised Land (Num. 34:20). [3] A Naphthalite whose son helped divide the Promised Land (Num. 34:28). [4] Father of Talmai, king of Geshur (2 Sam. 13:37). [5] A descendant of Pharez (1 Chron. 9:4).

Amminadab [Aminadab] ("my people are willing or noble"). [1] Aaron's father-in-law (Exod.

6:23). **[2]** A prince of Judah and ancestor of Christ (Num. 1:7; 2:3; Ruth 4:19–20; Matt. 1:4). **[3]** A son of Kohath (1 Chron. 6:22). **[4]** One who helped to bring the ark of the covenant from the house of Obed-edom (1 Chron. 15:10–11).

Ammi-shaddai ("the Almighty is my kinsman; my people are mighty"), father of Ahiezer, a captain of Dan during the wilderness journey (Num. 1:12; 2:25).

Ammizabad ("my people are endowed; my kinsman has a present"), one of David's captains (1 Chron. 27:6).

Ammon. *See* Ben-ammi.

Amnon ("upbringing; faithful"). **[1]** Eldest son of David, by Ahinoam, slain by Absalom (2 Sam. 3:2; 13:1–39). **[2]** A son of Shimon of the family of Caleb (1 Chron. 4:20).

Amok ("deep"), a priest who returned to Jerusalem with Zerubbabel (Neh. 12:7, 20).

Amon ("workman" or "trustworthy"). **[1]** Governor of Samaria in Ahab's time (1 Kings 22:26; 2 Chron. 18:25). **[2]** Son and successor of Manasseh to the throne of Judah; an ancestor of Christ (2 Kings 21:19–25; Jer. 1:2; Zeph. 1:1; Matt. 1:10). **[3]** *See* Ami.

Amos ("burden-bearer; burdensome"). [1] A prophet during the reigns of Uzziah and Jeroboam (Amos 1:1; 7:10–12, 14). [2] An ancestor of Christ (Luke 3:25).

Amos proclaimed God's message, "I will punish Israel" (Amos 2:1—3:15).

Amoz ("strong"), father of the prophet Isaiah (2 Kings 19:2, 20; Isa. 1:1; 2:1; 13:1).

Amplias ("large"), a Roman Christian to whom Paul sent greetings (Rom. 16:8).

Amram ("people exalted; red"). [1] A descendant of Levi and father or ancestor of Aaron,

Moses, and Miriam (Exod. 6:18, 20; Num. 3:19; 26:58–59). **[2]** One who had taken a foreign wife (Ezra 10:34). **[3]** *See* Hemdan.

Amraphel ("powerful people"), a king of Shinar who warred against Sodom (Gen. 14:1, 9).

Amzi ("my strength"). **[1]** A Levite of the family of Merari (1 Chron. 6:46). **[2]** An ancestor of returned exiles (Neh. 11:12).

Anah ("answering"). **[1]** The mother (father?) of one of Esau's wives (Gen. 36:2, 14, 18, 25). If the father, he is the same as Beeri the Hittite (Gen. 26:34). *See* Esau's Wives. **[2]** A son of Seir and a chief of Edom (Gen. 36:20, 29; 1 Chron. 1:38). **[3]** A son of Zibeon (Gen. 36:24; 1 Chron. 1:40–41).

Anaiah ("Jehovah has covered; Jehovah answers"). **[1]** One who stood with Ezra at the reading of the Law (Neh. 8:4). **[2]** One who sealed the new covenant with God after the Exile (Neh. 10:22).

Anak ("giant; long necked"), ancestor of the giant Anakim (Num. 13:22, 28, 33; Josh. 15:14).

Anamim ("rockmen"), a descendant of Mizraim (Gen. 10:13; 1 Chron. 1:11). Possibly an unknown Egyptian tribe.

Anan ("he beclouds; cloud"), one who sealed the new covenant with God after the Exile (Neh. 10:26).

Anani ("my cloud"), a descendant of David who lived after the Babylonian Captivity (1 Chron. 3:24).

Ananiah ("Jehovah is a cloud [i.e., protector]"), ancestor of a returned exile (Neh. 3:23).

Ananias ("Jehovah is gracious"). [1] A disciple struck dead for trying to deceive the apostles (Acts 5:1, 3, 5). [2] A disciple of Damascus who helped Paul after receiving a vision (Acts 9:10–17; 22:12). [3] A high priest in Jerusalem who opposed Paul (Acts 23:2; 24:1).

Anath ("answer"), father of the judge Shamgar (Judg. 3:31; 5:6).

Anathoth ("answers"). [1] A son of Becher (1 Chron. 7:8). [2] One who sealed the new covenant with God after the Exile (Neh. 10:19).

Andrew ("manly; conqueror"), the brother of Peter and one of the twelve apostles (Matt. 4:18; 10:2; John 1:40, 44; 6:8).

Andronicus ("conqueror"), a kinsman of Paul at Rome, to whom Paul sent greetings (Rom. 16:7).

Aner ("sprout; waterfall"), an Amorite chief (Gen. 14:13, 24).

Aniam ("lamentation of the people"), a descendant of Manasseh (1 Chron. 7:19).

Anna ("grace"), a prophetess of the tribe of Asher in Christ's time (Luke 2:36).

Annas ("grace of Jehovah"), high priest of the Jews who first tried Christ (Luke 3:2; John 18:13, 24; Acts 4:6).

Antipas, a Christian martyr of Pergamos (Rev. 2:13).

Anto-thijah ("answers of Jehovah; belonging to Anathoth"), a son of Shashak (1 Chron. 8:24).

Anub ("strong; high"), descendant of Judah through Caleb (1 Chron. 4:8).

Apelles, a Roman Christian to whom Paul sent greetings (Rom. 16:10).

Aphiah ("striving"), an ancestor of Saul (1 Sam. 9:1).

Aphses ("the dispersed"), chief of the eighteenth temple chorus (1 Chron. 24:15).

Apollos ("a destroyer"), a Jewish Christian, mighty in the Scripture, who came to Ephesus and was instructed by Aquila and Priscilla (Acts 18:24; 19:1; 1 Cor. 1:12; 3:4-6; Titus 3:13).

Appaim ("face; presence; nostrils"), a son of Nadab (1 Chron. 2:30).

Apphia, a female Christian Paul mentioned when writing Philemon (Philem. 2).

Aquila ("eagle"), a pious Jewish Christian, husband of Priscilla and friend of Paul (Acts 18:2, 18, 26; Rom. 16:3; 1 Cor. 16:19).

Ara ("strong"), a son of Jether (1 Chron. 7:38).

Arad ("fugitive"), one of the chief men of Aijalon (1 Chron. 8:15).

Arah ("wayfarer"). [1] A son of Ulla; member of the tribe of Asher (1 Chron. 7:39). [2] Ancestor of a family returned from the Exile (Ezra 2:5; Neh. 7:10). [3] Grandfather of the wife of Tobiah, who opposed Nehemiah in rebuilding the temple (Neh. 6:18).

Aram ("high; exalted"). [1] A son of Shem (Gen. 10:22–23; 1 Chron. 1:17). The Aramean people possibly are referred to. [2] A son of Abraham's nephew Kemuel (Gen. 22:21). [3] a descendant from Asher (1 Chron. 7:34). [4] The Greek form of Ram (also see).

Aran ("firmness"), a son of Seir (Gen. 36:28; 1 Chron. 1:42).

Araunah ("Jehovah is firm"). *See also* Ornan.

Arba ("four; strength of Baal"), an ancestor of the Anakim (Josh. 14:15; 15:13; 21:11).

Archelaus ("people's chief"), the son of Herod the Great who succeeded his father as the ruler of Idumea, Judea, and Samaria (Matt. 2:22).

Archippus ("chief groom"), a "fellow-soldier" whom Paul addresses (Col. 4:17; Philem. 2).

Ard ("sprout; descent"). [1] A son of Benjamin (Gen. 46:21). [2] A son of Bela listed in Numbers 26:40. Possibly identical with the Adar of 1 Chronicles 18:3.

Ardon ("descendant"), a son of Caleb of Judah mentioned in Chronicles (1 Chron. 2:18).

Areli ("valiant; heroic; God's hearth"), one of the sons of Gad (Gen. 46:16; Num. 26:17).

Aretas ("pleasing; virtuous"), Aretas IV, Philopatris. King of the Nabataeans whose deputy tried to seize Paul (2 Cor. 11:32).

Argob ("mound"), an officer of Pekahiah slain by Pekah (2 Kings 15:25).

Aridai ("delight of Hari"), a son of Haman slain by the Jews (Esther 9:9).

Aridatha ("given by Hari"), a son of Haman, hanged with his father (Esther 9:8).

Arieh ("lion of Jehovah"), a man of Israel killed by Pekah (2 Kings 15:25).

Ariel ("lion of God"), one sent by Ezra to secure the temple ministers (Ezra 8:16).

Arioch ("lion-like"). [1] A king of Ellasar in Assyria who took part in the expedition against Sodom and Gomorrah (Gen. 14:1, 9). [2] A captain of Nebuchadnezzar's guard commanded to slay the "wise men" (Dan. 2:14–15, 24–25).

Arisai, a son of Haman slain by the Jews (Esther 9:9).

Aristarchus ("the best ruler"), a faithful companion who accompanied Paul on his third missionary journey (Acts 19:29; 20:4; Col. 4:10).

Aristobulus ("best counselor"), a person in Rome whose household Paul saluted (Rom. 16:10).

Armoni ("of the palace"), a son of Saul by Rizpah (2 Sam. 21:8).

Arnan ("joyous; strong"), a descendant of David and founder of a family (1 Chron. 3:21).

Arod ("descent; posterity"), a son of Gad, progenitor of the tribe of Arodi (Num. 26:17; see Gen. 46:16).

Arphaxad, a son of Shem and an ancestor of Christ (Gen. 10:22, 24; 1 Chron. 1:17–18; Luke 3:36). Possibly the reference is to a tribe or people. Formerly identified with the mountainous land north of Nineveh.

Artaxerxes ("fervent to spoil"). **[1]** A king of Persia, Artaxerxes I Longimanus, at whose court Ezra and Nehemiah were officials (Ezra 7:1, 7, 11–12; Neh. 2:1; 5:14). **[2]** Some suppose that Ezra 4:7 uses "Artaxerxes" to refer to the pseudo-Smerdis king of Persia, but the reference is probably to [1].

Artemas ("whole; sound"), a friend of Paul's at Nicopolis (Titus 3:12).

Arza ("firm"), a steward of King Elah of Israel (1 Kings 16:9).

Asa ("physician; healer"). [1] The third king of Judah and an ancestor of Christ (1 Kings 15:8—16:29; Matt. 1:7–8). [2] Head of a Levite family (1 Chron. 9:16).

Asahel ("God is doer; God has made"). [1] A son of David's sister, Zeruiah. He was slain by Abner (2 Sam. 2:18–32; 3:27, 30). [2] A Levite sent to teach the Law (2 Chron. 17:8). [3] A Levite employed as an officer of the offerings and tithes (2 Chron. 31:13). [4] Father of Jonathan, appointed to take a census of foreign wives (Ezra 10:15).

Asahiah [Asaiah] ("Jehovah is doer; Jehovah has made"), one sent to inquire of the Lord concerning the Book of the Law (2 Kings 22:12, 14; 2 Chron. 34:20).

Asaiah ("Jehovah is doer; Jehovah has made"). [1] A prince of Simeon who helped defeat the people of Gedor (1 Chron. 4:36). [2] A descendant of Merari who helped bring up the ark

(1 Chron. 6:30; 15:6, 11). **[3]** A resident of Jerusalem (1 Chron. 9:5). **[4]** *See also* Asahiah.

Asaph ("collector; gatherer"). **[1]** One of David's three chief musicians (1 Chron. 6:39; 15:17, 19). Author of Psalms 50, 73—83. **[2]** Father of Joah the recorder to Hezekiah (2 Kings 18:18, 37; 2 Chron. 29:13). **[3]** A Levite whose descendants lived in Jerusalem (1 Chron. 9:15). **[4]** One whose descendants were porters in David's time (1 Chron. 26:1). The text should possibly read Abiasaph (also see). **[5]** A keeper of the royal forests in Judah (Neh. 2:8).

Asareel ("God is joined or ruler"), a descendant of Judah through Caleb (1 Chron. 4:16).

Asarelah ("Jehovah is joined; whom God has bound"), one appointed to the temple service by David (1 Chron. 25:2). He is called Jesharelah ("of Jesharel") in verse 14. This may be another name for Azarael [2].

Asenath ("dedicated to [the deity] Neit"), the Egyptian wife of Joseph (Gen. 41:45, 50; 46:20).

Aser, Greek form of Asher (also see).

Ashbea ("man of Baal"), a family of linen-workers that sprang from Shelah, son of Judah (1 Chron. 4:21).

Ashbel ("man of Baal"), son of Benjamin (Gen. 46:21; Num. 26:38; 1 Chron. 8:1).

Ashchenaz [Ashkenaz] ("a fire that spreads"), a son of Gomer (Gen. 10:3; 1 Chron. 1:6). Possibly a race or tribe who dwelt near Ararat and Minni in eastern Armenia.

Asher [Aser] ("happy"), the eighth son of Jacob and an ancestor of one of the twelve tribes of Israel (Gen. 30:13; 35:26; 46:17; 49:20; 1 Chron. 2:2).

Ashkenaz. *See* Ashchenaz.

Ashpenaz, prince of Nebuchadnezzar's eunuchs who had charge of the captives from Judah (Dan. 1:3).

Ashriel. *See* Asriel.

Ashur ("free man; man of Horus"), a son of Hezron and head of the inhabitants of Tekoa (1 Chron. 2:24; 4:5).

Ashvath ("made; wrought"), a son of Japhlet; a descendant of Asher (1 Chron. 7:33).

Asiel ("God is doer or maker"), a descendant of Simeon and grandfather of Jehu (1 Chron. 4:35).

Asnah ("thornbush"), one whose descendants returned from Exile (Ezra 2:50).

Asnapper (alternative form of Osnapper), one who brought men from Susa and Elam to Samaria (Ezra 4:9). Formerly believed to be Esarhaddon, he is now believed to have been Ashurbanipal, king of Assyria and Esarhaddon's son.

Aspatha ("horse-given"), son of Haman, slain by the Jews (Esther 9:7).

Asriel [Ashriel] ("God is joined; vow of God"), a son of Manasseh (Num. 26:31; 1 Chron. 7:14).

Asshur [Assur] ("level plain"). [1] A son of Shem (Gen. 10:22; 1 Chron. 1:17). Possibly the people of Assyria are intended. [2] Genesis 10:11, if denoting a person, refers to a son of Ham or to [1]. However, many scholars translate: "From that land he (Nimrod) went into Assyria (Asshur)."

Assir ("prisoner"). [1] A son of Korah (Exod. 6:24; 1 Chron. 6:22). [2] A son of Ebiasaph (1 Chron. 6:23, 37). [3] A son of Jeconiah (Jehoiachin), king of Judah (1 Chron. 3:17).

Assur. *See* Asshur.

Asuppim, a word which should be translated "storehouse" as in Nehemiah 12:25. First Chronicles 26:15 should read: "The lot for the South Gate (southward) fell to Obed-edom, and the lot for the storehouse fell to his sons."

Asyncritus ("incomparable"), one at Rome whom Paul salutes (Rom. 16:14).

Atarah ("crown; ornament"), a wife of Jerahmeel (1 Chron. 2:26).

Ater ("bound; lame"). [1] One who sealed the new covenant with God after the Exile (Neh. 10:17). [2] Ancestor of a family of gatekeepers (Ezra 2:42; Neh. 7:45). [3] Ancestor of a family that returned from the Exile (Ezra 2:16; Neh. 7:21).

Athaiah ("Jehovah is helper"), a descendant of Judah dwelling in Jerusalem (Neh. 11:4).

Athaliah ("whom Jehovah has afflicted; Jehovah is strong"). [1] The daughter of Jezebel, wife of King Jehoram, and afterwards ruler of Judah for six years (2 Kings 8:26; 11:1–20; 2 Chron. 22:2–23:21). [2] A son of Jeroham (1 Chron. 8:26). [3] Father of a returned exile (Ezra 8:7).

Athlai ("Jehovah is strong"), one who married a foreign wife (Ezra 10:28).

Attai ("seasonable; timely"). [1] One who joined David at Ziklag (1 Chron. 12:11). [2] A son of

King Rehoboam (2 Chron. 11:20). **[3]** Descendant of Pharez (1 Chron. 2:35–36).

Augustus (i.e., "consecrated" or "holy"). Acts 25:21, 25; 27:1 use the Greek rendering of the title "reverend" in this fashion, since Augustus had been dead many years.

Augustus Caesar. The imperial name of Octavian, a nephew of Julius Caesar who became emperor of Rome. During his reign, Christ was born (Luke 2:1).

Azaliah ("Jehovah is noble"), father of Shaphan the scribe (2 Kings 22:3; 2 Chron. 34:8).

Azaniah ("Jehovah is hearer"), father of one who signed the new covenant with God after the Exile (Neh. 10:9).

Azarael [Azareel] ("God is helper"). **[1]** One who joined David at Ziklag (1 Chron. 12:6). **[2]** One who ministered in the song service of the temple (1 Chron. 25:18). **[3]** A prince of Dan (1 Chron. 27:22). **[4]** One who took a foreign wife (Ezra 10:41). **[5]** A priest of the family of Immer (Neh. 11:13). **[6]** One who played the trumpet at the dedication of the new temple (Neh. 12:36).

Azariah ("Jehovah has helped"). **[1]** *See* Uzziah. **[2]** A ruler of Solomon's officers (1 Kings 4:5). **[3]** A descendant of David's high priest

(1 Kings 4:2). **[4]** A descendant of Judah (1 Chron. 2:8). **[5]** A descendant of Jerahmeel (1 Chron. 2:38–39). **[6]** A son of Ahimaaz (1 Chron. 6:9). **[7]** A high priest and grandson of [6] (1 Chron. 6:10–11). **[8]** A son of Hilkiah the high priest under Josiah (1 Chron. 6:13–14; 9:11; Ezra 7:1). **[9]** An ancestor of Samuel the prophet (1 Chron. 6:36). **[10]** A prophet who went to Asa (2 Chron. 15:1). **[11]**, **[12]** Two sons of King Jehoshaphat (2 Chron. 21:2). **[13]** *See* Ahaziah [2]. **[14]** A captain who helped to place Joash on the throne (2 Chron. 23:1). **[15]** Another man who helped Joash (2 Chron. 23:1). **[16]** A high priest who opposed Uzziah (2 Chron. 26:17, 20). **[17]** A chief of Ephraim (2 Chron. 28:12). **[18]** A descendant of Kohath and father of Joel (2 Chron. 29:12). **[19]** One who helped cleanse the temple (2 Chron. 29:12). **[20]** A chief of the family of Zadok, priest in Hezekiah's time (2 Chron. 31:10, 13). **[21]** Ancestor of Zadok and Ezra (Ezra 7:3). **[22]** One who repaired the wall of Jerusalem (Neh. 3:23–24). **[23]** One who came up to Jerusalem with Zerubbabel (Neh. 7:7). Perhaps this is another name of Seraiah (Ezra 2:2); if not, his name is omitted in this passage. **[24]** A priest who explained the Law (Neh. 8:7). **[25]** *See* Ezra [1]. **[26]** A

prince of Judah (Neh. 12:33). **[27]** One who charged Jeremiah with false prophecy (Jer. 43:2). **[28]** A captive carried to Babylon with Daniel (Dan. 1:6–7, 11, 19; 2:17). *See* Abednego.

Azaz ("strong; powerful"), a descendant of Reuben (1 Chron. 5:8).

Azaziah ("Jehovah is strong"). **[1]** A Levite who took part in the musical service when the ark was brought to the temple (1 Chron. 15:21). **[2]** Father of a prince of Ephraim in David's time (1 Chron. 27:20). **[3]** A Levite who had the oversight of the dedicated things of the temple under Hezekiah (2 Chron. 31:13).

Azbuk ("pardon"), the father of a man named Nehemiah (Neh. 3:16).

Azel ("noble"), a descendant of King Saul (1 Chron. 8:37–38; 9:43–44).

Azgad ("worship; supplication; Gad is strong"). **[1]** One whose descendants returned from the Exile with Zerubbabel (Ezra 2:12; Neh. 7:17). **[2]** One who came back to Jerusalem with Ezra (Ezra 8:12). **[3]** One who sealed the new covenant with God after the Exile (Neh. 10:15).

Aziel ("God is might"). *See* Jaaziel.

Aziza ("strong"), one who married a foreign wife (Ezra 10:27).

Azmaveth ("counsel or strength of death"). [1] One of David's mighty men (2 Sam. 23:31; 1 Chron. 11:33). [2] A descendant of Saul (1 Chron. 8:36; 9:42). [3] Father of two men who joined David at Ziklag (1 Chron. 12:3). [4] A treasury officer of David's (1 Chron. 27:25).

Azor ("helper"), an ancestor of Christ (Matt. 1:13–14).

Azriel ("God is helper"). [1] A chief of the tribe of Manasseh (1 Chron. 5:24). [2] Father of a ruler of Naphtali in David's time (1 Chron. 27:19). [3] Father of an officer sent to capture Baruch (Jer. 36:26).

Azrikam ("my help has risen"). [1] One of the family of David (1 Chron. 3:23). [2] A son of Azel of the family of Saul (1 Chron. 8:38; 9:44). [3] A descendant of Merari (1 Chron. 9:14; Neh. 11:15). [4] The governor of Ahaz's house (2 Chron. 28:7).

Azubah ("forsaken"). [1] The mother of King Jehoshaphat (1 Kings 22:42; 2 Chron. 20:31). [2] Wife of Caleb, the son of Hezron (1 Chron. 2:18–19).

Azur ("helper; helpful"). [1] Father of a prince that Ezekiel saw in a vision (Ezek. 11:1).

[2] Father of the false prophet Hananiah (Jer. 28:1). *See also* Azzur.

Azzan ("sharp; thorn"), father of a chief of Issachar (Num. 34:26).

Azzur ("helper; helpful"), one who sealed the covenant (Neh. 10:17). *See also* Azur.

B

Baal ("master; lord"). **[1]** A descendant of Reuben (1 Chron. 5:5). **[2]** The fourth of ten sons of Jehiel (1 Chron. 8:29, 30; 9:36).

Baal-hanan ("the lord is gracious"). **[1]** The seventh of the kings of Edom (Gen. 36:38–39; 1 Chron. 1:49–50). **[2]** A tender of olive and sycamore trees in David's time (1 Chron. 27:28).

Baalis ("lord of joy"), the king of the Ammonites after Jerusalem was taken (Jer. 40:14).

Baana [Baanah] ("son of grief; patient"). **[1]** One of Solomon's royal merchants (1 Kings 4:12). **[2]** Another merchant of Solomon, responsible for Asher (1 Kings 4:16). **[3]** Father of Zadok, the builder of the temple (Neh. 3:4). **[4]** Father of one of David's mighty men (2 Sam. 23:29; 1 Chron. 11:30). **[5]** A captain in Ish-bosheth's army (2 Sam. 4:2, 5–6, 9). **[6]** One who returned from the Exile with Zerubbabel (Ezra 2:2; Neh. 7:7; 10:27).

Baara ("a wood; the burning one"), a wife of Sha-haraim (1 Chron. 8:8).

Baaseiah ("Jehovah is bold"), an ancestor of Asaph (1 Chron. 6:40).

Baasha ("boldness"), the third king of Israel; war and wickedness characterized his reign (1 Kings 15:16—16:13).

Bakbakkar ("diligent; searcher"), a Levite who returned from the Babylonian Captivity (1 Chron. 9:15). *See* Bakbukiah [1].

Bakbuk ("waste; hollow"), one whose descendant returned from the Exile (Ezra 2:51; Neh. 7:53).

Bakbukiah ("wasted by Jehovah"). [1] A Levite who lived in Jerusalem (Neh. 11:17). Perhaps identical with Bakbakkar (also see). [2] A Levite who returned with Zerubbabel (Neh. 12:9). [3] A Levite and guard of the temple storehouse (Neh. 12:25).

Balaam ("a pilgrim; lord [Baal] of the people"), a prophet that the king of Moab induced to curse Israel. Instead, God put words of blessing in his mouth (Num. 22—24; 31:8).

Balac, Greek form of Balak (also see).

Baladan ("having power"), father of the king of Babylon in Hezekiah's time (2 Kings 20:12; Isa. 39:1).

Balak [Balac] ("void; empty"), the king of Moab that hired Balaam to curse Israel (Num. 22—24; Josh. 24:9).

Bani ("posterity"). **[1]** One of David's mighty men (2 Sam. 23:36). **[2]** A descendant of Merari (1 Chron. 6:46). **[3]** A descendant of Pharez (1 Chron. 9:4). **[4]** Father of a family that returned from the Babylonian Captivity (Ezra 2:10; 10:29). In Nehemiah 7:15, he is called Binnui. **[5]** One whose descendants had taken

Balaam's donkey had good reason for being stubborn (Num. 22:22–35).

foreign wives during the Exile (Ezra 10:34).
[6] A descendant of [5] who took a foreign wife
during the Exile (Ezra 10:38). [7] A Levite
who helped to repair the wall of Jerusalem
(Neh. 3:17; 8:7). [8] A Levite who assisted in
the devotions of the people (Neh. 9:4; 10:13).
[9] One who sealed the new covenant with God
after the Exile (Neh. 10:14). [10] A Levite
whose son was an overseer of the Levites after
the Exile. Perhaps the same as [7] or [8] (Neh.
11:22). [11], [12], [13] Three Levites who par-
ticipated in the temple worship (Neh. 9:4–5).

Bar (Aramaic for the Hebrew "bēn," "son.")
"Bar" and "ben" are frequently prefixed to
names to indicate direct relationship. Thus
Peter is called Bar-jonah (son of Jonah) because his father was named Jonah (Matt.
16:17) and perhaps Nathanael was called Bartholomew (son of Tolmai) because his father
was named Tolmai. It can also designate characteristics or conditions. For example, Joses
was called Barnabas ("son of consolation") because of the aid he rendered the apostles (Acts
4:36).

Barabbas ("father's son"), a murderer whom the
people demanded that Pontius Pilate should
release instead of Christ (Matt. 27:17, 20–21,
26; Mark 15:7). *See* Bar.

Barachel ("blessed of God"), father of Elihu, a figure in Job (Job 32:2, 6).

Barachias (Greek form of Barachiah), the father of a prophet whom the Jews killed (Matt. 23:35). It is quite possible the reference is to the author of the Book of Zechariah, Zechariah [11], or else an unknown prophet. *See* Berechiah.

Barak ("lightning"), the general of the judge Deborah; he helped to defeat Sisera (Judg. 4:6—5:15).

Bariah ("fugitive"), a descendant of David (1 Chron. 3:22).

Bar-jesus. *See* Elymas; Bar.

Bar-jonah. *See* Peter; Bar.

Barkos ("partly colored"), an ancestor of captives returning from the Exile (Ezra 2:53; Neh. 7:55).

Barnabas ("son of consolation"), a Jewish Christian who traveled widely with Paul (Acts 4:36; 9:27; 11:22–30; Gal. 2:1). His original name was Joses, but he was named Barnabas by the apostles (Acts 4:36); obviously they considered him to be *their* consoler. *See* Bar.

Barsabas ("son of Saba"). *See* Bar; Joseph [11]; Juda [12].

Bartholomew ("son of Tolmai"), one of Jesus' twelve apostles (Matt. 10:3; Mark 3:18; Acts 1:13). He is probably the same as Nathanael (also see). *See* Bar.

Bartimaeus, (Aramaic *bar* "son" and Greek *timaios,* "honorable"), a blind beggar healed by Christ (Mark 10:46–52). *See* Bar.

Baruch ("blessed"). [1] Jeremiah's friend and scribe (Jer. 32:12–13, 16; 36). [2] One who helped to rebuild the wall of Jerusalem (Neh. 3:20; 10:6). [3] A descendant of Perez who returned from the Exile (Neh. 11:5).

Barzillai ("strong"). [1] One who befriended David when he fled from Absalom (2 Sam. 17:27; 19:31–39). [2] Husband of Merab, Saul's eldest daughter, and father of Adriel (2 Sam. 21:8). [3] A priest whose genealogy was lost during the Exile (Ezra 2:61; Neh. 7:63).

Bashemath [Basmath] ("fragrant"). [1] A daughter of Solomon (1 Kings 4:15). [2] A wife of Esau (Gen. 26:34). *See also* Esau. [3] Another wife of Esau, whom he married to appease his father (Gen. 36:3–4, 10, 13). *See also* Esau's Wives.

Basmath. *See* Bashemath.

Bath-sheba ("the seventh daughter; daughter of the oath"), the beautiful wife of Uriah the

Hittite, and afterward the wife of David (2 Sam. 11:3; 12:24; 1 Kings 1:11–2:19). She was the mother of Solomon and an ancestor of Christ (Matt. 1:6). She is called Bath-shua in 1 Chronicles 3:5.

Bath-shua ("daughter of prosperity"). [1] Another name of Bath-sheba (also see). [2] The wife of Judah. In Genesis 38:2 and 1 Chronicles 2:3, the KJV incorrectly renders her name as "daughter of Shua"; Bath-shua is really a proper name.

Bavai ("wisher"), one who helped to rebuild the wall of Jerusalem (Neh. 3:18).

Bazlith [Bazluth] ("asking"), one whose descendants returned from the Exile (Ezra 2:52; Neh. 7:54).

Bealiah ("Jehovah is lord"), a man who joined David at Ziklag (1 Chron. 12:5).

Bebai ("fatherly"). [1] An ancestor of captives returning from the Exile (Ezra 2:11; Neh. 7:16). [2] An ancestor of some returning from the Exile with Ezra (Ezra 8:11; 10:28); perhaps the same as [1]. [3] One who sealed the new covenant with God after the Exile (Neh. 10:15).

Becher ("youth; firstborn"). [1] A son of Benjamin (Gen. 46:21). [2] A son of Ephraim (Num.

26:35); perhaps the same as Bered in 1 Chronicles 7:20.

Bechorath ("first birth"), an ancestor of Saul (1 Sam. 9:1).

Bedad ("alone"), father of Hadad, fourth king of Edom (Gen. 36:35; 1 Chron. 1:46).

Bedan ("son of judgment"). [1] A leader of Israel mentioned as a deliverer of the nation (1 Sam. 12:11). The Septuagint, Syriac, and Arabic read *Barak* instead; however, many think this is a reference to Abdon. [2] A descendant of Manasseh (1 Chron. 7:17).

Bedeiah ("servant of Jehovah"), one who had married a foreign wife during the Exile (Ezra 10:35).

Beeliada ("the lord knows"), a son of David (1 Chron. 14:7) also known as Eliada (2 Sam. 5:16; 1 Chron. 3:8).

Beera [Beerah] ("expounder"). [1] A descendant of Asher (1 Chron. 7:37). [2] A prince of Reuben who was carried captive to Assyria (1 Chron. 5:6).

Beeri ("man of the springs; expounder"). [1] Father of Judith, a wife of Esau (Gen. 26:34). *See also* Esau's Wives. [2] Father of the prophet Hosea (Hos. 1:1).

Bela [Belah] ("consumption"). **[1]** A king of Edom, the first mentioned in Scripture (Gen. 36:32–33; 1 Chron. 1:43–44). **[2]** A son of Benjamin and one of the left-handed heroes (Gen. 46:21; 1 Chron. 7:6–7). **[3]** Descendant of Reuben (1 Chron. 5:8).

Belshazzar (Hebrew form of the Babylonian name Bel-shar-usur—"[the god] Bel has protected the king [ship]"), the son of Nabonidus and co-regent in Babylon. He witnessed strange handwriting on the wall of his palace before his kingdom was overthrown by Persia (Dan. 5; 7:1; 8:1).

Belteshazzar (Hebrew form of the Babylonian name, Balat-usu-usur—"Protect his life!"), the name given to Daniel in Babylon (Dan. 1:7). *See* Daniel.

Ben ("son"), an assistant in the temple musical service at the time of David (1 Chron. 15:18).

Benaiah ("Jehovah has built"). **[1]** The third leader of David's army, counselor to the kings, and loyal friend of both David and Solomon (2 Sam. 8:18; 20:23; 1 Kings 1:8—2:46). **[2]** One of David's mighty men (2 Sam. 23:30; 1 Chron. 11:31). **[3]** Head of a family of the tribe of Simeon (1 Chron. 4:36). **[4]** One of David's priests (1 Chron. 15:18, 20, 24; 16:5–6). **[5]** Father of one of David's counselors

(1 Chron. 27:34). **[6]** The grandfather of Jahaziel (2 Chron. 20:14). **[7]** An overseer of the
temple during Hezekiah's reign (2 Chron.
31:13). **[8]**, **[9]**, **[10]**, **[11]** Four men who married foreign wives during the Exile (Ezra
10:25, 30, 35, 43). **[12]** Father of Pelatiah, a
prince of Judah (Ezek. 11:1, 13).

Ben-ammi ("son of my people"), the ancestor of
the Ammonites (Gen. 19:38), born to Lot and
his daughter.

Ben-hadad ("son of [the god] Hadad"). **[1]** Ben-
hadad I, the king of Syria who made a league
with Asa of Judah and invaded Israel
(1 Kings 15:18, 20; 2 Chron. 10:2, 4). **[2]** Ben-
hadad II, another king of Syria defeated by
Ahab; he eventually laid siege to Samaria it-
self (1 Kings 20; 2 Kings 6:24; 8:7, 9. **[3]** The
son of Hazael who reigned over Syria as the
empire disintegrated (2 Kings 13:3, 24–25;
Amos 1:4). **[4]** Possibly a general title of the
Syrian kings (Jer. 49:27).

Ben-hail ("strong; son of strength"), a prince of
Judah under Jehoshaphat (2 Chron. 17:7).

Ben-hanan ("son of grace"), a son of Shimon of
the tribe of Judah (1 Chron. 4:20).

Beninu ("our son"), one who sealed the new covenant with God after the Exile (Neh. 10:13).

Benjamin ("son of the right hand"). [1] The youngest son of Jacob; his descendants became one of the twelve tribes of Israel (Gen. 35:18, 24; 42:4, 36; 43–45. [2] A descendant of Benjamin (1 Chron. 7:10). [3] A descendant of Harim (Ezra 10:32). [4] One who helped to repair the wall of Jerusalem (Neh. 3:23). [5] One who helped to dedicate the wall of Jerusalem (Neh. 12:34).

Beno ("his son"), a descendant of Merari (1 Chron. 24:26–27).

Benoni ("son of my sorrow"), name given to Rachel's child as she died bearing him; Jacob changed his name to Benjamin (also see).

Ben-zoheth ("son of Zoheth; corpulent; strong"), a descendant of Judah through Caleb (1 Chron. 4:20).

Beor [Bosor] ("shepherd"). [1] Father of Bela, the king of Edom (Gen. 36:32; 1 Chron. 1:43). [2] Father of the prophet Balaam (Num. 22:5; 24:3, 15; 31:8).

Bera ("gift"), a king of Sodom in the time of Abram (Gen. 14:2).

Berachah ("blessing"), one who joined David at Ziklag (1 Chron. 12:3).

Berachiah. *See* Berechiah [2].

Beraiah ("unfortunate"), a chief of Benjamin (1 Chron. 8:21).

Berechiah [Berachiah] ("Jehovah is blessing"). **[1]** A descendant of Jehoiakim (1 Chron. 3:20). **[2]** Father of Asaph, the chief singer (1 Chron. 6:39; 15:17). **[3]** A Levite who lived near Jerusalem (1 Chron. 9:16). **[4]** One of the tabernacle doorkeepers (1 Chron. 15:23). **[5]** A descendant of Ephraim in the time of Pekah (2 Chron. 28:12). **[6]** Father of one who repaired the wall of Jerusalem (Neh. 3:4, 30; 6:18). **[7]** The father of the prophet Zechariah (Zech. 1:1, 7). *See* Barachias.

Bered ("seed place"), a descendant of Ephraim (1 Chron. 7:20); perhaps the same as Becher (Num. 26:35).

Beri ("expounder"), a descendant of Asher (1 Chron. 7:36).

Beriah ("unfortunate"). **[1]** A descendant of Asher (Gen. 46:17; Num. 26:44–45; 1 Chron. 7:30–31). **[2]** A descendant of Ephraim (1 Chron. 7:23). **[3]** A descendant of Benjamin (1 Chron. 8:13, 16). **[4]** A descendant of Levi (1 Chron. 23:10–11).

Bernice ("victorious"), the immoral daughter of Herod Agrippa I. She and her brother Agrippa (with whom she was living in incest) sat in judgment on Paul (Acts 25:13, 23; 26:30).

Berodach-baladan, a copyist's mistake or another form of Merodach-baladan (also see).

Besai ("treading down"), one who returned to Jerusalem with Zerubbabel (Ezra 2:49; Neh. 7:52).

Besodeiah ("given to trust in Jehovah"), one of the repairers of the old gate of Jerusalem (Neh. 3:6).

Beth-rapha ("place of fear"), a descendant of Judah or a city Eshton built (1 Chron. 4:12).

Bethuel ("dweller in God"), a son of Nahor, Abraham's brother (Gen. 22:22–23; 28:5).

Bezai ("shining; high"). [1] An ancestor of 323 captives returning from the Exile (Ezra 2:17; Neh. 7:23). [2] One who sealed the new covenant with God after the Exile (Neh. 10:18).

Bezaleel ("God is protection"). [1] A chief worker and designer of the tabernacle (Exod. 31:2; 35:30; 36:1–2). [2] One who had married a foreign wife (Ezra 10:30).

Bezer ("strong"), one of the heads of Asher (1 Chron. 7:37).

Bichri ("youth; firstborn"), an ancestor of Sheba, who rebelled against David (2 Sam. 20:1).

Bidkar ("servant of Ker [Kar]"), a captain in the service of Jehu who executed the sentence on Ahab's son (2 Kings 9:25).

Bigtha ("given by fortune"), a chamberlain of Ahasuerus (Esther 1:10).

Bigthan [Bigthana] ("given by fortune"), a chamberlain who conspired against Ahasuerus (Esther 2:21; 6:2).

Bigvai ("happy; of the people"). [1] Head of one of the families who returned with Zerubbabel (Ezra 2:2, 14; 8:14; Neh. 7:7, 19). [2] One who sealed the covenant with Nehemiah (Neh. 10:16).

Bildad ("lord Adad; son of contention"), one of Job's three "friends" (Job 2:11; 8:1; 18:1; 25:1; 42:9).

Bilgah ("bursting forth; firstborn"). [1] A priest in the tabernacle service (1 Chron. 24:14). [2] A priest who came up to Jerusalem with Zerubbabel (Neh. 12:5, 18).

Bilgai ("bursting forth"), one who sealed the new covenant with God after the Exile (Neh. 10:8); perhaps the same as Bilgah [2].

Bilhah ("tender"), the handmaid of Rachel and mother of Dan and Naphtali (Gen. 29:29; 30:3–5, 7).

Bilhan ("tender"). [1] A descendant of Seir (Gen. 36:27; 1 Chron. 1:42). [2] A descendant of Benjamin (1 Chron. 7:10).

Bilshan ("searcher"), a prince who returned from the Exile (Ezra 2:2; Neh. 7:7).

Bimhal ("circumcised"), a descendant of Asher (1 Chron. 7:33).

Binea ("wanderer"), a descendant of Saul (1 Chron. 8:37; 9:43).

Binnui ("being a family"). [1] A Levite appointed by Ezra to weigh gold and silver (Ezra 8:33). [2],[3] Two men who married foreign wives during the Exile (Ezra 10:30, 38). [4] One who repaired the wall of Jerusalem (Neh. 3:24; 10:9). [5] A Levite who came up with Zerubbabel (Neh. 12:8). [6] *See* Bani [4].

Birsha ("thick; strong"), a king of Gomorrah in the days of Abraham (Gen. 14:2).

Birzavith ("olive well"), descendant of Asher (1 Chron. 7:31).

Bishlam ("peaceful"), a foreign colonist who wrote a letter of complaint against the Jews (Ezra 4:7).

Bithiah ("daughter of Jehovah"), a daughter of the pharaoh and wife of Mered (1 Chron. 4:18); her name implies her conversion.

Biztha ("eunuch"), one of Ahasuerus' eunuchs (Esther 1:10).

Blastus ("a bud"), the chamberlain of Herod Agrippa I (Acts 12:20).

Boanerges ("sons of thunder"), the surname bestowed upon James and John, the sons of Zebedee (Mark 3:17).

Boaz [Booz] ("fleetness; strength"), a Bethlehemite of Judah who became the husband of Ruth and an ancestor of Christ (Ruth 2—4; Matt. 1:5; Luke 3:32).

Bocheru ("youth"), a descendant of King Saul (1 Chron. 8:38; 9:44).

Bohan ("stumpy"), a descendant of Reuben for whom a boundary stone between Judah and Benjamin was named (Josh. 15:6; 18:17).

Booz, Greek form of Boaz (also see).

Bosor, Greek form of Beor (also see).

Bukki ("proved of Jehovah; mouth of Jehovah"). [1] An ancestor of Ezra and descendant of Aaron (1 Chron. 6:5, 51; Ezra 7:4). [2] A prince of the tribe of Dan (Num. 34:22).

Bukkiah ("proved of Jehovah; mouth of Jehovah"), a son of Heman and musician in the temple (1 Chron. 25:4, 13).

Bunah ("understanding"), a son of Jerahmeel (1 Chron. 2:25).

Bunni ("my understanding"). [1] An ancestor of Shemaiah the Levite (Neh. 11:15). [2] A Levite who helped Ezra in teaching the Law

(Neh. 9:4). **[3]** One who sealed the new covenant with God after the Exile (Neh. 10:15).

Buz ("contempt"). **[1]** The second son of Nahor, the brother of Abraham (Gen. 22:21). **[2]** A descendant of Gad (1 Chron. 5:14).

Buzi ("despised by Jehovah"), a descendant of Aaron and father of Ezekiel (Ezek. 1:3).

C

Caesar, the name of a branch of the aristocratic family of the Julii, which gained control of the Roman government; afterward it became a formal title of the Roman emperors. *See* Augustus Caesar; Tiberius Caesar; Claudius Caesar.

Caiaphas ("depression"), the high priest who took a leading role in the trial of Jesus (Matt. 26:3, 57–68; John 11:49).

Cain ("acquired; spear"), the eldest son of Adam who killed his brother Abel (Gen. 4:1–25).

Cainan [Kenan] ("acquired"). **[1]** A son of Enosh and ancestor of Christ (Gen. 5:9; Luke 3:37). The KJV inconsistently spells the same name *Kenan* in 1 Chronicles 1:2. **[2]** A son of Arphaxad and an ancestor of Christ (Luke 3:36). It should be noted that this name occurs in

Cain's anger against his brother Abel led to the first murder (Gen. 4:8, see page 59).

the Septuagint text and not in the Hebrew of Genesis 10:24; 11:12. The presence of this name shows that the early lists in Genesis were not meant to be complete.

Calcol ("sustaining" or "nourishment"), a descendant of Judah (1 Chron. 2:6). *See also* Chalcol.

Caleb [Chelubai] ("impetuous; raging with madness"). **[1]** One of the spies sent out by Moses to see the Promised Land (Num. 13:6;

Josh. 14—15). **[2]** A son of Hezron and grandfather of [1] (1 Chron. 2:18–19, 42).

Canaan ("low"), a son of Ham and grandson of Noah (Gen. 10:6–19; 1 Chron. 1:8, 13). Possibly a reference to the inhabitants of Canaan.

Candace ("contrite one"), a dynastic title of Ethiopian queens (Acts 8:27).

Caphtorim [Caphthorim], a son of Mizraim (Gen. 10:14; 1 Chron. 1:12). Possibly a reference to the people from Caphtor.

Carcas ("severe"), a chamberlain of Ahasuerus (Esther 1:10).

Careah. *See* Kareah.

Carmi ("fruitful; noble"). **[1]** A son of Reuben who went to Egypt with him (Gen. 46:9; Exod. 6:14; 1 Chron. 5:3). **[2]** A descendant of Judah (Josh. 7:1; 1 Chron. 2:7). **[3]** Another son of Judah (1 Chron. 4:1); some identify him with [2].

Carpus ("fruit; wrist"), a friend with whom Paul left his cloak (2 Tim. 4:13).

Carshena ("distinguished; lean"), one of the seven princes of Persia and Media during Ahasuerus' reign (Esther 1:14).

Casluhim ("fortified"), a son of Mizraim (Gen. 10:14; 1 Chron. 1:12). Possibly a people related to the Egyptians. They were the ancestors of the Philistines.

Cephas. *See* Peter.

Chalcol ("sustaining"), a wise man with whom Solomon was compared (1 Kings 4:31).

Chedorlaomer (Elamite, Kutir-Lakamar—"servant of [the goddess] Lakamar"), a king of Elam who came up against Sodom and Gomorrah (Gen. 14:1–24).

Chelal ("completeness"), a man who took a foreign wife during the Exile (Ezra 10:30).

Chelluh ("robust"), a man who married a foreign wife during the Exile (Ezra 10:35).

Chelub ("boldness"). [1] A descendant of Judah (1 Chron. 4:11). [2] Father of Ezri (1 Chron. 27:26).

Chelubai. *See* Caleb [2].

Chenaanah ("flat; low"). [1] A son of Bilhan (1 Chron. 7:10). [2] Father of the false prophet Zedekiah (1 Kings 22:11, 24).

Chenani ("Jehovah, creator"), a Levite in the time of Ezra (Neh. 9:4).

Chenaniah ("established by Jehovah"). [1] A head Levite when David brought the ark of the covenant to the temple (1 Chron. 15:22,

27). **[2]** An officer of David (1 Chron. 26:29). *See also* Conaniah.

Cheran ("lyre; lamb; union"), a son of Dishon (Gen. 36:26).

Chesed ("gain"), son of Nahor and Milcah and nephew of Abraham (Gen. 22:22).

Chidon. *See* Nachon.

Chileab ("restraint of father"), a son of David (2 Sam. 3:3); probably also called Daniel (1 Chron. 3:1).

Chilion ("pining"), son of Naomi and husband of Orpah (Ruth 1:2, 5).

Chimham ("pining"), a friend and political supporter of David (2 Sam. 19:37–38, 40; Jer. 41:17).

Chislon ("strength"), a prince of the tribe of Benjamin (Num. 34:21).

Chloe ("a tender sprout"), a Corinthian woman or an Ephesian woman who knew of the problems at Corinth (1 Cor. 1:11).

Christ. *See* Jesus.

Chushan-rishathaim ("man of Cush; he of the twofold crime"), a king of Mesopotamia that God chose to punish Israel (Judg. 3:8, 10).

Chuza ("seer"), steward of Herod Antipas whose wife ministered to Christ and the apostles (Luke 8:3).

Cis, Greek form of Kish (also see).

Claudia ("lame"), a Roman Christian who sent greetings to Timothy (2 Tim. 4:21).

Claudius Caesar ("lame ruler"), Roman emperor who banished the Jews from Rome (Acts 18:2).

Claudius Lysias ("lame dissolution"), a Roman officer, chief captain in Jerusalem (Acts 23:26).

Clement ("mild"), a co-worker with Paul at Philippi (Phil. 4:3).

Cleopas ("renowned father"), one of the disciples whom Jesus met on the way to Emmaus (Luke 24:18). *See also* Cleophas.

Cleophas ("renowned"), the husband of one of the Marys who followed Jesus (John 19:25); possibly the same as Alphaeus (also see). *See also* Cleopas.

Col-hozeh ("wholly a seer"). [1] Father of Shallum, who helped to rebuild the wall of Jerusalem (Neh. 3:15). [2] A man of Judah (Neh. 11:5); possibly the same as [1].

Conaniah [Cononiah] ("Jehovah has founded"). [1] A Levite appointed to be overseer of the tithes and offerings at the temple (2 Chron. 31:12–13). [2] A chief of the Levites (2 Chron. 35:9). *See also* Chenaniah.

Coniah. *See* Jehoiachin.

Cononiah. *See* Conaniah.

Core Greek form of Korah (also see).

Cornelius ("of a horn"), a Roman centurion who was converted to Christianity (Acts 10:1–31).

Cosam ("diviner"), an ancestor of Christ (Luke 3:28).

Coz ("thorn; nimble"), a descendant of Judah through Caleb (1 Chron. 4:8).

Cozbi ("deceitful"), a Midianite woman slain by Phinehas at Shittim (Num. 25:6–18).

Crescens ("increasing"), an assistant with Paul at Rome (2 Tim. 4:10).

Crispus ("curled"), a ruler of the Jewish synagogue at Corinth who was converted to Christ (Acts 18:7–8; 1 Cor. 1:14).

Cush ("black"). [1] Eldest son of Ham (Gen. 10:6–8; 1 Chron. 1:8–10). [2] A descendant of Benjamin and enemy of David (Ps. 7, title).

Cushi ("black"). [1] Father of Zephaniah (Zeph. 1:1). [2] Great-grandfather of Jehudi (Jer. 36:14). [3] The messenger that told David of the defeat of Absalom (2 Sam. 18:21–32).

Cyrenius [Quirinius] ("of Cyrene"), the governor of Syria (Luke 2:2).

King Cyrus of Persia allowed the Jews to return home (2 Chron. 36:22–23).

Cyrus, founder of the Persian Empire; he returned the Jews to their land (Ezra 1:1–4, 7; 3:7; Isa. 44:28; 45:1–4; Dan. 6:28).

D

Dalaiah ("Jehovah is deliverer" or "Jehovah has raised"), a descendant of Judah (1 Chron. 3:24). *See also* Delaiah.

Dalphon ("swift"), a son of Haman slain by the Jews (Esther 9:6–7, 10).

Damaris ("heifer"), an Athenian woman converted by Paul (Acts 17:34).

Dan ("judge"), the fifth son of Jacob and ancestor of one of the twelve tribes of Israel (Gen. 30:6; 49:16–17).

Daniel ("God is my judge"). **[1]** Hero of the prophetic book bearing his name, Daniel is most famous for surviving a night in a den of hungry

Daniel's faith in God was proven again in the lion's den (Dan. 6:28).

lions. How he got there and what happened afterward enhance his fascinating story.

When Babylonians defeated the southern nation of Judah in 597 B.C., and before they destroyed the cities a decade later, they peeled away the top layer of society—the most educated and influential—taking them to Babylon to serve the empire. Daniel, a wise young noble, was among this group. He became the elite of the elite, chosen to work in the palace, as were his friends Shadrach, Meshach, and Abednego. They are remembered for surviving a fiery furnace after refusing to worship an idol.

Daniel was a gifted sage, and a visionary who interpreted dreams for King Nebuchadnezzar. The king became so impressed that he put Daniel in charge of all sages of the empire. Jealous rivals later tricked a subsequent king (of the conquering Persian Empire) into issuing a decree for all people to pray only to him for thirty days. When Daniel continued praying to God, he was punished by facing the lions. After surviving, Daniel was promoted to the number two position in the empire, second only to the king.

[2] One of the sons of David (1 Chron. 3:1). *See* Chileab. [3] A Levite of the line of Ithamar (Ezra 8:2; Neh. 10:6).

Dara ("bearer [pearl] of wisdom"), a son of Zerah (1 Chron. 2:6). Possibly the same as Darda (also see).

Darda ("bearer [pearl] of wisdom"), a wise man with whom Solomon was compared (1 Kings 4:31). *See also* Dara.

Darius ("he that informs himself"). **[1]** The sub-king of Cyrus who received the kingdom of Belshazzar (Dan. 5:30—6:28); also known as Darius the Mede. **[2]** The fourth king of Persia (Ezra 4:5; Hag. 1:1; Zech. 1:1); also called Hystaspis. **[3]** Darius II (Nothus) who ruled Persia and Babylon (Neh. 12:22).

Darkon ("carrier"), a servant of Solomon whose descendants returned to Palestine after the Exile (Ezra 2:56; Neh. 7:58).

Dathan ("fount"), a chief of the tribe of Reuben who tried to overthrow Moses and Aaron (Num. 16; 26:9; Deut. 11:6).

David ("beloved"). Israel's greatest king had a humble start in life. David was born into a Bethlehem shepherd's family, as the youngest of eight sons. But even as a lad he showed signs of greatness. He killed bears and lions that raided his flock. And with only a slingshot he defeated the Philistine champion, Goliath.

God's creation drew the young David close to God (Ps. 8).

Invited to live in King Saul's palace, David calmed the moody ruler by playing a harp. When Saul erupted over David's growing popularity and tried to kill him, David fled and lived as a fugitive. David immediately began attracting an army of followers. After Saul died in a battle with the Philistines, Israel rallied around the still popular giant-slayer and crowned him king.

David chose Jerusalem as his capital, expanded the nation's borders, and launched Israel's Golden Age, which spanned his reign

After David became king, he brought the ark of the covenant to Jerusalem (1 Chron. 13:1–14; 15:1—16:6).

as well as Solomon's, his son. Yet David had failings: he committed adultery with Bathsheba and had her husband killed. And he raised an incredibly dysfunctional family—one son led a coup against him. Still, David never grew too proud to repent.

His dynasty began in 1000 B.C. and endured for nearly 500 years. Early Christians believed his dynasty was resurrected in Jesus, the Messiah promised from David's family and hometown.

Debir ("oracle"), a king of Eglon defeated by Joshua (Josh. 10:3).

Deborah ("bee"). [1] The nurse of Rebekah (Gen. 24:59; 35:8). [2] Prophetess and judge of Israel who helped to deliver her people from Jabin and Sisera (Judg. 4:4–14; 5).

Deborah, a prophetess and judge, reluctantly led Israel into battle (Judg. 4:1–24).

Dedan. [1] A descendant of Cush (Gen. 10:7). Possibly a people of Arabia in the neighborhood of Edom. [2] A son of Jokshan and grandson of Abraham (Gen. 25:3).

Dekar ("lancer"), father of one of Solomon's commissaries (1 Kings 4:9).

Delaiah ("Jehovah has raised; Jehovah is deliverer"). [1] One of David's priests (1 Chron. 24:18). [2] A prince who urged Jehoiakim not to destroy the roll containing Jeremiah's prophecies (Jer. 36:12, 25). [3] Ancestor of a postexilic family that had lost its genealogy (Ezra 2:60; Neh. 7:62). [4] The father of Shemaiah (Neh. 6:10). *See also* Dalaiah.

Delilah ("longing; dainty one"), a woman whom the Philistines paid to find Samson's source of strength (Judg. 16).

Demas ("popular"), a friend of Paul at Rome who later forsook him (Col. 4:14; 2 Tim. 4:10; Philem. 24).

Demetrius ("belonging to Demeter"). [1] A Christian praised by John (3 John 12). [2] A silversmith who led the opposition against Paul at Ephesus (Acts 19:24–41).

Deuel ("knowledge of God"), father of Eliasaph (Num. 1:14). He is called Reuel in Numbers 2:14; we do not know which name is original.

Diblaim ("two cakes; double embrace"), father-in-law of Hosea (Hos. 1:3).

Dibri ("eloquent; on the pasture born"), a descendant of Dan whose daughter married an

Egyptian; her son was stoned for blasphemy (Lev. 24:11).

Didymus. *See* Thomas.

Diklah ("place of palms"), a son of Joktan (Gen. 10:27; 1 Chron. 1:21). Possibly a people who dwelt in Arabia is intended.

Dinah ("justice"), the daughter of Jacob and Leah who was violated by Hamor; this resulted in a tribal war (Gen. 34).

Dionysius ("Bacchus"), a member of the supreme court at Athens converted by Paul (Acts 17:34).

Diotrephes ("nourished by Jupiter"), a person who opposed John's authority (3 John 9–10).

Diphath. *See* Riphath.

Dishan ("antelope; leaping"), a son of Seir (Gen. 36:21, 28, 30; 1 Chron. 1:38, 42). *See also* Dishon.

Dishon ("antelope; leaping"). **[1]** A son of Seir (Gen. 36:21, 30; 1 Chron. 1:38). **[2]** A grandson of Seir (Gen. 36:25; 1 Chron. 1:41). *See also* Dishan.

Dodai. *See* Dodo.

Dodanim [Rodanim], the son of Javan (Gen. 10:4). First Chronicles 1:7 states his name as Rodanim; many scholars consider Rodanim to be original. Possibly a reference to the inhabitants of Rhodes and the neighboring islands.

Dodavah ("loved of Jehovah"), father of Eliezer (2 Chron. 20:37).

Dodo [Dodai] ("beloved"). **[1]** The grandfather of Tola, a judge (Judg. 10:1). **[2]** A commander of one of the divisions of David's army and father of Eleazar [3] (2 Sam. 23:9; 1 Chron. 11:12; 27:4). **[3]** Father of Elhanan [2] (2 Sam. 23:24; 1 Chron. 11:26).

Doeg ("anxious; cared for"), a servant of King Saul who executed the priests of Nob on Saul's orders (1 Sam. 21:7; 22:9–19).

Dorcas. *See* Tabitha.

Drusilla ("watered by dew"), a Jewess, the daughter of Herod Agrippa I and wife of Felix; she and Felix heard a powerful message of Paul's (Acts 24:24–25).

Dumah ("silence"), a descendant of Ishmael (Gen. 25:14; 1 Chron. 1:30).

E

Ebal [Obal] ("bare; naked"). **[1]** A son of Shobal the Horite (Gen. 36:23; 1 Chron. 1:40). **[2]** A son of Joktan, descendant of Shem (1 Chron. 1:22). He is called Obal in Genesis 10:28. Possibly an Arabian people is meant.

Ebed ("servant"). [1] A companion of Ezra on his return to Jerusalem (Ezra 8:6). [2] Father of Gaal who rebelled against Abimelech (Judg. 9:26-35).

Ebed-Melech ("the king's servant"), an Ethiopian eunuch who rescued Jeremiah (Jer. 38:7-12; 39:16).

Eber ("the other side; across"). [1] A descendant of Shem and an ancestor of Christ (Gen. 10:21, 24-25; 11:14-17; Luke 3:35). His name occurs as Heber in Luke 3:35. Possibly the Hebrews and certain Aramean people are intended. [2] A descendant of Benjamin (1 Chron. 8:12). [3] Head of a priestly family (Neh. 12:20). *See* Heber.

Ebiasaph. *See* Abiasaph.

Eden ("delight"). [1] A descendant of Gershom (2 Chron. 29:12). [2] A Levite in the time of Hezekiah (2 Chron. 31:15).

Eder ("flock"), a grandson of Merari, son of Levi (1 Chron. 23:23; 24:30).

Edom ("red"), name given to Esau, the elder son of Isaac, because of his red skin (Gen. 25:30). *See* Esau; Obed-edom.

Eglah ("calf"), one of David's wives (2 Sam. 3:5; 1 Chron. 3:3).

Eglon ("circle"), a king of Moab who oppressed Israel in the days of the judges (Judg. 3:12–17).

Ehi. *See* Ahiram.

Ehud ("strong"). **[1]** A judge who delivered Israel from the oppression of Eglon of Moab (Judg. 3:15–30). **[2]** Great-grandson of Benjamin (1 Chron. 7:10; 8:6); perhaps the same as **[1]**.

Eker ("root"), a descendant of Judah (1 Chron. 2:27).

E

Eladah ("God is ornament"), a descendant of Ephraim (1 Chron. 7:20).

Elah ("oak"). **[1]** A chieftain of Edom (Gen. 36:41; 1 Chron. 1:52). **[2]** Father of a commissary officer under Solomon (1 Kings 4:18). **[3]** The son and successor of Baasha, king of Israel. He was murdered by Zimri (1 Kings 16:6–14). **[4]** The father of Hoshea, last king of Israel (2 Kings 15:30; 17:1). **[5]** A son of Caleb, son of Jephunneh (1 Chron. 4:15). **[6]** A descendant of Benjamin (1 Chron. 9:8).

Elam ("highland"). **[1]** A son of Shem (Gen. 10:22; 1 Chron. 1:17). Some consider the people of Elam, a region beyond the Tigris east of Babylonia, to be intended. It was bounded on the north by Assyria and Media, on the south by the Persian Gulf, and on the east and southeast by Persia. [2] A descendant of Benjamin (1 Chron. 8:24). [3] A descendant of Korah (1 Chron. 26:3). [4] A leader of the people who sealed the new covenant with God after the Exile (Neh. 10:14). [5] A priest of Nehemiah's time who helped to cleanse Jerusalem (Neh. 12:42). [6] One whose descendants returned from the Exile (Ezra 2:7). [7] Another whose descendants returned from the Exile (Ezra 2:31). [8] Yet another whose descendants returned from the Exile (Ezra 8:7). [9] Ancestor of some who married foreign wives during the Exile (Ezra 10:2).

Elasah ("God is doer"). [1] One who married a foreign wife (Ezra 10:22). [2] Ambassador of Zedekiah (Jer. 29:3). [3] See Eleasah.

Eldaah ("whom God calls"), a son of Midian (Gen. 25:4; 1 Chron. 1:33).

Eldad ("God is a friend"), one of two elders who received the prophetic powers of Moses (Num. 11:26–27).

Elead ("God is witness"), a descendant of Ephraim slain by invaders (1 Chron. 7:21).

Eleasah ("God is doer"). [1] A descendant of Judah (1 Chron. 2:39–40). [2] A descendant of King Saul (1 Chron. 8:37; 9:43). See Elasah.

Eleazar ("God is helper"). [1] Third son of Aaron and successor to the high priest's office (Exod.

6:23; Num. 3:32; 20:28). [2] One sanctified to keep the ark of the covenant (1 Sam. 7:1). [3] One of David's mighty men (2 Sam. 23:9; 1 Chron. 11:12). [4] A descendant of Merari who had no sons (1 Chron. 23:21–22; 24:28). [5] A priest who accompanied Ezra when he returned to Jerusalem (Ezra 8:33). [6] A priest who assisted at the dedication of the walls of Jerusalem (Neh. 12:42); possibly the same as [5]. [7] An ancestor of Jesus (Matt. 1:15).

Elhanan ("whom God gave; God is gracious"). [1] The warrior who killed Lahmi, the brother of Goliath (1 Chron. 20:5; 2 Sam. 21:19). [2] One of David's mighty men (2 Sam. 23:24; 1 Chron. 11:26).

Eli ("Jehovah is high"), high priest at Shiloh and judge of Israel. He is remembered for his lack of firmness (1 Sam. 1–4). *See also* Heli.

Eliab ("God is father"). [1] A prince of Zebulun (Num. 1:9; 2:7; 7:24, 29; 10:16). [2] Father of the wicked pair, Dathan and Abiram (Num. 16:1, 12; 26:8). [3] Son of Jesse and brother of David (1 Sam. 16:6); he is called Elihu in 1 Chronicles 27:18. [4] Ancestor of Samuel (1 Chron. 6:27); he is called Eliel in 1 Chronicles 6:34 and Elihu in 1 Samuel 1:1. [5] A warrior of David (1 Chron. 12:8–9, 14). [6] A

Levite musician in the time of David (1 Chron. 15:18, 20; 16:5). **[7]** *See* Eliel.

Eliada [Eliadah] ("God is knowing"). **[1]** A mighty man of Jehoshaphat (2 Chron. 17:17). **[2]** Father of Rezon (1 Kings 11:23). **[3]** *See* Beeliada.

Eliah. *See* Elijah.

Eliahba ("God hides"), one of David's thirty-man guard (2 Sam. 23:32; 1 Chron. 11:33).

Eliakim ("God is setting up"). **[1]** Successor of Shebna as master of Hezekiah's household (2 Kings 18:18, 26; Isa. 22:20). **[2]** Original name of King Jehoiakim (also see). **[3]** A priest in Nehemiah's time (Neh. 12:41). **[4]** An ancestor of Christ (Matt. 1:13).

Eliam ("my God is a kinsman; God is founder of the people"). **[1]** Father of Bathsheba (2 Sam. 11:3). By transposition of the two parts of the name he is called Ammiel (1 Chron. 3:5). **[2]** One of David's mighty men (2 Sam. 23:34).

Elias, Greek form of Elijah (also see).

Eliasaph ("God is gatherer"). **[1]** Head of the tribe of Gad (Num. 1:14; 2:14; 7:42, 47). **[2]** A prince of Gershon (Num. 3:24).

Eliashib ("God is requiter"). **[1]** A priest in the time of David (1 Chron. 24:12). **[2]** A descendant of David (1 Chron. 3:24). **[3]** The high

priest in Nehemiah's time (Neh. 3:1, 20–21).
[4], [5], [6] Three men who married foreign
wives during the Exile (Ezra 10:24, 27, 36).
[7] One who assisted Ezra in resolving the
matter of the foreign wives (Ezra 10:6; Neh.
12:10); possibly the same as [3].

Eliathah ("God is come"), one appointed for the
song service in the temple (1 Chron. 25:4, 27).

Elidad ("God is a friend"), a chief of the tribe of
Benjamin (Num. 34:21).

E

Eliel ("God, my God"). [1] Head of a family of
the tribe of Manasseh (1 Chron. 5:24). [2] A
descendant of Benjamin (1 Chron. 8:20).
[3] Another descendant of Benjamin in Chronicles (1 Chron. 8:22). [4] A captain of David's
army (1 Chron. 11:46). [5] One of David's
mighty men (1 Chron. 11:47). [6] One who
joined David at Ziklag (1 Chron. 12:11); perhaps the same as [4] or [5]. [7] A chief of Judah
(1 Chron. 15:9); perhaps [4]. [8] A chief Levite
whom David commissioned to bring the ark
of the covenant to the temple (1 Chron. 15:11).
[9] The Levite overseer of the dedicated things
of the temple under Hezekiah (2 Chron.
31:13). [10] *See* Eliab [4].

Elienai ("unto God are my eyes"), a chief of Benjamin (1 Chron. 8:20).

Eliezer ("God is help"). [1] Abraham's chief servant (Gen. 15:2). [2] The second son of Moses and Zipporah (Exod. 18:4; 1 Chron. 23:15, 17). [3] A descendant of Benjamin (1 Chron. 7:8). [4] A priest who assisted with bringing the ark of the covenant to the temple (1 Chron. 15:24). [5] A prince of Reuben in the time of David (1 Chron. 27:16). [6] A prophet who rebuked Jehoshaphat (2 Chron. 20:37). [7] A leader who induced others to return to Jerusalem (Ezra 8:16). [8], [9], [10] Three men who took foreign wives during the Exile (Ezra 10:18, 23, 31). [11] An ancestor of Christ (Luke 3:29).

Elihoenai ("to Jehovah are my eyes"), ancestor of some returned exiles (Ezra 8:4). *See also* Elioenai.

Elihoreph ("God of harvest grain"), a scribe of Solomon (1 Kings 4:3).

Elihu ("God himself"). [1] One who joined David at Ziklag (1 Chron. 12:20). [2] A porter at the tabernacle at the time of David (1 Chron. 26:7). [3] The youngest "friend" of Job (Job 32:2, 4–6). [4] *See* Eliab [3]. [5] *See* Eliab [4].

Elijah [Eliah; Elias] ("Jehovah is my God"). [1] A great prophet of God; he strenuously opposed idolatry and was caught up to heaven in a chariot of fire (1 Kings 17:1–2 Kings 2:11;

Elijah challenged the prophets of Baal to a contest on Mount Carmel (1 Kings 18:19–40).

Matt. 17:3). **[2]** A chief of the tribe of Benjamin (1 Chron. 8:27). **[3]** One who married a foreign wife during the Exile (Ezra 10:26). **[4]** Another who took a foreign wife during the Exile (Ezra 10:21).

Elika ("God is rejector"), one of David's warriors (2 Sam. 23:25).

Elimelech ("my God is King"), the husband of Naomi and father-in-law of Ruth. He died in Moab (Ruth 1:2–3; 2:1, 3; 4:3, 9).

Elioenai ("to Jehovah are my eyes"). [1] A descendant of David (1 Chron. 3:23–24). [2] A chief of the tribe of Simeon (1 Chron. 4:36). [3] A chief of Benjamin (1 Chron. 7:8). [4], [5] Two men who had married foreign wives during the Exile (Ezra 10:22, 27). [6] A priest in the days of Nehemiah (Neh. 12:41); possibly the same as [4]. [7] A doorkeeper of the temple (1 Chron. 26:3). [8] See Elihoenai.

Eliphal ("God is judge"), one of David's mighty men (1 Chron. 11:35).

Eliphalet [Eliphelet; Elpalet] ("God is escape"). [1] The last of David's thirteen sons (2 Sam. 5:16; 1 Chron. 3:8; 14:7). [2] Another of David's sons (1 Chron. 3:6); called Elpalet in 1 Chronicles 14:5. [3] One of David's mighty men (2 Sam. 23:34). [4] A descendant of Benjamin and Saul (1 Chron. 8:39). [5] One who came back to Jerusalem with Ezra (Ezra 8:13). [6] One who took a foreign wife during the Exile (Ezra 10:33).

Eliphaz ("God is dispenser"). [1] The leader of Job's three "friends" who confronted him (Job 2:11; 4:1; 15:1). [2] A son of Esau (Gen. 36:4, 10–12; 1 Chron. 1:35–36).

Elipheleh ("Jehovah is distinction"), a Levite set over the choral service of the temple when the ark of the covenant was returned (1 Chron. 15:18, 21).

Eliphelet. *See* Eliphalet.

Elisabeth ("God is swearer; oath of God"), the wife of Zacharias and mother of John the Baptist (Luke 1:5–57).

Eliseus, Greek form of Elisha (also see).

Elisha [Elishah; Eliseus] ("God is Savior"). [1] The disciple and successor of Elijah; he held the prophetic office for fifty-five years (1 Kings 19:16–17, 19; 2 Kings 2–6; Luke 4:27). [2] Eldest son of Javan and grandson of Noah (Gen. 10:4). Possibly the people of Cyprus or the inhabitants of Alasiya, a country near Cilicia. Others suggest it includes the Italians and Peloponnesians.

Elishama ("God is hearer"). [1] Grandfather of Joshua (Num. 1:10; 2:18; 1 Chron. 7:26). [2] A son of King David (2 Sam. 5:16; 1 Chron. 3:8). [3] Another son of David (1 Chron. 3:6); also called Elishua in 2 Samuel 5:15 and 1 Chronicles 14:5. [4] A descendant of Judah (1 Chron. 2:41). [5] One of the "royal seed" and grandfather of Gedaliah (2 Kings 25:25; Jer. 41:1). [6] A scribe or secretary of Jehoiakim (Jer. 36:12, 20, 21). [7] A priest sent by Jehoshaphat to teach the Law (2 Chron. 17:8).

Elishaphat ("God is judge"), one of the captains of hundreds commissioned by Jehoiada (2 Chron. 23:1).

Elisheba ("God is swearer; God is an oath"), the wife of Aaron and mother of Nadab, Abihu, Eleazar, and Ithamar (Exod. 6:23).

Elishua ("God is rich"). *See* Elishama [3].

Eliud ("God my praise"), an ancestor of Jesus (Matt. 1:14–15).

Elizaphan [Elzaphan] ("God is protector"). [1] A chief of the family of Kohath (Num. 3:30; 1 Chron. 15:8); he is also called Elzaphan (Exod. 6:22; Lev. 10:4). [2] A prince of the tribe of Zebulun (Num. 34:25).

Elizur ("God is a rock"), a chief of the tribe of Reuben who assisted Moses in taking the census (Num. 1:5; 2:10; 7:30, 35).

Elkanah [Elkonah] ("God is possessing"). [1] Grandson of Korah (Exod. 6:24; 1 Chron. 6:23). [2] Father of the prophet Samuel and a descendant of [1] (1 Sam. 1:1–23; 2:11, 20). [3] A descendant of Levi (1 Chron. 6:25, 36). [4] A descendant of Levi (1 Chron. 6:26, 35); perhaps the same as [3]. [5] A Levite ancestor of Berechiah (1 Chron. 9:16). [6] One who joined David at Ziklag (1 Chron. 12:6). [7] A doorkeeper of the ark of the covenant (1 Chron. 15:23); perhaps the same as [6]. **[8]** An officer of King Ahaz (2 Chron. 28:7).

Elmodam ("measure"), an ancestor of Christ (Luke 3:28).

Elnaam ("God is pleasant"), the father of two of David's warriors (1 Chron. 11:46).

Elnathan ("God is giving"). **[1]** Father of Nehushta, Jehoiakim's queen (2 Kings 24:8; Jer. 26:22). **[2]**, **[3]**, **[4]** Three Levites in the time of Ezra (Ezra 8:16).

Elon ("oak; strong"). **[1]** Father of a wife of Esau (Gen. 26:34; 36:2). **[2]** A son of Zebulun (Gen. 46:14; Num. 26:26). **[3]** A judge of Israel for ten years (Judg. 12:11–12).

Elpaal ("God is working"), a descendant of Benjamin (1 Chron. 8:11–12).

Elpalet. *See* Eliphalet [2].

Eluzai ("God is strong"), one who joined David at Ziklag (1 Chron. 12:5).

Elymas ("a sorcerer"), a false prophet who opposed Saul and Barnabas at Paphos (Acts 13:8); he was also called Bar-jesus (v. 6).

Elzabad ("God is endowing"). **[1]** One who joined David at Ziklag (1 Chron. 12:12). **[2]** A descendant of Levi (1 Chron. 26:7).

Elzaphan. *See* Elizaphan.

Emmor, Greek form of Hamor (also see).

Enan ("eyes; fountain"), father of a prince of Naphtali (Num. 1:15; 2:29).

Enoch [Henoch] ("teacher"). [1] The eldest son of Cain (Gen. 4:17–18). [2] A son of Jared and an ancestor of Christ (Gen. 5:18–19, 21; 1 Chron. 1:3; Luke 3:37; Heb. 11:5).

Enos [Enosh] ("mortal"), son of Seth and ancestor of Christ (Gen. 4:26; 5:6–11; 1 Chron. 1:1; Luke 3:38).

Enosh. *See* Enos.

Epaenetus ("praised"), a Christian at Rome to whom Paul sent greetings (Rom. 16:5).

Epaphras (shortened form of *Epaphroditus*— *"lovely"*), a Christian worker with Paul who served as missionary to Colossae (Col. 1:7; 4:12; Philem. 23).

Epaphroditus ("lovely"), a Philippian Christian who worked so strenuously that he lost his health (Phil. 2:25; 4:18).

Ephah ("obscurity"). [1] A concubine of Caleb (1 Chron. 2:46). [2] A descendant of Judah (1 Chron. 2:47). [3] A grandson of Abraham (Gen. 25:4; 1 Chron. 1:33).

Ephai ("obscuring"), one whose children were left in Judah after the Exile (Jer. 40:8).

Epher ("calf; young deer"). **[1]** A grandson of Abraham and son of Midian (Gen. 25:4; 1 Chron. 1:33). **[2]** One of the descendants of Judah (1 Chron. 4:17). **[3]** A chief of the tribe of Manasseh east of the Jordan River (1 Chron. 5:24).

Ephlal ("judging"), a descendant of Pharez through Jerahmeel (1 Chron. 2:37).

Ephod ("oracular"), father of a prince of the tribe of Manasseh (Num. 34:23).

Ephraim ("doubly fruitful"), the second son of Joseph by Asenath. Although Ephraim was the younger of the two sons of Joseph, he received the firstborn's blessing. He was an ancestor of one of the twelve tribes of Israel (Gen. 41:52; 46:20; 48; 50:23).

Ephratah [Ephrath] ("fertility"), the second wife of Caleb (1 Chron. 2:19, 50; 4:4).

Ephron ("strong"), a Hittite from whom Abraham bought a field with a cave, which became Sarah's burial place (Gen. 23:8, 10, 13–14; 49:30).

Er ("watcher"). **[1]** Eldest son of Judah, slain by God (Gen. 38:3, 6–7; 1 Chron. 2:3). **[2]** A son

E

of Shelah (1 Chron. 4:21). [3] An ancestor of Jesus (Luke 3:28).

Eran ("watcher; watchful"), the son of Ephraim's oldest son (Num. 26:36).

Erastus ("beloved"). [1] Christian sent with Timothy into Macedonia while Paul stayed in Asia (Acts 19:22). [2] An important person in Corinth sending greetings to Rome (Rom. 16:23). [3] One who remained at Corinth (2 Tim. 4:20). Perhaps some or all of the above are identical.

Eri ("watcher"), a son of Gad (Gen. 46:16; Num. 26:16).

Esaias, Greek form of Isaiah (also see).

Esarhaddon ("Ashur has given a brother"), the son of Sennacherib and a powerful king of Assyria (2 Kings 19:37; Ezra 4:2; Isa. 37:38).

Esau ("hairy"), eldest son of Isaac and twin brother of Jacob. He is the progenitor of the tribe of Edom (Gen. 25:25). He sold his birthright to Jacob (Gen. 25:26–34; 27; 36).

Esau's Wives: There are two lists of Esau's wives—Genesis 26:34; 28:9 list them in this fashion: [1] Judith, the daughter of Beeri the Hittite. [2] Bashemath, daughter of Elon the

Hittite, and [3] Mahalath, the daughter of Ishmael, Abraham's son. The other list in Genesis 36:2–3 runs thus: [1] Aholibamah, the daughter of Anah the daughter of Zibeon. [2] Adah, the daughter of Elon the Hittite, and [3] Bashemath, the daughter of Ishmael. Some scholars suppose we are dealing with six women, but this seems unlikely. In the ancient world, many women received new names at marriage and this fact would account for the different names. Thus, [1] Judith is Aholibamah, [2] Bashemath is Adah, and [3] Mahalath is Bashemath. As far as Judith is concerned, Beeri might be her father and Anah her mother; or perhaps Anah is another name of Beeri. Some even think Beeri ("man of the springs") is a nickname rather than a proper name.

Esh-baal ("man or servant of Baal"), altered to a curse. *See* Ishbosheth.

Eshban ("man of understanding"), son of Dishon (Gen. 36:26; 1 Chron. 1:41).

Eshcol ("a cluster of grapes"), the brother of Mamre and Aner who helped Abraham defeat Chedorlaomer (Gen. 14:13–24).

Eshek ("oppressor"), a descendant of King Saul (1 Chron. 8:39).

Eshtemoa ("bosom of women"), a Maacathite, a son of Ishbah (1 Chron. 4:17, 19).

Eshton ("rest"), a descendant of Judah through Caleb (1 Chron. 4:11–12).

Esli ("reserved"), an ancestor of Christ (Luke 3:25).

Esrom, Greek form of Hezron (also see).

Esther ("star; [the goddess] Ishtar"), the Persian name of Hadassah, who was chosen by Ahasu-

Esther risked her own life to ask the king to spare her people (Esther 4:8–5).

erus to be his queen. The book of Esther tells her story.

Etam ("wild beast's lair"), a name occurring in Judah's genealogy list (1 Chron. 4:3). It may be a place name.

Ethan ("ancient"). [1] A wise man in the days of Solomon (1 Kings 4:31; Ps. 89 title). [2] A descendant of Judah (1 Chron. 2:6, 8). He is possibly identical with [1]. [3] *See* Jeduthun. [4] A descendant of Levi (1 Chron. 6:42).

Ethbaal ("Baal's man; with Baal"), king of Sidon and father of Ahab's wife Jezebel (1 Kings 16:31).

Ethnan ("gift"), grandson of Ashur through Caleb, son of Hur (1 Chron. 4:7).

Ethni ("my gift"), one whom David set over the song service of the temple (1 Chron. 6:41).

Eubulus ("of good counsel"), one of the Roman Christians that remained loyal to Paul (2 Tim. 4:21).

Eunice ("conquering well"), the pious mother of Timothy (2 Tim. 1:5; see Acts 16:1).

Euodias ("fragrant"), a Christian woman at Philippi (Phil. 4:2). The KJV is mistaken at this point, giving a man's name for a woman's. The name should read *Euodia.*

Eutychus ("fortunate"), a young man at Troas whom Paul restored to life (Acts 20:6–12).

Eve ("life; life-giving"), the first woman, Adam's wife (Gen. 3:20; 4:1; 2 Chron. 11:3).

Eve tasted the forbidden fruit in spite of God's command (Gen. 3:1–6).

Evi ("desire"), one of the five kings of Midian slain by Israel (Num. 31:8; Josh. 13:21).

Evil-merodach (Babylonian, Arvil-Marduk— "the man of [the god] Marduk"), the king of

Babylon who released Jehoiachin from imprisonment. He succeeded his father, Nebuchadnezzar (2 Kings 25:27–30; Jer. 52:31).

Ezar. *See* Ezer [6].

Ezbai ("shining; beautiful"), the father of one of David's mighty men (1 Chron. 11:37).

Ezbon ("bright"). [1] A son of Gad (Gen. 46:16), called Ozni ("Jehovah hears") in Numbers 26:16. [2] A descendant of Benjamin (1 Chron. 7:7).

Ezekias, Greek form of Hezekiah (also see).

Ezekiel ("God strengthens"), a prophet of a priestly family carried captive to Babylon. He prophesied to the exiles in Mesopotamia by the river Chevar, and is the author of the book bearing his name (Ezek. 1:3; 24:24).

Ezer ("help"). [1] A son of Ephraim slain by the inhabitants of Gath (1 Chron. 7:21). [2] A priest in Nehemiah's time (Neh. 12:42). [3] A descendant of Judah through Caleb (1 Chron. 4:4); perhaps the same as Ezra [2]. [4] A valiant man who joined David at Ziklag (1 Chron. 12:9). [5] A Levite who assisted in repairing the wall of Jerusalem (Neh. 3:19). [6] ("union"), a son of Seir (Gen. 36:21, 27, 30; 1 Chron. 1:42); he is also called Ezar (1 Chron. 1:38). *See* Abi-ezer; Romamti-ezer.

Ezra ("help"). **[1]** Head of one of the courses of priests that returned from the Exile (Neh. 12:1). The full form of his name, *Azariah,* occurs in Nehemiah 10:2. **[2]** A descendant of Judah through Caleb (1 Chron. 4:17). *See* Ezer [3]. **[3]** A prominent scribe and priest descended from Hilkiah the high priest (Ezra 7:1–12; 10:1; Neh. 8:1–13). *See* Azariah.

Ezri ("my help"), one of David's superintendents of farm workers (1 Chron. 27:26).

In one of Ezekiel's visions, he found himself in a valley of dry bones (Ezek. 37:1–14, see page 95).

Ezra the scribe read God's Law to the returned Jews in Jerusalem (Neh. 8:1–18)

F

Felix ("happy"), Roman governor of Judea that presided over the trial of Paul at Caesarea (Acts 23:23–27; 24:22–27).

Festus ("swine-like"), successor of Felix to the governorship of Judea. He continued the trial of Paul begun under Felix (Acts 25; 26).

The Roman governor Felix heard Paul's defense against the charges of the Jewish leaders (Acts 24:1-27, see page 97).

Fortunatus ("fortunate"), a Corinthian Christian who cheered and comforted Paul at Ephesus (1 Cor. 16:17–18).

G

Gaal ("rejection"), a son of Ebed. He tried to lead a rebellion against Abimelech (Judg. 9:26–41).

Gabbai ("collector"), a chief of the tribe of Benjamin after the return from the Exile (Neh. 11:8).

Gad ("fortune"). [1] The seventh son of Jacob and an ancestor of one of the twelve tribes (Gen. 30:11; 49:19). [2] David's seer who frequently advised him (1 Sam. 22:5; 1 Chron. 21:9–19).

Gaddi ("my fortune"), one of those sent to spy out Canaan (Num. 13:11).

Gaddiel ("fortune of God"), one of the spies (Num. 13:10).

Gadi ("fortunate"), father of King Menahem of Israel (2 Kings 15:14, 17).

Gaham ("blackness"), a son of Nahor (Gen. 22:24).

Gahar ("prostration; concealment"), one whose family returned from captivity (Ezra 2:47; Neh. 7:49).

Gaius ("lord"). [1] One to whom John's third epistle is addressed (3 John 1). [2] A native of Macedonia and a companion of Paul (Acts 19:29). [3] A man of Derbe who accompanied Paul as far as Asia (Acts 20:4). [4] The host to Paul when he wrote to the Romans (Rom. 16:23). [5] A convert whom Paul baptized at Corinth (1 Cor. 1:14); some think he is identical with [4].

Galal ("great; rolling"). [1] A returned exile (1 Chron. 9:15). [2] A Levite who returned from the Exile (1 Chron. 9:16; Neh. 11:17).

Gallio, Roman proconsul of Achaia before whom Paul was tried in Corinth (Acts 18:12–17).

Gamaliel ("reward or recompense of God"). **[1]** A prince of the tribe of Manasseh (Num. 1:10; 2:20). **[2]** A great Jewish teacher of the Law. He persuaded his fellow Jews to let the apostles go free (Acts 5:33–40; 22:3).

Gamul ("weaned"), a chief priest (1 Chron. 24:17).

Gareb ("reviler; despiser"), one of David's mighty men (2 Sam. 23:38; 1 Chron. 11:40).

Gashmu. *See* Geshem.

Gatam ("burnt valley"), an Edomite chief, grandson of Esau (Gen. 36:11, 16; 1 Chron. 1:36).

Gazez ("shearer"). **[1]** A son of Caleb (1 Chron. 2:46). **[2]** A grandson of Caleb (1 Chron. 2:46).

Gazzam ("devourer; swaggerer"), one whose descendants returned (Ezra 2:48; Neh. 7:51).

Geber ("man; strong one"). **[1]** The father of one of Solomon's officers (1 Kings 4:13). **[2]** One of Solomon's commissaries (1 Kings 4:19).

Gedaliah ("Jehovah is great"). **[1]** Governor of Jerusalem after the Exile (2 Kings 25:22; Jer. 40:5–6). **[2]** A Levite musician (1 Chron. 25:3, 9). **[3]** A priest who had married a foreign wife during the Exile (Ezra 10:18). **[4]** A chief of Jerusalem that imprisoned Jeremiah (Jer.

20:1-6). **[5]** Grandfather of the prophet Zephaniah (Zeph. 1:1).

Gedeon, Greek form of Gideon (also see).

Gedor ("wall"). **[1]** An ancestor of Saul (1 Chron. 8:31). **[2]** A descendant of Judah (1 Chron. 4:4). **[3]** A descendant of Judah (1 Chron. 4:18).

Gehazi ("valley of vision; diminisher"), the dishonest servant of Elisha (2 Kings 4:12-37; 5:20-27; 8:4).

Gemalli ("camel owner"), father of Ammiel (Num. 13:12).

Gemariah ("Jehovah has accomplished"). **[1]** One who sought to stop Jehoiakim from burning Jeremiah's prophecies (Jer. 36:10-11, 12, 25). **[2]** One of Zedekiah's ambassadors to Babylon (Jer. 29:3).

Genubath ("theft"), a son of Hadad the Edomite (1 Kings 11:20).

Gera ("enmity" or "grain"). **[1]** A son of Benjamin (Gen. 46:21). **[2]** A son of Bela (1 Chron. 8:3, 5, 7). **[3]** Father of Ehud (Judg. 3:15). **[4]** Father or ancestor of Shimei (2 Sam. 16:5; 19:16, 18; 1 Kings 2:8). [Note: All of these may be identical.]

Gershom ("exile"). **[1]** Firstborn son of Moses and Zipporah (Exod. 2:22; 18:3). **[2]** See Gershon. **[3]** A descendant of Phinehas (Ezra 8:2).

[4] Father of Jonathan, a Levite during the time of the judges (Judg. 18:30).

Gershon [Gershom] ("exile"), an important priest, the eldest son of Levi (Gen. 46:11; Exod. 6:16; 1 Chron. 6:1). He is also called Gershom (1 Chron. 6:16–17, 20; 15:7).

Gesham ("firm"), a descendant of Caleb (1 Chron. 2:47).

Geshem [Gashmu] ("rainstorm; corporealness"), an Arabian opponent of Nehemiah (Neh. 2:19; 6:1–2).

Gether. [1] A descendant of Shem (1 Chron. 1:17). Possibly an unknown family of Arameans is meant. [2] The third of Aram's sons (Gen. 10:23).

Geuel ("salvation of God"), the spy sent out from Gad to bring back word about Canaan (Num. 13:15).

Gibbar ("high; mighty"), one who returned to Jerusalem with Zerubbabel (Ezra 2:20).

Gibea ("highlander"), a descendant of Caleb (1 Chron. 2:49).

Giddalti ("I have magnified"), a son of Heman in charge of one of the courses at the temple (1 Chron. 25:4).

Giddel ("very great"). [1] One whose descendants returned to Jerusalem with Zerubbabel

(Ezra 2:47; Neh. 7:49). [2] Head of a family of Solomon's servants (Ezra 2:56; Neh. 7:58).

Gideon [Gedeon] ("feller [i.e., great warrior]"), the great judge of Israel who delivered his people from Midian (Judg. 6—8); he was given the name Jerubbaal (also see).

Gideoni ("feller"), a descendant of Benjamin (Num. 1:11; 2:22).

Gilalai ("rolling; weighty"), one of a party of priests who played on David's instruments at the consecration of the Jerusalem walls under Ezra (Neh. 12:36).

Gilead ("strong; rocky"). [1] A son of Machir (Num. 26:29–30). [2] Father of Jephthah the judge (Judg. 11:1–2). [3] A descendant of Gad (1 Chron. 5:14).

Ginath ("protection"), father of Tibni (1 Kings 16:21–22).

Ginnetho [Ginnethon] ("great protection"), a prince or priest who sealed the new covenant with God after the Exile (Neh. 10:6; 12:4, 16).

Ginnethon. See Ginnetho.

Gispa ("listening; attentive"), an overseer of the Nethinim (Neh. 11:21).

Gog ("high; mountain"). [1] A descendant of Reuben (1 Chron. 5:4). [2] A prince of Rosh, Meshech, and Tubal (Ezek. 38:2; 39:1, 11). In

Revelation 20:8 Gog appears to have become a nation as is Magog, thus indicating the name is to be understood symbolically. *See also* Magog.

Goliath ("an exile or soothsayer"). [1] The Philistine giant who was slain by David (1 Sam. 17:4–54). [2] Another giant, possibly the son of [1] (2 Sam. 21:19).

Gomer. [1] Eldest son of Japheth (Gen. 10:2–3; 1 Chron. 1:5–6). Possibly a people inhabiting the north, probably including or identical with the Cimmerians of classical history. [2] The immoral wife of Hosea (Hos. 1:3; 3:1–4).

Guni ("protected"). [1] Son of Naphtali found in three lists (Gen. 46:24; Num. 26:48; 1 Chron. 7:13). [2] Father of Abdiel (1 Chron. 5:15).

H

Haahashtari ("the courier"), a son of Ashur listed in the descendants of Judah (1 Chron. 4:6).

Habaiah ("Jehovah is protection"), ancestor of a priestly family (Ezra 2:61; Neh. 7:63).

Habakkuk ("love's embrace"), a prophet during the reigns of Jehoiakim and Josiah (Hab. 1:1; 3:1).

Habaziniah ("Jehovah's light"), the grandfather of Jaazaniah, the founder of a Jewish sect (Jer. 35:3).

Hachaliah ("Jehovah is hidden"), the father of Nehemiah the governor of Israel (Neh. 1:1).

Hachmoni ("the wise"), father of Jehiel, the royal tutor (1 Chron. 27:32).

Hadad ("thunderer"). **[1]** One of the twelve sons of Ishmael and grandson of Abraham (1 Chron. 1:30). He is called Hadar, due to a copyist's mistake or a dialectal variant, in Genesis 25:15. **[2]** A king of Edom who fought Midian (Gen. 36:35–36; 1 Chron. 1:46). **[3]** The last of Edom's early kings (1 Chron. 1:50–51). Due to a copyist's mistake or dialectal variant, he is called Hadar in Genesis 36:39. **[4]** A member of the royal family of Edom who opposed Israel's rule of Edom (1 Kings 11:14–22, 25).

Hadadezer [Hadarezer] ("[the god] Hadad is my help"), the king of Zobah in Syria that warred against David and Joab (2 Sam. 8:3–12). His name is also written Hadarezer; perhaps this is a dialectal variant (2 Sam. 10:16; 1 Chron. 18:3–10).

Hadar. *See* Hadad [1], [3].

Hadarezer. *See* Hadadezer.

Hadassah ("myrtle"), the Hebrew name of Esther (also see).

Hadlai ("resting"), the father of Amasa, a chief man of the tribe of Ephraim (2 Chron. 28:12).

Hadoram ("Hadad is high"). [1] The son of Joktan, a descendant of Noah (Gen. 10:27; 1 Chron. 1:21). Possibly the name denotes an Arabian tribe. [2] The son of the king of Hamath; he bore presents to David (1 Chron. 18:10). He is called Joram in 2 Samuel 8:9–10, perhaps as a token to honor David's God (i.e., Joram means "Jehovah is high"). [3] The superintendent of forced labor under David, Solomon, and Rehoboam. He is variously called Adoniram ("my lord is exalted"), and Adoram, a contraction of the former (2 Sam. 20:24; 1 Kings 4:6; 12:18; 2 Chron. 10:18). *See also* Jehoram.

Hagab ("locust"), an ancestor of captives returning with Zerubbabel (Ezra 2:46). *See* Hagaba.

Hagaba [Hagabah] ("locust"), an ancestor of some of the captives returning with Zerubbabel (Ezra 2:45; Neh. 7:48). *See* Hagab.

Hagabah. *See* Hagaba.

Hagar [Agar] ("wandering"), an Egyptian servant of Sarah; she became the mother of Ishmael by Abraham (Gen. 16:1–16; 21:14–17).

Haggai ("festive"), the first of the prophets who prophesied after the Babylonian Captivity (Ezra 5:1; Hag. 1:1, 3, 12).

Haggeri ("wanderer"), the father of one of David's mighty men (1 Chron. 11:38).

Haggi ("festive"), the second son of Gad (Gen. 46:16; Num. 26:15).

Haggiah ("feast of Jehovah"), a descendant of Levi (1 Chron. 6:30).

Haggith ("festal"), the fifth wife of David and mother of Adonijah (2 Sam. 3:4; 1 Kings 1:5, 11).

Hakkatan ("the little one"), the father of Johanan, who returned with Ezra (Ezra 8:12).

Hakkoz ("the nimble"), a priest and chief of the seventh course of service in the sanctuary (1 Chron. 24:10). *See* Koz [1].

Hakupha ("incitement"), ancestor of a family returning from captivity (Ezra 2:51; Neh. 7:53).

Hallohesh [Halohesh] ("the whisperer; the slanderer"). [1] The father of one who repaired the wall (Neh. 3:12). [2] A man or family that sealed the new covenant with God after the Exile (Neh. 10:24); some identify him with [1].

Halohesh. *See* Hallohesh.

Ham ("hot"), the youngest son of Noah. Because of his wickedness, his son Canaan was cursed (Gen. 5:32; 9:22–27).

Haman ("celebrated Human [Humban]"), the prime minister of Ahasuerus who plotted against the Jews (Esther 3—9).

Hamath. *See* Hemath.

Hammedatha ("given by the moon"), the father of Haman (Esther 3:1).

Hammelech. This is not a proper name. It is a general title that means "the king" (Jer. 36:26; 38:6).

Hammoleketh ("the queen"), an ancestor of Gideon. It may be a proper name or title (1 Chron. 7:18).

Hamor [Emmor] ("ass"), the prince of Shechem whose son Shechem brought destruction on himself and his family (Gen. 33:19; 34:2–26).

Hamran. *See* Hemdan.

Hamuel ("wrath of God"), a descendant of Simeon (1 Chron. 4:26).

Hamul ("pity"), the younger son of Pharez (Gen. 46:12; 1 Chron. 2:5).

Hamutal ("kinsman of the dew"), one of King Josiah's wives (2 Kings 23:31; 24:18; Jer. 52:1).

Hanameel ("gift or grace of God"), a cousin of Jeremiah's who sold him a field (Jer. 32:6–9).

Hanan ("merciful"). [1] A descendant of Benjamin (1 Chron. 8:23). [2] A descendant of Benjamin through Saul (1 Chron. 8:38; 9:44). [3] One of David's heroes (1 Chron. 11:43). [4] A returned captive (Ezra 2:46; Neh. 7:49). [5] A Levite who assisted Ezra when reading the Law (Neh. 8:7). [6] A Levite who sealed the covenant with Nehemiah (Neh. 10:10; 13:13). Perhaps identical with [5]. [7] A chief or family who sealed the covenant with Nehemiah (Neh. 10:22). [8] A chief or family who also sealed the covenant (Neh. 10:26). [9] A temple officer whose sons had a chamber in the temple (Jer. 35:4). [Note: This name should not be confused with Baal-hanan.]

Hanani ("gracious"). [1] A musician and head of one of the courses of the temple services (1 Chron. 25:4, 25). [2] The father of the prophet Jehu; cast into prison by Asa (1 Kings 16:1, 7; 2 Chron. 16:7–10). [3] A priest who married a foreign wife (Ezra 10:20). [4] A brother of Nehemiah and a governor of Jerusalem under him (Neh. 1:2; 7:2). [5] A priest and musician who helped to purify the walls of Jerusalem (Neh. 12:36).

H

Hananiah ("Jehovah is gracious"). **[1]** A descendant of Benjamin (1 Chron. 8:24). **[2]** An officer of Uzziah (2 Chron. 26:11). **[3]** The father of a prince under Jehoiakim (Jer. 36:12). **[4]** The leader of the sixteenth division of David's musicians (1 Chron. 25:4, 23). **[5]** The grandfather of Irijah (Jer. 37:13). **[6]** A false prophet who opposed Jeremiah (Jer. 28). **[7]** One of Daniel's friends at Babylon (Dan. 1:7, 11, 19). *See also* Shadrach. **[8]** A son of Zerubbabel (1 Chron. 3:19, 21). **[9]** A Levite who married a foreign wife during the Exile (Ezra 10:28). **[10]** A druggist and priest who helped to rebuild the wall of Jerusalem (Neh. 3:8). **[11]** One who helped to rebuild the gate of Jerusalem (Neh. 3:30); perhaps the same as [10]. **[12]** A faithful Israelite placed in charge of Jerusalem (Neh. 7:2). **[13]** One who sealed the new covenant with God after the Exile (Neh. 10:23). **[14]** A priest present at the dedication of the walls of Jerusalem (Neh. 12:12, 41).

Haniel [Hanniel] ("God is gracious"). **[1]** A prince of the tribe of Manasseh (Num. 34:23). **[2]** A hero of Asher (1 Chron. 7:39).

Hannah ("grace"), a prophetess, the mother of Samuel (1 Sam. 1).

Hanniel. *See* Haniel.

Hanoch [Henoch] ("dedicated"). [1] A grandson of Abraham (Gen. 25:4), called Henoch in 1 Chronicles 1:33. [2] The eldest son of Reuben, and founder of the Hanochite clan (Gen. 46:9; 1 Chron. 5:3). [3] Enoch, the son of Jared (1 Chron. 1:3).

Hanun ("gracious"). [1] A king of Ammon who involved the Ammonites in a disastrous war with David (2 Sam. 10:1–6). [2] One who repaired the wall (Neh. 3:30). [3] One who repaired the valley gate of Jerusalem (Neh. 3:13).

Haran ("strong; enlightened"). [1] A brother of Abraham who died before his father (Gen. 11:26–31). [2] A descendant of Levi (1 Chron. 23:9). [3] A son of Caleb (1 Chron. 2:46).

Harbona [Harbonah] ("ass-driver"), a chamberlain under Ahasuerus (Esther 1:10; 7:9).

Hareph ("early born"), a son of Caleb (1 Chron. 2:51), not to be confused with Hariph (also see).

Harhaiah ("Jehovah is protecting"), father of Uzziel, a builder of the wall of Jerusalem (Neh. 3:8).

Harhas [Hasrah] ("glitter"), grandfather of Shallum, the husband of the prophetess Huldah (2 Kings 22:14). Another form of the name is Hasrah (2 Chron. 34:22).

Harhur ("nobility; distinction"), ancestor of returned captives (Neh. 7:53; Ezra 2:51).

Harim ("snub-nosed"). **[1]** A priest in charge of the third division of temple duties (1 Chron. 24:8; Ezra 2:39; 10:21; Neh. 3:11). **[2]** An ancestor of some returning from captivity (Ezra 2:32; Neh. 7:35). **[3]** One whose descendants took foreign wives during the Exile (Ezra 10:31). **[4]** One who sealed the new covenant with God after the Exile (Neh. 10:5). **[5]** A family that sealed the new covenant with God after the Exile (Neh. 10:27). **[6]** An ancestor of a family, perhaps [4] (Neh. 12:15). [Note: Many of those named Harim may be identical; there are many uncertainties.]

Hariph ("early born"). **[1]** An ancestor of returning captives (Neh. 7:24). **[2]** Head of a family who sealed the new covenant with God after the Exile (Neh. 10:19). He is called Jorah in Ezra 2:18.

Harnepher ("panting"), a descendant of Asher (1 Chron. 7:36).

Haroeh ("the seer"), a descendant of Judah (1 Chron. 2:52); perhaps Reaiah (1 Chron. 4:2).

Harsha ("artificer"), an ancestor of returning captives (Ezra 2:52; Neh. 7:54).

Harum ("elevated"), a descendant of Judah (1 Chron. 4:8).

Harumaph ("slit-nosed"), father of Jedaiah the wall-builder (Neh. 3:10).

Haruz ("industrious"), mother of King Amon (2 Kings 21:19).

Hasadiah ("Jehovah is kind"), a descendant of Jehoiakim (1 Chron. 3:20).

Hasenuah ("the violated"), a descendant of Benjamin (1 Chron. 9:7). The original name was probably Senuah, to which the Hebrew definite article (Ha-) is prefixed. *See also* Se-nuah.

Hashabiah ("Jehovah is associated"). [1] A descendant of Levi (1 Chron. 6:45). [2] Another descendant of Levi (1 Chron. 9:14). [3] A son of Jeduthun (1 Chron. 25:3). [4] A descendant of Kohath (1 Chron. 26:30). [5] A son of Kemuel who was a prince of the Levites (1 Chron. 27:17). [6] A chief of a Levite clan (2 Chron. 35:9). [7] A Levite who returned with Ezra from Babylon (Ezra 8:19). [8] A chief of the family of Kohath (Ezra 8:24). [9] One who repaired the wall of Jerusalem (Neh. 3:17). [10] One who sealed the covenant with Nehemiah (Neh. 10:11). [11] A Levite in charge of certain temple functions (Neh. 11:15). [12] An attendant of the temple (Neh. 11:22). [13] A priest in the days of Jeshua (Neh. 12:21). [14] A chief Levite (Neh. 12:24). [Note: It is

H

quite possible that [9], [12], and [14] refer to the same person.]

Hashabnah ("Jehovah is a friend"), one who sealed the new covenant with God after the Exile (Neh. 10:25).

Hashabniah ("Jehovah is a friend"). [1] Father of Hattush who helped to rebuild the wall of Jerusalem (Neh. 3:10). [2] A Levite who officiated at the fast under Ezra and Nehemiah when the covenant was sealed (Neh. 9:5).

Hashbadana ("judge"), an assistant to Ezra at the reading of the Law (Neh. 8:4).

Hashem ("shining"), father of several of David's guards (1 Chron. 11:34).

Hashub [Hasshub] ("associate"). [1] A Levite chief (1 Chron. 9:14; Neh. 11:15). [2] A builder of the wall of Jerusalem (Neh. 3:11). [3] One of the signers of the new covenant with God after the Exile (Neh. 10:23). [4] One who repaired the wall of Jerusalem (Neh. 3:23).

Hashubah ("association"), a descendant of Jehoiakim (1 Chron. 3:20).

Hashum ("shining"). [1] One whose descendants returned from the Babylonian Captivity (Ezra 2:19; 10:33; Neh. 7:22). [2] One who sealed the covenant (Neh. 8:4; 10:18).

Hashupha [Hasupha] ("stripped"), an ancestor of returning captives (Ezra 2:43; Neh. 7:46).

Hasrah. *See* Harhas.

Hassenaah ("the thorn hedge"), an ancestor of those who rebuilt the Fish Gate at Jerusalem (Neh. 3:3). The name is probably identical with the Senaah of Ezra 2:35 and Nehemiah 7:38, which most English translators have understood to have the Hebrew definite article (Ha-) prefixed.

Hasshub. *See* Hashub.

Hasupha. *See* Hashupha.

Hatach, a chamberlain of Ahasuerus (Esther 4:5–10).

Hathath ("terror"), son of Othniel (1 Chron. 4:13).

Hatipha ("taken; captive"), an ancestor of returning captives (Ezra 2:54; Neh. 7:56).

Hatita ("exploration"), a temple gatekeeper or porter whose descendants returned from the Babylonian Captivity (Ezra 2:42; Neh. 7:45).

Hattil ("decaying"), an ancestor of some who returned from the Babylonian Captivity (Ezra 2:57; Neh. 7:59).

Hattush ("contender"). **[1]** Descendant of the kings of Judah, perhaps of Shechaniah

H

(1 Chron. 3:22). [2] A descendant of David who returned from the Exile with Ezra (Ezra 8:2). [3] A priest who returned from the Exile with Zerubbabel (Neh. 12:2). [4] One who helped to rebuild the wall of Jerusalem (Neh. 3:10). [5] A priest who signed the covenant (Neh. 10:1, 4). [Note: entries [1], [2], [3], and [5] may refer to the same person.]

Havilah (perhaps "sandy"). [1] Son of Cush (Gen. 10:7; 1 Chron. 1:9). Possibly an unknown tribe is intended. [2] A descendant of Shem in two genealogies (Gen. 10:29; 1 Chron. 1:23). Possibly a tribe of Arabians who inhabited central or south Arabia is meant.

Hazael ("God sees"), the murderer of Benhadad II who usurped the throne of Syria (1 Kings 19:15, 17; 2 Kings 8:8–29).

Hazaiah ("Jehovah is seeing"), a descendant of Judah (Neh. 11:5).

Hazar-maveth ("court of death"), the third son of Joktan (Gen. 10:26; 1 Chron. 1:20). Possibly the name refers to a people who dwelt in the peninsula of Arabia.

Hazelelponi ("protection of the face of"), a daughter of Etam in the genealogy of Judah (1 Chron. 4:3).

Haziel ("God is seeing"), a descendant of Levi in the time of David (1 Chron. 23:9).

Hazo ("vision; seer"), a son of Nahor and nephew of Abraham (Gen. 22:22).

Heber (properly Eber—"the other side; across"). [1] Head of a family of Gad (1 Chron. 5:13). [2] A descendant of Benjamin (1 Chron. 8:22). See Eber.

Heber ("companion"). [1] A descendant of Asher (Gen. 46:17; 1 Chron. 7:31–32). [2] The husband of Jael, who killed Sisera (Judg. 4:11, 17, 21; 5:24). [3] Head of a clan of Judah (1 Chron. 4:18). [4] A descendant of Benjamin (1 Chron. 8:17). [5] Used in Luke 3:35 to refer to Eber [1].

Hebron ("ford; company"). [1] A son of Kohath (Exod. 6:18; Num. 3:19; 1 Chron. 6:2, 18). [2] A descendant of Caleb (1 Chron. 2:42–43).

Hegai [Hege], a chamberlain of Ahasuerus (Esther 2:3, 8, 15).

Helah ("tenderness"), a wife of Asher (1 Chron. 4:5, 7).

Heldai ("enduring"). [1] A captain of the temple service (1 Chron. 27:15). [2] An Israelite who returned from the Babylonian Captivity and was given special honors (Zech. 6:10); he is called Helem in verse 14.

Heleb [Heled] ("fat"), one of David's mighty men (2 Sam. 23:29; 1 Chron. 11:30).

Heled. *See* Heleb.

Helek ("portion"), a descendant of Manasseh (Num. 26:30; Josh. 17:2).

Helem ("strength"). [1] A descendant of Asher (1 Chron. 7:35). [2] Another name for Heldai [2] (also see).

Helez ("vigor"). [1] One of David's mighty men (2 Sam. 23:26; 1 Chron. 11:27; 27:10). [2] A descendant of Judah (1 Chron. 2:39).

Heli ("high," perhaps a contracted form of "God is high." Heli is the Greek form of Eli.), the father of Joseph in Luke's genealogy (Luke 3:23).

Helkai ("Jehovah is my portion"), the head of a priestly family (Neh. 12:15).

Helon ("valorous"), the father of Eliab, the prince of Zebulun (Num. 1:9; 2:7; 7:24; 10:16).

Hemam. *See* Homam.

Heman ("faithful"). [1] A musician and seer appointed by David as a leader in the temple's vocal and instrumental music (1 Chron. 6:33; 15:17; 2 Chron. 5:12; 35:15). [2] A wise man with whom Solomon was compared (1 Kings 4:31; 1 Chron. 2:6). He composed a meditative Psalm (Ps. 88, title).

Hemath ("warmth"), father of the house of Rechab (1 Chron. 2:55); also called Hamath (Amos 6:14).

Hemdan ("pleasant"), a descendant of Seir (Gen. 36:26). The KJV wrongly rendered his name *Amram* in 1 Chronicles 1:41—the reading there is Hamran, possibly a copyist's mistake.

Hen ("favor"), a son of Zephaniah (Zech. 6:14); he is probably the same as *Josiah* in verse 10.

Henadad ("Hadad is gracious"), a head of a Levite family that helped to rebuild the temple (Ezra 3:9; Neh. 3:18, 24; 10:9).

Henoch. *See* Hanoch [1] and Enoch [2].

Hepher ("a digging; a well"). [1] The youngest son of Gilead and founder of the Hepherites (Num. 26:32; Josh. 17:2). [2] A man of Judah (1 Chron. 4:6). [3] One of David's heroes (1 Chron. 11:36).

Hephzi-bah ("my delight is in her"), the mother of King Manasseh (2 Kings 21:1).

Heresh ("work; silence"), head of a Levite family (1 Chron. 9:15).

Hermas ("Mercury; interpreter"), a Christian to whom Paul sent greetings (Rom. 16:14).

Hermes ("Mercury [the god]; interpreter"), a Greek Christian in Rome to whom Paul sent greetings (Rom. 16:14).

H

Hermogenes ("born of Hermes"), a Christian who deserted Paul at Rome or Ephesus (2 Tim. 1:15).

Herod ("heroic"). [1] Herod the Great, the sly king of Judea when Christ was born. In order to maintain power, he murdered the children of Bethlehem, thinking that he would be killing the Messiah (Matt. 2:1–22; Luke 1:5). [2] Herod Antipas, son of the former, was tetrarch of Galilee and Perea. He was the murderer of John the Baptist (Matt. 14:1–10; Luke 13:31–32; Luke 23:7–12). [3] Herod Philip, son of Herod the Great, was tetrarch of Iturea and Trachonitis (Luke 3:1). [4] Herod Philip, another son of Herod the Great, is the Philip whose wife Herod Antipas lured away (Matt. 14:3). [5] Herod Agrippa I, tetrarch of Galilee and eventual ruler of his grandfather's (i.e., Herod the Great's) old realm. He bitterly persecuted Christians (Acts 12:1–23). [6] Herod Agrippa II, son of Agrippa I and king of various domains, witnessed the preaching of Paul (Acts 25:13–26; 26:1–32).

Herodias ("heroic"), granddaughter of Herod the Great, wife of Antipas, and ultimate cause of John the Baptist's death (Matt. 14:3–9; Luke 3:19).

Herodion ("heroic"), a Jewish Christian to whom Paul sent greetings (Rom. 16:11).

Hesed ("kindness; [God has kept] faithfulness"), father of one of Solomon's officers (1 Kings 4:10); not to be confused with Jushab-hesed (also see).

Heth, a son of Canaan (Gen. 10:15; 1 Chron. 1:13). Possibly a reference to the Hittite people.

Hezeki ("Jehovah is strength"), a descendant of Benjamin (1 Chron. 8:17).

Hezekiah [Ezekias; Hizkijah] ("Jehovah is strength"). **[1]** One who returned from Babylon (Ezra 2:16; Neh. 7:21). He, or his representative, is called Hizkijah (a form of Hezekiah) in Nehemiah 10:17. **[2]** The twelfth king of Judah; an ancestor of Christ. He instituted religious reform and improved the overall safety and prosperity of the nation (2 Kings 18—20; 2 Chron. 29—32; Matt. 1:9–10). **[3]** A son of Neariah, a descendant of the royal family of Judah (1 Chron. 3:23).

Hezion ("vision"), the grandfather of Ben-hadad, king of Syria (1 Kings 15:18). Many scholars identify him with Rezon (also see).

Hezir ("returning home"). **[1]** A Levite in the time of David (1 Chron. 24:15). **[2]** A chief of

H

the people that sealed the new covenant with God after the Exile (Neh. 10:20).

Hezrai [Hezro] ("blooming; beautiful"), one of David's warriors (2 Sam. 23:35). He is also called Hezro (1 Chron. 11:37).

Hezro. *See* Hezrai.

Hezron [Esrom] ("blooming"). [1] A son of Perez and an ancestor of Christ (Gen. 46:12; 1 Chron. 2:5, 9, 18, 21, 24–25; Matt. 1:3; Luke 3:33). [2] A son of Reuben (Gen. 46:9; Exod. 6:14).

Hiddai [Hurai] ("mighty; chief"), one of David's mighty men (2 Sam. 23:30). He is called Hurai ("free; noble") in 1 Chronicles 11:32.

Hiel ("God is living"), a man who rebuilt Jericho (1 Kings 16:34) and sacrificed his sons, in fulfillment of Joshua's curse (Josh. 6:26).

Hilkiah ("Jehovah is protection; my portion"). [1] One who stood with Ezra at the reading of the Law (Neh. 8:4). [2] A Levite who kept the children of the temple officials (1 Chron. 6:45). [3] A gatekeeper of the tabernacle (1 Chron. 26:11). [4] Master of the household of King Hezekiah (2 Kings 18:18, 26; Isa. 22:20; 36:3). [5] A priest of Anathoth and father of Jeremiah (Jer. 1:1). [6] High priest and the discoverer of the Book of the Law in the days of Josiah (2 Kings 22:4, 8; 23:4). [7] The father of Gemariah (Jer. 29:3). [8] A chief of priests who returned from captivity (Neh. 12:7) and his later descendants (Neh. 12:12, 21).

Hillel ("praised greatly"), the father of Abdon, one of the judges (Judg. 12:13, 15).

Hinnom, an unknown person who had a son(s) after whom a valley near Jerusalem was named. Human sacrifices took place there in Jeremiah's day, and garbage was later incinerated in this defiled place (Josh. 15:8; 18:16; Neh. 11:30; Jer. 7:31–32).

Hirah ("distinction"), a friend of Judah (Gen. 38:1, 12).

Hiram [Huram] (abbreviated form of Ahiram, "My brother is the exalted"). [1] A king of Tyre who befriended David and Solomon (2 Sam. 5:11; 1 Kings 5; 9:11; 10:11). [2] The skillful worker in brass whom Solomon secured from King Hiram (1 Kings 7:13, 40, 45; 2 Chron. 4:11, 16). [3] A descendant of Benjamin (1 Chron. 8:5).

Hizkiah [Hizkijah] ("Jehovah is strength"). [1] An ancestor of the prophet Zephaniah (Zeph. 1:1). *See* Hezekiah [1].

Hobab ("beloved"), the father-in-law or brother-in-law of Moses (Num. 10:29; Judg. 4:11). The

H

phrase "father-in-law" in Judges 4:11 may possibly mean nothing more than "in-law," or perhaps Jethro was also named Hobab; but the identity is uncertain. *See also* Jethro.

Hod ("majesty"), one of the sons of Zophah (1 Chron. 7:37).

Hodaiah ("honorer of Jehovah"), a descendant of the royal line of Judah (1 Chron. 3:24); possibly an alternate spelling of Hodaviah (also see).

Hodaviah ("honorer of Jehovah"). [1] A chief of the tribe of Manasseh (1 Chron. 5:24). [2] A descendant of Benjamin (1 Chron. 9:7). [3] An ancestor of returning captives (Ezra 2:40). He is also called Hodevah ("Jehovah is honor") in Nehemiah 7:43. *See also* Hodaiah.

Hodesh ("new moon"), a wife of Shaharaim (1 Chron. 8:9).

Hodevah. *See* Hodaviah.

Hodiah [Hodijah] ("splendor [or honor] of Jehovah"). [1] A brother-in-law of Naham (1 Chron. 4:19). The KJV incorrectly identifies him as the "wife" of Naham. [2] One of the Levites who explained the Law (Neh. 8:7; 10:10, 13). [3] One who sealed the new covenant with God after the Exile (Neh. 10:18).

Hodijah. *See* Hodiah.

Hoglah ("partridge"), a daughter of Zelophehad (Num. 26:33; 27:1; Josh. 17:3).

Hoham ("whom Jehovah impels; Jehovah protects the multitude"), an Amorite king slain by Joshua (Josh. 10:1–27).

Homam [Hemam] ("raging"), a Horite descendant of Esau (1 Chron. 1:39). He is called Hemam in Genesis 36:22 (probably a copyist's error).

Hophni ("strong"), the unholy son of Eli slain at the battle of Aphek (1 Sam. 1:3; 2:22–24, 34).

Horam ("height"), a king of Gezer defeated by Joshua (Josh. 10:33).

Hori ("free; noble"). [1] A descendant of Esau (Gen. 36:22; 1 Chron. 1:39). [2] The father of one of the men sent to spy out the Promised Land (Num. 13:5).

Hosah ("refuge"), one of the first doorkeepers of the ark of the covenant (1 Chron. 16:38; 26:10–11, 16).

Hosea [Osee] ("help; i.e., Jehovah is help"), a prophet of Israel; he denounced the idolatries of Israel and Samaria (Hos. 1:1–2).

Hoshaiah ("whom Jehovah helps"). [1] The father of Jezaniah or Azariah (Jer. 42:1; 43:2). [2] A man who led half of the princes of Judah in procession at the dedication of the walls (Neh. 12:32).

Hoshama ("whom Jehovah heareth"), a son or descendant of Jeconiah or Jehoiakim (1 Chron. 3:18).

Hoshea [Hosea] ("Jehovah is help or salvation"). **[1]** A chief of the tribe of Ephraim in the days of David (1 Chron. 27:20). **[2]** The last king of Israel; he was imprisoned by Sargon of Assyria (2 Kings 15:30; 17:1, 4, 6; 18:1). **[3]** One who sealed the covenant with Nehemiah (Neh. 10:23). **[3]** The original name of Joshua (also see).

Hotham [Hothan] ("determination"). **[1]** A descendant of Asher (1 Chron. 7:32). **[2]** Father of two of David's best men (1 Chron. 11:44).

Hothan. *See* Hotham.

Hothir ("abundance"), son of Heman in charge of the twenty-first course of the tabernacle service (1 Chron. 25:4, 28).

Hul ("circle"), grandson of Shem (Gen. 10:23; 1 Chron. 1:17). Possibly an Aramean tribe is referred to; some have suggested the people of Hūlīa near Mount Masius.

Huldah ("weasel"), a prophetess in the days of King Josiah (2 Kings 22:14; 2 Chron. 34:22).

Hupham ("coast-inhabitant; protected"), the head of a family descendant from Benjamin (Num. 26:39). In Genesis 46:21 and 1 Chronicles 7:12, his name is listed as Huppim ("coast-people" or "protection").

Huppah ("protection"), a priest in the time of David who had charge of one of the courses of service in the sanctuary (1 Chron. 24:13).

Huppim. *See* Hupham.

Hur ("free; noble"). [1] One of the men who held up Moses' arms during the battle with Amalek (Exod. 17:10, 12; 24:14). [2] A son of Caleb (Exod. 31:2; 35:30; 38:22; 1 Chron. 2:19, 50; 4:1, 4). [3] A Midianite king slain by Israel (Num. 31:8; Josh. 13:21). [4] An officer of Solomon on Mount Ephraim (1 Kings 4:8). [5] The ruler of half of Jerusalem under Nehemiah (Neh. 3:9).

Hurai ("free; noble"). *See* Hiddai.

Huram. *See* Hiram.

Huri ("linen weaver"), a descendant of Gad (1 Chron. 5:14).

Hushah ("haste"), a descendant of Judah (1 Chron. 4:4).

Hushai ("quick"), a friend and counselor of David (2 Sam. 15:32, 37; 16:16–18; 17:5–15).

H

Husham ("hasting; alert"), a descendant of Esau who became king of Edom (Gen. 36:34–35; 1 Chron. 1:45–46).

Hushim ("hasting; hasters"). [1] A son of Dan (Gen. 46:23); in Numbers 26:42, his name is Shuham. [2] A descendant of Benjamin (1 Chron. 7:12). [3] One of the two wives of Shaharaim (1 Chron. 8:8, 11).

Huz. *See* Uz.

Hymenaeus ("nuptial"), an early Christian who fell into apostasy and error (1 Tim. 1:20; 2 Tim. 2:17).

——————— **I** ———————

Ibhar ("chooser; Jehovah chooses"), one of David's sons born at Jerusalem (2 Sam. 5:15; 1 Chron. 3:6).

Ibneiah [Ibnijah] ("Jehovah builds up"). [1] A descendant of Benjamin (1 Chron. 9:8). [2] A man of Benjamin whose descendants lived in Jerusalem (1 Chron. 9:8).

Ibnijah. *See* Ibneiah.

Ibri ("one who passes over; a Hebrew"), a descendant of Merari in the time of David (1 Chron. 24:27).

Ibzan ("famous; splendid"), a Bethlehemite who judged Israel for seven years (Judg. 12:8–10).

Ichabod ("inglorious"), son of Phinehas, born after his father's death and after the ark was taken (1 Sam. 4:19–22).

Idbash ("honey-sweet"), one of the sons of Abi-etam (1 Chron. 4:3).

Iddo ("honorable; happy"), the official of Casiphia who provided Levites for Ezra (Ezra 8:17).

Iddo ("beloved"). [1] Captain of the tribe of Manasseh in Gilead (1 Chron. 27:21). [2] A descendant of Gershon (1 Chron. 6:21); called Adaiah in 1 Chronicles 6:41.

Iddo ("timely"). [1] Father of Abinadab (1 Kings 4:14). [2] Grandfather of the prophet Zechariah (Ezra 5:1; Zech 1:7).

Iddo ("adorned"). [1] A prophet who wrote about the kings of Israel (2 Chron. 9:29; 2 Chron. 12:15). [2] A priest who returned to Jerusalem with Zerubbabel (Neh. 12:4); perhaps the same as [1].

Igal [Igeal] ("Jehovah redeems"). [1] One of the twelve spies sent to search out Canaan (Num. 13:7). [2] One of David's heroes (2 Sam. 23:36). [3] A descendant of the royal house of Judah (1 Chron. 3:22).

Igdaliah ("Jehovah is great"), ancestor of persons who had a "chamber" in the temple (Jer. 35:4).

Igeal. *See* Igal.

Ikkesh ("subtle" or "crooked"), father of Ira, one of David's mighty men (2 Sam. 23:26; 1 Chron. 11:28; 27:9).

Ilai ("exalted"). *See* Zalmon.

Imla [Imlah] ("fullness"), father of Micaiah (2 Chron. 18:7–8).

Imlah. *See* Imla.

Immer ("loquacious; prominent"). [1] A priest in the time of David (1 Chron. 24:14). [2] A priest of Jeremiah's time (Jer. 20:1). [3] The father of Zadok (Neh. 3:29). [4] A family of priests who gave their name to the sixteenth course of the temple service (1 Chron. 9:12; Ezra 2:37; Neh. 7:40).

Imna [Jimna; Jimnah; Imnah] ("lugging"). [1] A descendant of Asher (Gen. 46:17; 1 Chron. 7:35). [2] A son of Asher (Num. 26:44; 1 Chron. 7:30). [3] Father of Kore in Hezekiah's reign (2 Chron. 31:14).

Imnah. *See* Imna.

Imrah ("height of Jehovah" or "stubborn"), a descendant of Asher (1 Chron. 7:36).

Imri ("talkative; projecting"). [1] A descendant of Judah (1 Chron. 9:4). [2] Father of Zaccur, one of Nehemiah's assistants (Neh. 3:2).

Iphedeiah ("Jehovah redeems"), a descendant of Benjamin (1 Chron. 8:25).

Ir ("watcher; city"), a descendant of Benjamin (1 Chron. 7:12); possibly the same as Iri (v. 7). Not to be confused with Ir-nahash.

Ira ("watchful"). [1] A priest to David (2 Sam. 20:26). [2] One of David's thirty mighty men (1 Chron. 11:28; 2 Sam. 23:38) and a captain of the temple guard (1 Chron. 27:9). [3] Another of David's thirty (1 Chron. 11:40; 2 Sam. 23:26).

Irad ("fleet"), a descendant of Enoch (Gen. 4:18).

Iram ("citizen"), a duke of Edom (Gen. 36:43).

Iri ("watchful"), a descendant of Benjamin (1 Chron. 7:7); possibly the same as Ir (v. 12).

Irijah ("seen of Jehovah"), a captain of the gate who arrested Jeremiah (Jer. 37:13–14).

Ir-nahash ("serpent city"), a descendant of Judah (1 Chron. 4:12).

Iru ("watch"), a son of Caleb (1 Chron. 4:15).

Isaac ("laughter"), the son of Abraham and Sarah, born to them in their old age. He was the father of Jacob and Esau and an ancestor of Christ (Gen. 21–25; Matt. 1:2).

Isaiah ("salvation of Jehovah"). The prophet Isaiah lived 750 years before Christ, but his

In an overwhelming vision, God called Isaiah to be his prophet (Isa. 6:1–13).

predictions about the Messiah—a deliverer who would save Israel—read as though he was an eyewitness to Jesus: "He was wounded and crushed because of our sins. . . . He was condemned to death without a fair trial" (Isa. 53:5, 8).

Isaiah was an educated noble living in Jerusalem when, at age twenty, he saw a phenomenal vision. In this vision God called him to become a prophet who would deliver messages of warning and hope to the Jewish people—a ministry Isaiah performed for forty years. His style of delivery, preserved in the book of Isaiah, was dramatic and often symbolic. He even walked naked for three years to predict that the Egyptians would become slaves. This encouraged the Jews to trust in God rather than in an alliance with Egypt against Assyria.

During Isaiah's lifetime, Assyria crushed the northern Jewish nation of Israel. Isaiah warned his native Judah, in the south, that a similar fate awaited it. But he also offered hope, promising that God would one day send a messiah—promises the New Testament says were fulfilled in Jesus.

Iscah ("Jehovah is looking; who looks"), daughter of Haran, sister of Milcah, and niece of Abraham (Gen. 11:29).

Iscariot. *See* Juda(s) [8].

Ishbah ("praising; appeaser"), a descendant of Judah (1 Chron. 4:17).

Ishbak ("leaning; free"), son of Abraham and father of a northern Arabian tribe (Gen. 25:2; 1 Chron. 1:32).

Ishbi-benob ("dweller at Nob"), one of the sons of Rapha the Philistine; he attacked David but was killed by Abishai (2 Sam. 21:15–22).

Ishbosheth ("man of shame"), son and successor of King Saul. He reigned two years before being defeated by David (2 Sam. 2:8–15; 3:8, 14–15; 4:5–12). He also was known as Eshbaal (1 Chron. 8:33; 9:39).

Ishi ("my husband; salutary"). [1] A descendant of Pharez, son of Judah (1 Chron. 2:31). [2] A descendant of Judah (1 Chron. 4:20). [3] A descendant of Simeon (1 Chron. 4:42). [4] A chief of the tribe of Manasseh (1 Chron. 5:24).

Ishiah. *See* Isshiah.

Ishijah. *See* Isshiah.

Ishma ("high; desolate"), a brother of Jezreel and Idbash, all descendants of Caleb (1 Chron. 4:3).

Ishmael ("God hears"). [1] Son of Abraham and Hagar; his descendants are the Arabian nomads (Gen. 16:11–16; 17:18–26; 25:9–17; 28:9; 36:3). [2] The cunning son of Nethaniah and traitor of Israel (Jer. 40:8—41:18). [3] A descendant of Benjamin (1 Chron. 8:38). [4] Father of Zebadiah (2 Chron. 19:11). [5] A captain in the time of Jehoiada and Joash (2 Chron. 23:1). [6] A Levite who married a foreign wife during the Exile (Ezra 10:22).

Ishmaiah [Ismaiah] ("Jehovah hears"). [1] A chief of Zebulun in David's time (1 Chron. 27:19). [2] A chief of Gibeon who joined David at Ziklag (1 Chron. 12:4).

Ishmerai ("Jehovah is keeper; to guard"), a descendant of Benjamin (1 Chron. 8:18).

Ishod ("man of majesty"), a man of Manasseh (1 Chron. 7:18).

Ish-pan ("he will hide"), a chief man of Benjamin (1 Chron. 8:22).

Ishuah [Isuah] ("he will level; even"), second son of Asher (Gen. 46:17; 1 Chron. 7:30).

Ishui [Ishuai; Isui; Jesui] ("equal"). [1] Third son of Asher (Gen. 46:17; Num. 26:44; 1 Chron. 7:30). [2] A son of King Saul by Ahinoam (1 Sam. 14:49). Some believe he is identical with Ishbosheth.

Ismachiah ("Jehovah will sustain"), an overseer under King Hezekiah (2 Chron. 31:13).

Ismaiah. *See* Ishmaiah.

Ispah ("firm"), a descendant of Benjamin (1 Chron. 8:16).

Israel. *See* Jacob.

Issachar ("reward"). [1] Ninth son of Jacob and ancestor of one of the twelve tribes of Israel (Gen. 30:17–18; 49:14–15). [2] A tabernacle porter (1 Chron. 26:5).

Isshiah [Ishiah; Ishijah] ("Jehovah exists"). [1] One of David's chiefs (1 Chron. 7:3). [2] *See*

Jesiah [2]. [3] A man who took a foreign wife during the Exile (Ezra 10:31). [4] A descendant of Moses (1 Chron. 24:21). *See* Isaiah.

Isuah. *See* Ishuah.

Isui. *See* Ishui.

Ithai ("being"), one of David's thirty mighty men (1 Chron. 11:31). He is called Ittai in 2 Samuel 23:29.

Ithamar ("land; island of palms"), a son of Aaron (Exod. 6:23; 28:1); Eli was high priest of his line (1 Chron. 24:6).

Ithiel ("God is"), a man of the tribe of Benjamin (Neh. 11:7).

Ithiel and **Ucal** ("signs of God"; or verb meaning "to be weary"), the names of two wise men to whom Agur spoke his words. Some scholars believe these are not proper names, but two verbs. If so, the last part of Proverbs 30:1 would read: "The man said, I have wearied myself, O God, I have wearied myself, O God, and am consumed."

Ithmah ("purity"), a Moabite, one of David's guards (1 Chron. 11:46).

Ithra ("abundance"), the father of Amasa, Absalom's captain (2 Sam. 17:25). He was also known as Jether (1 Kings 2:5, 32).

Ithran ("excellent"). [1] A descendant of Seir (Gen. 36:26). [2] A son of Zophah of Asher (1 Chron. 7:37).

Ithream ("residue of the people"), a son of David probably by Eglah (2 Sam. 3:5).

Ittai ("timely"). [1] A Philistine friend and general of David (2 Sam. 15:11–22; 18:2, 4, 12). [2] *See* Ithai.

Izehar [Izhar] ("shining"), a Levite, the father of Korah (Exod. 6:18–21; Num. 3:19).

Izrahiah ("Jehovah shines"), a descendant of Issachar (1 Chron. 7:3).

Izri ("creator"), leader of the fourth musical course (1 Chron. 25:11); perhaps the same as Zeri (v. 3).

------------------------ **J** ------------------------

Jaakan [Jakan] ("intelligent"), a son of Ezer, son of Seir (Deut. 10:6; 1 Chron. 1:42). In Genesis 36:27, he is called Akan. Many scholars believe the reference in the Deuteronomy passage is to a city.

Jaakobah ("to Jacob"), a descendant of Simeon (1 Chron. 4:36).

Jaalah [Jaala] ("elevation"), a servant of Solomon whose descendants returned from the Exile (Ezra 2:56; Neh. 7:58).

J

Jaalam ("hidden"), a duke of Edom (Gen. 36:5, 14, 18; 1 Chron. 1:35).

Jaanai ("answerer"), a descendant of Gad (1 Chron. 5:12).

Jaare-oregim ("foresters"), father of Elhanan, slayer of Goliath the Gittite (2 Sam. 21:19). Some suggest this is a copyist's error for Jair (see 1 Chron. 20:5), the "oregim" ("weavers") being a mistaken repetition of the last word in the verse.

Jaasau ("maker"), one who married a foreign wife (Ezra 10:37).

Jaasiel [Jasiel] ("God is maker"). [1] One of David's mighty men (1 Chron. 11:47). [2] A cousin of Saul's (1 Chron. 27:21).

Jaazaniah ("Jehovah is hearing"). [1] A captain of the forces who joined Gedaliah (2 Kings 25:23). He is the Jezaniah ("Jehovah determines; Jehovah hears") of Jeremiah 40:8; 42:1, and possibly the Azariah of Jeremiah 43:2. [2] A chief of the tribe of Reuben, a son of a certain man named Jeremiah but not the prophet (Jer. 35:3). [3] One enticing the people to idolatry (Ezek. 8:11). [4] A wicked prince of Judah seen in Ezekiel's vision (Ezek. 11:1).

Jaaziah ("Jehovah is determining"), a descendant of Merari living in Solomon's day (1 Chron. 24:26–27).

Jaaziel ("God is determining"), a temple musician in David's time (1 Chron. 15:18). He is called Aziel in verse 20.

Jabal ("moving"), son of Lamech, a nomad (Gen. 4:20).

Jabesh ("dry place"), father of Shallum, who killed Zechariah and reigned in his place (2 Kings 15:10–14).

Jabez ("height"), head of a family of Judah (1 Chron. 4:9–10).

Jabin ("intelligent; observed"). [1] A king of Hazor defeated by Joshua (Josh. 11:1). [2] Another king of Hazor who oppressed Israel and was defeated by Deborah (Judg. 4).

Jachan ("afflicting"), a descendant of Gad (1 Chron. 5:13).

Jachin ("founding; he will establish"). [1] A son of Simeon (Gen. 46:10; Exod. 6:15; Num. 26:12). He is called Jarib in 1 Chronicles 4:24. [2] A priest in Jerusalem after the Babylonian Captivity (1 Chron. 9:10; Neh. 11:10). [3] Head of a family of Aaron (1 Chron. 24:17). *See* Jarib.

Jacob ("supplanter; following after"). [1] Son of Isaac, twin of Esau, and an ancestor of Christ. He bought Esau's birthright and became the father of the Jewish nation (Gen. 25—50;

Matt. 1:2). God changed his name from Jacob to Israel ("God strives"; Gen. 32:28; 35:10). **[2]** The father of Joseph, the husband of Mary (Matt. 1:15–16). *See also* Heli.

Jada ("knowing"), a descendant of Judah (1 Chron. 2:28, 32).

Jadau ("friend"), one who married a foreign wife (Ezra 10:43).

Jaddua ("very knowing; known"). **[1]** One who sealed the covenant (Neh. 10:21). **[2]** The last high priest mentioned in the Old Testament (Neh. 12:11, 22).

Jadon ("judging"), one who helped repair the wall (Neh. 3:7).

Jael ("a wild goat"), wife of Heber who killed Sisera (Judg. 4:17–22; 5:6, 24).

Jahath ("comfort; revival"). **[1]** A descendant of Judah (1 Chron. 4:2). **[2]**, **[3]**, **[4]**, **[5]** Four descendants of Levi (1 Chron. 6:30, 43; 23:10–11; 24:22). **[5]** An overseer of temple repair (2 Chron. 34:12).

Jahaziah ("Jehovah reveals"), one who assisted in recording those who had foreign wives (Ezra 10:15).

Jahaziel ("God reveals"). **[1]** One who joined David at Ziklag (1 Chron. 12:4). **[2]** A priest who helped bring the ark of the covenant into the temple (1 Chron. 16:6). **[3]** Son of Hebron (1 Chron. 23:19; 24:23). **[4]** A Levite who encouraged Jehoshaphat's army against the Moabites (2 Chron. 20:14). **[5]** A chief man whose son returned from Babylon (Ezra 8:5).

Jahdai ("Jehovah leads; leader; guide"), one of the family of Caleb the spy (1 Chron. 2:47).

Jahdiel ("union of God; God gives joy"), head of a family of Manasseh east of the Jordan (1 Chron. 5:24).

Jahdo ("union"), descendant of Gad (1 Chron. 5:14).

Jahleel ("God waits; wait for God"), a son of Zebulun (Gen. 46:14; Num. 26:26).

Jahmai ("Jehovah protects"), head of a clan of Issachar (1 Chron. 7:2).

Jahzeel [Jahziel] ("God apportions"), a son of Naphtali listed three times (Gen. 46:24; Num. 26:48; 1 Chron. 7:13).

Jahzerah ("Jehovah protects"), a priest of the family of Immer whose descendants dwelt in Jerusalem (1 Chron. 9:12). Perhaps another name for Ahasai (also see).

Jahziel. *See* Jahzeel.

Jair ("Jehovah enlightens"). **[1]** A descendant of Judah through his father and of Manasseh through his mother (Num. 32:41; Deut. 3:14;

J

1 Kings 4:13; 1 Chron. 2:22). **[2]** Judge of Israel for twenty-three years (Judg. 10:3–5). **[3]** The father of Mordecai, Esther's cousin (Esther 2:5). **[4]** *See* Jaare-oregim.

Jairus ("enlightened"), a ruler of a synagogue near Capernaum whose daughter Jesus raised from the dead (Luke 8:41).

Jakan. *See* Jaakan.

Jakeh ("hearkening"), the father of Agur, the wise man (Prov. 30:1).

Jakim ("a setter up"). **[1]** Descendant of Benjamin (1 Chron. 8:19). **[2]** Head of a family descended from Aaron (1 Chron. 24:12).

Jalon ("Jehovah abides"), a descendant of Caleb the spy (1 Chron. 4:17).

Jambres, one of the Egyptian magicians who opposed Moses (Exod. 7:9–13; 2 Tim. 3:8; see Exod. 8:7; 9:11).

James (Greek form of Jacob). **[1]** The son of Zebedee and brother of John called to be one of the Twelve. He was slain by Herod Agrippa I (Matt. 4:21; Mark 5:37; Luke 9:54; Acts 12:2). **[2]** The son of Alpheus, another of the twelve apostles. He is probably the same as James "the less," the son of Mary. By "the less" is meant his age or height in relation to James the son of Zebedee (Matt. 10:3; Mark 15:40;

Acts 1:13). **[3]** The brother of Jesus (Matt. 13:55). After Christ's resurrection, he became a believer (1 Cor. 15:7) and a leader of the church at Jerusalem (Acts 12:17; Gal. 1:19; 2:9). He wrote the Epistle of James (James 1:1). **[4]** Unknown person mentioned as "the brother of Judas." Most view this as an incorrect translation and would render ". . . Judas, the son of James" (Luke 6:16; Acts 1:13).

Jamin ("right hand; favor"). **[1]** A son of Simeon (Gen. 46:10; Exod. 6:15; Num. 26:12; 1 Chron. 4:24). **[2]** A descendant of Ram (1 Chron. 2:27). **[3]** A priest who explained the Law (Neh. 8:7).

Jamlech ("Jehovah rules"), a prince of Simeon (1 Chron. 4:34).

Janna, an ancestor of Christ (Luke 3:24).

Jannes ("he who seduces"), an Egyptian magician who opposed Moses (2 Tim. 3:8–9; see Exod. 7:9–13).

Japheth ("the extender; fair; enlarged"), second son of Noah, considered the father of the Indo-European races (Gen. 5:32; 6:10; 7:13; 9:18, 23, 27; 1 Chron. 1:4–5).

Japhia ("high"). **[1]** Amorite king of Lachish defeated by Joshua (Josh. 10:3). **[2]** A son of David (2 Sam. 5:15; 1 Chron. 3:7; 14:6).

J

Japhlet ("Jehovah causes to escape"), a descendant of Asher (1 Chron. 7:32–33).

Jarah ("unveiler; honey"), a son of Ahaz of the family of Saul (1 Chron. 9:42). He is called Jehoadah in 1 Chronicles 8:36.

Jareb ("contender; avenger"), a king of Assyria (Hos. 5:13; 10:6); surely a nickname.

Jared [Jered] ("descending"), a descendant of Seth and ancestor of Christ (Gen. 5:15–20; 1 Chron. 1:2; Luke 3:37).

Jaresiah ("Jehovah gives a couch"), a descendant of Benjamin (1 Chron. 8:27).

Jarha, an Egyptian servant who married his master's daughter (1 Chron. 2:34–35).

Jarib ("striving"). **[1]** A chief man under Ezra (Ezra 8:16). **[2]** A priest who took a foreign wife during the Exile (Ezra 10:18). **[3]** *See* Jachin [1].

Jaroah ("new moon"), a descendant of Gad (1 Chron. 5:14).

Jashen ("shining"), the father of some, or one, of David's mighty men (2 Sam. 23:32). But the text probably should read thus: ". . . Jashen, Jonathan the son of Shammah the Hararite." Thus, Jashen would be one of the mighty men, and Shage (1 Chron. 11:34) is the same as Shammah (2 Sam. 23:33). *See also* Hashem.

Jasher ("upright"), one who wrote a now lost book (Josh. 10:13; 2 Sam. 1:18).

Jashobeam ("the people return"). [1] One of David's mighty men (1 Chron. 11:11; 27:2). [2] One who joined David at Ziklag (1 Chron. 12:6). *See* Adino.

Jashub ("turning back"). [1] One who took a foreign wife (Ezra 10:29). *See* Jashubi-lehem. [2] *See* Job [2].

Jashubi-lehem ("turning back to Bethlehem"), a descendant of Judah (1 Chron. 4:22).

Jasiel. *See* Jaasiel.

Jason ("healing"). [1] Paul's host during his stay at Thessalonica (Acts 17:5–9). [2] A Jewish Christian kinsman of Paul who sent salutations to Rome (Rom. 16:21). Both are possibly identical.

Jathniel ("God is giving"), a gatekeeper of the tabernacle (1 Chron. 26:2).

Javan, fourth son of Japheth (Gen. 10:2, 4; 1 Chron. 1:5, 7). The name corresponds etymologically with Ionia and may denote the Greeks (see Isa. 66:19).

Jaziz ("shining"), David's chief shepherd (1 Chron. 27:31).

Jeaterai ("steadfast"), a descendant of Gershon (1 Chron. 6:21).

Jeberechiah ("Jehovah is blessing"), the father of the Zechariah whom Isaiah took as a witness (Isa. 8:2).

Jecamiah [Jekamiah] ("may Jehovah establish"). [1] A descendant of Judah (1 Chron. 2:41). [2] A son of King Jeconiah (Jehoiachin; 1 Chron. 3:18).

Jecholiah [Jecoliah] ("Jehovah is able"), mother of Uzziah (or Azariah), king of Judah (2 Kings 15:2; 2 Chron. 26:3).

Jechonias, Greek form of Jeconiah. *See* Jehoiachin.

Jecoliah. *See* Jecholiah.

Jeconiah. *See* Jehoiachin.

Jedaiah ("Jehovah is praise"). [1] A descendant of Simeon (1 Chron. 4:37). [2] One who helped repair the wall (Neh. 3:10).

Jedaiah ("Jehovah is knowing"). [1] A priest of Jerusalem (1 Chron. 9:10; 24:7; Ezra 2:36; Neh. 7:39). [2] A priest who returned with Zerubbabel (Neh. 11:10; 12:6, 19). [3] Another priest who came up with Zerubbabel (Neh. 12:7, 21). [4] One who brought gifts to the temple (Zech. 6:10, 14).

Jediael ("God knows"). [1] A son of Benjamin (1 Chron. 7:6, 10–11). Possibly the same as Ashbel (1 Chron. 8:1). [2] One of David's mighty men (1 Chron. 11:45). **[3]** One who joined David at Ziklag (1 Chron. 12:20). **[4]** A descendant of Korah, son of Meshele-miah (1 Chron. 26:2).

Jedidah ("beloved"), mother of King Josiah (2 Kings 22:1).

Jedidiah ("beloved of Jehovah"), the name God gave Solomon through Nathan (2 Sam. 12:25).

Jeduthun ("a choir of praise"). **[1]** One of the three chief musicians of the service of song (1 Chron. 9:16; 25:1–6; Neh. 11:17). He was also named Ethan (1 Chron. 6:44; 15:17, 19). **[2]** The father of Obed-edom (1 Chron. 16:38). Some believe him identical with [1].

Jeezer (contracted form of Abiezer, "father of help"), a descendant of Manasseh (Num. 26:30). Probably the same as the Abiezer of Joshua's time (Josh. 17:2; 1 Chron. 7:18).

Jehaleleel [Jehalelel] ("God is praised"). **[1]** A descendant of Judah through Caleb the spy (1 Chron. 4:16). **[2]** A descendant of Me-rari in the time of Hezekiah (2 Chron. 29:12).

Jehdeiah ("union of Jehovah"). **[1]** A descendant of Levi in David's time (1 Chron. 24:20). **[2]** An overseer of David (1 Chron. 27:30).

J

Jehezekel ("God is strong"), a priest with sanctuary duty (1 Chron. 24:16).

Jehiah ("Jehovah is living"), a Levite gatekeeper of the ark (1 Chron. 15:24). He was also called Jeiel (1 Chron. 15:18; 2 Chron. 20:14).

Jehiel ("God is living"). **[1]** A singer in the tabernacle in David's time (1 Chron. 15:18; 16:5). **[2]** A descendant of Gershon (1 Chron. 23:8; 29:8). **[3]** A companion of the sons of David (1 Chron. 27:32). **[4]** A son of Jehoshaphat (2 Chron. 21:2). **[5]** A son of Heman the singer (2 Chron. 29:14). **[6]** A Levite in charge of the dedicated things in the temple (2 Chron. 31:13). **[7]** A chief priest in Josiah's day (2 Chron. 35:8). **[8]** Father of one who returned from the Exile (Ezra 8:9). **[9]** Father of the one who first admitted taking a foreign wife during the Exile (Ezra 10:2). **[10]**, **[11]** Two who had taken foreign wives (Ezra 10:21, 26).

Jehieli, a Levite set over the treasures of the sanctuary in David's time (1 Chron. 26:21-22). *See* Jehiel.

Jehizkiah ("Jehovah is strong; Jehovah strengthens"), an opponent of those who would have made fellow Jews slaves (2 Chron. 28:12). *See* Hezekiah.

Jehoadah ("Jehovah unveils; Jehovah has numbered"). *See* Jarah.

Jehoaddan ("Jehovah gives delight"), mother of King Amaziah and wife of King Joash (2 Kings 14:2; 2 Chron. 25:1).

Jehoahaz ("Jehovah upholds"). [1] Son and successor of Jehu on the throne of Israel. His reign was one of disaster (2 Kings 10:35; 13:2–25). [2] The son of Josiah and ruler of Judah for three months before he was deposed by Pharaoh Necho (2 Kings 23:30–34; 2 Chron. 36:1–4). He was also called Shallum before becoming king (1 Chron. 3:15; Jer. 22:11). [3] *See* Ahaziah [2].

Jehoash [Joash] ("Jehovah has given; Jehovah supports"). [1] The ninth king of Judah. Until the time of Jehoiada the priest's death, Jehoash followed God; afterwards, he brought idolatry and disaster to his country (2 Kings 11:21—12:21). He is more frequently called by the shortened form of his name, Joash. [2] The twelfth king of Israel; he was successful in many military campaigns (2 Kings 13:9—14:16). He is most frequently called Joash, an abbreviated form of his name.

Jehohanan ("Jehovah is gracious"). [1] A gatekeeper of the tabernacle in David's time (1 Chron. 26:3). [2] A chief captain of Judah (2 Chron. 17:15). [3] Father of one who aided Jehoiada (2 Chron. 23:1). [4] One who married a foreign wife during the Exile (Ezra 10:28). [5] A priest who returned to Jerusalem with Zerubbabel (Neh. 12:13). [6] A singer at the purification of the wall of Jerusalem (Neh. 12:42). [7] Son of Tobiah the Ammonite (Neh. 6:17–18).

Jehoiachin ("Jehovah establishes"), ruler of Judah when it was captured by Nebuchadnezzar. He was an ancestor of Christ (2 Kings 24:8–16; 2 Chron. 36:9–10; Matt. 1:11–12). Jeconiah [Jechonias] ("Jehovah is able") is an altered form of his name (1 Chron. 3:16–17; Jer. 24:1) as is Coniah ("Jehovah is creating"; Jer. 22:24, 28; 37:1).

Jehoiada ("Jehovah knows"). [1] The father of one of David's officers (2 Sam. 8:18; 1 Kings 1:8, 26). [2] The chief priest of the temple for many years of the monarchy. He hid Joash from Athaliah for six years (2 Kings 11–12:9). [3] One who joined David at Ziklag (1 Chron. 12:27). [4] A counselor of David (1 Chron. 27:34). [5] One who helped to repair a gate of Jerusalem (Neh. 3:6). [6] A priest replaced by Zephaniah (Jer. 29:26). *See* Joiada.

Jehoiakim ("Jehovah sets up; Jehovah has established"), the name given to Eliakim by Pharaoh Necho when he made him king of

Judah. The name probably means that Necho claimed Jehovah had authorized him to put Eliakim on the throne (2 Kings 23:34—24:6). Not to be confused with Joiakim.

Jehoiarib ("Jehovah contends"). [1] Head of a family of Aaron (1 Chron. 24:7). [2] *See* Joiarib [3].

Jehonadab [Jonadab] ("Jehovah is liberal"). [1] Descendant of Rechab, who forbade his followers and descendants to drink wine and live in houses (Jer. 35:6–19; 2 Kings 10:15, 23). [2] The sly son of David's brother, Shimeah (2 Sam. 13:3, 5, 32, 35).

Jehonathan ("Jehovah gives"). [1] An overseer of David's storehouses (1 Chron. 27:25). [2] One sent by Jehoshaphat to teach the Law (2 Chron. 17:8). [3] A priest (Neh. 12:18). He is called Jonathan in Nehemiah 12:35.

Jehoram [Joram] ("Jehovah is high"). Joram is a shortened form of the name. [1] Son and successor of Jehoshaphat to the throne of Judah and an ancestor of Christ (2 Kings 8:16–24; Matt. 1:8). [2] The ninth king of Israel, slain by Jehu (2 Kings 1:17; 3:1–6; 9:24). [3] A priest commissioned to teach the people (2 Chron. 17:8).

Jehoshabeath [Jehosheba] ("Jehovah makes oath"), a daughter of Jehoram, king of Judah, who helped conceal Joash (2 Chron. 22:11). In 2 Kings 1:2, she is called Jehosheba.

Jehoshaphat [Josaphat] ("Jehovah is judge"). **[1]** The recorder of David (2 Sam. 8:16; 20:24; 1 Kings 4:3). **[2]** An officer of Solomon (1 Kings 4:17). **[3]** Father of Jehu, who conspired against Joram (2 Kings 9:2, 14). **[4]** A priest who helped to bring the ark of the covenant from Obed-edom (1 Chron. 15:24). **[5]** Faithful king of Judah and an ancestor of Christ (1 Kings 22:41–50; Matt. 1:8).

Jehosheba. *See* Jehoshabeath.

Jehoshua. *See* Joshua.

Jehozabad ("Jehovah endows"). **[1]** A servant who killed Jehoash (2 Kings 12:21; 2 Chron. 24:26). **[2]** A gatekeeper descended from Korah (1 Chron. 26:4). **[3]** A chief captain of Jehoshaphat (2 Chron. 17:18). Not to be confused with Jozabad.

Jehozadak. *See* Josedech.

Jehu ("Jehovah is he"). **[1]** The prophet who brought tidings of disaster to Baasha of Israel (1 Kings 16:1–12; 2 Chron. 19:2). **[2]** The tenth king of Israel (1 Kings 19:16–17; 2 Kings 9–10). His corrupt leadership weakened the nation. **[3]** A descendant of Hezron (1 Chron. 2:38). **[4]** A descendant of Simeon (1 Chron.

4:35). **[5]** One who joined David at Ziklag (1 Chron. 12:3).

Jehubbah ("hidden"), a descendant of Asher (1 Chron. 7:34).

Jehucal [Jucal] ("Jehovah is able"), a messenger of Zedekiah (Jer. 37:3; 38:1).

Jehudi ("a Jew"), a man who brought Baruch to the princes and read Jeremiah's prophecies to the king (Jer. 36:14, 21, 23).

Jehudijah ("the Jewess"), the wife of Ezra and descendant of Caleb (1 Chron. 4:18).

Jehush ("collector"), a man of the family of Saul (1 Chron. 8:39).

Jeiel [Jehiel] ("God snatches away"). **[1]** A chief of the tribe of Reuben (1 Chron. 5:7). **[2]** An ancestor of Saul (1 Chron. 9:35). **[3]** One of David's mighty men (1 Chron. 11:44). **[4]** A singer and gatekeeper of the tabernacle (1 Chron. 15:18, 21; 16:5). **[5]** A descendant of Asaph (2 Chron. 20:14). **[6]** A scribe or recorder of Uzziah (2 Chron. 26:11). **[7]** A Levite in Hezekiah's time (2 Chron. 29:13). **[8]** A chief Levite in the days of Josiah (2 Chron. 35:9). **[9]** One who returned to Jerusalem with Ezra (Ezra 8:13). **[10]** One who married a foreign wife during the Exile (Ezra 10:43).

J

Jekameam ("standing of the people"), a descendant of Levi (1 Chron. 23:19; 24:23).

Jekamiah. *See* Jecamiah.

Jekuthiel ("God is mighty"), a descendant of the spy Caleb (1 Chron. 4:18).

Jemima ("little dove"), first daughter of Job to be born after his restoration from affliction (Job 42:14).

Jemuel ("God is light"). *See* Nemuel.

Jephthae, Greek form of Jephthah (also see).

Jephthah [Jephthae] ("an opposer"), a judge of Israel who delivered his people from Ammon (Judg. 11—12:7).

Jephunneh ("appearing"). [1] A man of Judah and father of Caleb the spy (Num. 13:6; 14:6; Deut. 1:36). [2] Head of a family of the tribe of Asher (1 Chron. 7:38).

Jerah ("moon"), a son of Joktan (Gen. 10:26; 1 Chron. 1:20). Possibly an Arabian tribe is intended.

Jerahmeel ("God is merciful"). [1] A son of Hezron, grandson of Judah (1 Chron. 2:9, 25–27, 33, 42). [2] A son of Kish (1 Chron. 24:29). [3] An officer of Jehoiakim (Jer. 36:26).

Jered ("low; flowing"). [1] A son of Ezra, a descendant of Caleb (1 Chron. 4:18). [2] *See* Jared.

Jeremai ("Jehovah is high"), one who took a foreign wife during the Exile (Ezra 10:33).

Jeremiah [Jeremias; Jeremy] ("Jehovah is high"). **[1]** A dweller of Libnah whose daughter married King Josiah (2 Kings 23:31; Jer. 52:1). **[2]** Head of a family of the tribe of Manasseh (1 Chron. 5:24). **[3]** One who joined David at Ziklag (1 Chron. 12:4). **[4]** A man

For warning against the threat of Babylon, Jeremiah was imprisoned in a muddy cistern (Jer. 38:1-13).

J

of Gad who joined David at Ziklag (1 Chron. 12:10). **[5]** Another who joined David at Ziklag (1 Chron. 12:13). **[6]** A priest who sealed the new covenant with God after the Exile (Neh. 10:2; 12:1, 12). **[7]** A descendant of Jonadab (Jer. 35:3). **[8]** A prophet whose activity covered the reigns of the last five kings of Judah. He denounced the policies and idolatries of his nation (Jer. 1; 20; 26; 36).

Jeremias, Greek form of Jeremiah (also see).

Jeremoth ("elevation"). **[1]** A son of Beriah (1 Chron. 8:14). **[2]**, **[3]** Two who married foreign wives (Ezra 10:26–27). **[4]** A son of Mushi, descendant of Levi (1 Chron. 23:23). He is called Jerimoth in 1 Chronicles 24:30. **[5]** One appointed by David to the song service of the temple (1 Chron. 25:22). He is called Jerimoth in 1 Chronicles 25:4.

Jeriah [Jerijah] ("Jehovah is foundation"), a descendant of Hebron in the days of David (1 Chron. 23:19; 24:23; 26:31).

Jeribai ("Jehovah contends"), one of David's mighty men (1 Chron. 11:46).

Jeriel ("foundation of God"), a descendant of Issachar (1 Chron. 7:2).

Jerijah. *See* Jeriah.

Jerimoth ("elevation"). [1] A son of Bela (1 Chron. 7:7). [2] A son of Becher, son of Benjamin (1 Chron. 7:8). [3] One who joined David at Ziklag (1 Chron. 12:5). [4] A ruler of the tribe of Naphtali (1 Chron. 27:19). [5] A son of David (2 Chron. 11:18). [6] *See* Jeremoth [4], [5].

Jerioth ("tremulousness"), a wife or concubine of Caleb (1 Chron. 2:18).

Jeroboam ("enlarger; he pleads the people's cause"). [1] The first king of Israel after the division of the kingdom. He reigned for twenty-two years (1 Kings 11:26–40; 12:1–14:20). [2] The thirteenth king of Israel; his Israel was strong but overtly idolatrous (2 Kings 14:23–29).

Jeroham ("loved"). [1] A Levite, the grandfather of Samuel (1 Sam. 1:1; 1 Chron. 6:27). [2] A descendant of Benjamin (1 Chron. 9:8). [3] Head of a family of Benjamin (1 Chron. 8:27). [4] A priest whose son lived in Jerusalem after the Exile (1 Chron. 9:12; Neh. 11:12). [5] Father of two who joined David at Ziklag (1 Chron. 12:7). [6] Father of Azareel, prince of Dan (1 Chron. 27:22). [7] Father of one who helped Jehoiada to set Joash on the throne of Judah (2 Chron. 23:1).

J

Jerubbaal ("let Baal contend" or possibly "let Baal show himself great"), the name given to Gideon by his father (Judg. 6:32; 7:1; 8:29).

Jerubbesheth ("contender with the idol"), name given to Jerubbaal (Gideon) by those who wanted to avoid pronouncing Baal (2 Sam. 11:21).

Jerusha [Jerushah] ("possession"), the wife of King Uzziah (2 Kings 15:33; 2 Chron. 27:1).

Jesaiah [Jeshaiah] ("Jehovah is helper"). [1] A grandson of Zerubbabel (1 Chron. 3:21). [2] One appointed to the song service (1 Chron. 25:3, 15). [3] A grandson of Moses (1 Chron. 26:25). [4] One who returned from the Babylonian Captivity (Ezra 8:7). [3] A descendant of Merari who returned from Exile (Ezra 8:19). [6] One whose descendants dwelled in Jerusalem (Neh. 11:17).

Jesharelah. *See* Asarelah.

Jeshebeab ("seat of the father"), head of the fourteenth course of priests (1 Chron. 24:13).

Jesher ("rightness"), a son of Caleb (1 Chron. 2:18).

Jeshishai ("Jehovah is ancient; aged"), a descendant of Gad (1 Chron. 5:14).

Jeshohaiah ("humbled by Jehovah"), a descendant of Simeon (1 Chron. 4:36).

Jeshua [Jeshuah] ("Jehovah is deliverance").
[1] A priest of the sanctuary (1 Chron. 24:11;
Ezra 2:36; Neh. 7:39). [2] A Levite in charge
of various offerings to the temple (2 Chron.
31:15). [3] A priest who returned to Jerusalem
with Zerubbabel (Ezra 2:2; 3:2–9; 4:3; Neh.
7:7; 12:1–26). [4] Father of Jozabad the Levite
(Ezra 8:33). [5] One whose descendants returned from the Exile (Ezra 2:6; Neh. 7:11).
[6] Father of one who repaired the wall of Jerusalem (Neh. 3:19). [7] A Levite who explained
the Law to the people (Neh. 8:7; 9:4–5).
[8] One who sealed the new covenant with God
after the Exile (Ezra 2:40; Neh. 7:43; 10:9).
Some believe he is identical with [6]. [9] *See*
Joshua.

Jesiah ("Jehovah exists"). [1] One who joined
David at Ziklag (1 Chron. 12:6). [2] A descendant of Uzziel and a Levite (1 Chron.
23:20). He is called Isshiah in 1 Chronicles
24:25.

Jesimiel ("God sets"), a descendant of Simeon
(1 Chron. 4:36).

Jesse ("Jehovah exists; wealthy"), father of David and an ancestor of Christ (Ruth 4:17, 22;
1 Sam. 17:17; Matt. 1:5–6).

J

Jesui. *See* Ishui.

Many of Jesus' teachings are included in His Sermon on the Mount (Matt. 5:1—7:29).

Jesus (Greek form of Joshua). **[1]** A Christian who, with Paul, sent greetings to the Colossians (Col. 4:11); he was also called Justus. **[2]** *See* Joshua.

Jesus Christ (*Jesus*—"Jehovah is salvation," *Christ*—"the anointed one"), the son of the Virgin Mary who came to earth to fulfill the prophecies of the King who would die for the sins of His people. The account of His ministry is found in the Gospels of Matthew, Mark, Luke, and John. (*See also* page vii.)

Less than a week before His crucifixion, Jesus was welcomed into Jerusalem with palm branches and shouts of praise (Matt. 21:1–11).

Jether ("pre-eminent"). **[1]** The firstborn son of Gideon (Judg. 8:20). **[2]** A son of Jerahmeel (1 Chron. 2:32). **[3]** A descendant of Caleb the spy (1 Chron. 4:17). **[4]** A descendant of Asher (1 Chron. 7:38). **[5]** *See* Ithra.

Jetheth ("subjection"), a duke of Edom (Gen. 36:40; 1 Chron. 1:51).

Jethro ("pre-eminence"), the father-in-law of Moses. He advised Moses to delegate the administration of justice (Exod. 3:1; 4:18; 18:1–

J

12). He is called Reuel in Exodus 2:18. In Numbers 10:29, the KJV calls him Raguel; but the Hebrew text reads Reuel.

Jetur, a son of Ishmael (Gen. 25:15; 1 Chron. 1:31).

Jeuel ("snatching away"), a descendant of Judah (1 Chron. 9:6).

Jeush ("collector"). **[1]** A son of Esau (Gen. 36:5, 14, 18; 1 Chron. 1:35). **[2]** A descendant of Benjamin (1 Chron. 7:10). **[3]** A descendant of Gershon and the head of a clan (1 Chron. 23:10–11). **[4]** A son of Rehoboam (2 Chron. 11:19).

Jeuz ("counselor"), son of Shaharaim, a descendant of Benjamin (1 Chron. 8:10).

Jezaniah. *See* Jaazaniah [1].

Jezebel ("unexalted; unhusbanded"). **[1]** The wicked, idolatrous queen of Israel (1 Kings 16:31; 18:4—21:25; 2 Kings 9:7–37). **[2]** A false prophetess at Thyatira (Rev. 2:20). Possibly the name is symbolic and not the prophetess's real name.

Jezer ("formation"), the third son of Naphtali (Gen. 46:24; Num. 26:49; 1 Chron. 7:13).

Jeziah ("Jehovah unites"), one who took a foreign wife (Ezra 10:25).

Jeziel ("God unites"), man of valor who joined David at Ziklag (1 Chron. 12:3).

Jezliah ("Jehovah delivers"), a descendant of Benjamin (1 Chron. 8:18).

Jezoar, a descendant of Caleb, the son of Hur (1 Chron. 4:7).

Jezrahiah ("Jehovah is shining"), an overseer of the singers at the purification of the people (Neh. 12:42). *See* Izrahiah.

Jezreel ("God sows"). **[1]** A descendant of Etam (1 Chron. 4:3). **[2]** The symbolic name of a son of Hosea (Hos. 1:4).

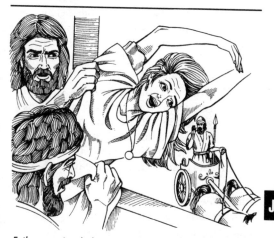

Evil queen Jezebel met a violent end (2 Kings 9:30–37).

J

Jibsam ("lovely scent"), a son of Tola (1 Chron. 7:2).

Jidlaph ("melting away"), son of Nahor and nephew of Abraham (Gen. 22:22).

Jimna. *See* Imna.

Joab ("Jehovah is father"). [1] A son of Zeruiah, David's sister. He was captain of David's army (2 Sam. 2:13–32; 3:23–31; 18; 1 Kings 2:22–23). [2] A descendant of Judah (1 Chron. 2:54). Some scholars believe a city of Judah is referred to here. The name would include the four words that follow in the KJV and be written: Atroth-beth-joab. [3] One of the tribe of Judah (1 Chron. 4:14). [4] An ancestor of returned captives (Ezra 2:6; 8:9; Neh. 7:11).

Joah ("Jehovah is brother"). [1] A son of Asaph, the recorder in the time of Hezekiah (2 Kings 18:18, 26; Isa. 36:3, 11, 22). [2] A descendant of Gershom (1 Chron. 6:21; 2 Chron. 29:12). [3] A porter in the tabernacle (1 Chron. 26:4). [4] A Levite commissioned to repair the Lord's house (2 Chron. 34:8).

Joahaz ("Jehovah helps"), father of Joah, Josiah's recorder (2 Chron. 34:8).

Joanna ("God-given"). [1] An ancestor of Christ (Luke 3:27). [2] The wife of Chuza, Herod's steward, who ministered to Christ and the apostles (Luke 8:3; 24:10).

Joash (abbreviated form of Jehoash). **[1]** A man of Judah (1 Chron. 4:22). **[2]** Father of Gideon the judge (Judg. 6:11–32). **[3]** A son of Ahab (1 Kings 22:26; 2 Chron. 18:25). **[4]** One who joined David at Ziklag (1 Chron. 12:3). **[5]** *See* Jehoash [1]. **[6]** *See* Jehoash [2].

Joash ("Jehovah has aided"). **[1]** A son of Becher, a descendant of Benjamin (1 Chron. 7:8). **[2]** The keeper of David's stores of oil (1 Chron. 27:28). *See* Jehoash.

Joatham, Greek form of Jotham (also see).

Job ("hated; persecuted"). **[1]** A pious man of Uz. His endurance in fierce trial resulted in marvelous blessing (Job 1–3; 42; Ezek. 14:14, 20). **[2]** The third son of Issachar (Gen. 46:13); he is also called Jashub (Num. 26:24; 1 Chron. 7:1).

Jobab. **[1]** A son of Joktan (Gen. 10:29; 1 Chron. 1:23). The name may possibly refer to an unknown Arabian tribe. **[2]** A king of Edom (Gen. 36:33–34; 1 Chron. 1:44–45). **[3]** A king of Canaan conquered by Joshua (Josh. 11:1). **[4]** A descendant of Benjamin (1 Chron. 8:9). **[5]** Another descendant of Benjamin (1 Chron. 8:18).

J

Jochebed ("Jehovah is honor or glory"), a descendant of Levi and mother of Moses (Exod. 6:20; Num. 26:59).

Joed ("Jehovah is witness"), a son of Pedaiah, a descendant of Benjamin (Neh. 11:7).

Joel ("Jehovah is God"). **[1]** The firstborn son of Samuel the prophet (1 Sam. 8:2; 1 Chron. 6:33; 15:17). *See also* Vashni. **[2]** A descendant of Simeon (1 Chron. 4:35). **[3]** The father of Shemaiah, a descendant of Reuben (1 Chron. 5:4, 8). **[4]** A chief of the tribe of Gad (1 Chron. 5:12). **[5]** An ancestor of the prophet Samuel

Three friends came to comfort Job after his many losses (Job 2:11–13, see page 165).

(1 Chron. 6:36). **[6]** A descendant of Tola (1 Chron. 7:3). **[7]** One of David's mighty men (1 Chron. 11:38). **[8]** A Levite in David's time (1 Chron. 15:7, 11; 23:8). **[9]** A keeper of the treasures of the Lord's house (1 Chron. 26:22). **[10]** A prince of Manasseh west of the Jordan (1 Chron. 27:20). **[11]** A Levite who aided in cleansing the temple (2 Chron. 29:12). **[12]** One who married a foreign wife during the Exile (Ezra 10:43). **[13]** An overseer of the descendants of Benjamin in Jerusalem (Neh. 11:9). **[14]** A prophet in the days of Uzziah (Joel 1:1; Acts 2:16).

Joelah ("God is snatching; may he avail!"), one who joined David at Ziklag (1 Chron. 12:7).

Joezer ("Jehovah is help"), a warrior who joined David at Ziklag (1 Chron. 12:6).

Jogli ("exiled"), a prince of Dan (Num. 34:22).

Joha ("Jehovah is living"). **[1]** A descendant of Benjamin (1 Chron. 8:16). **[2]** One of David's valiant men (1 Chron. 11:45).

Johanan ("Jehovah is gracious"). **[1]** A captain who allied with Gedaliah after the fall of Jerusalem (2 Kings 25:23; Jer. 40:8, 13). **[2]** Eldest son of Josiah, king of Judah (1 Chron. 3:15). **[3]** A son of Elionai (1 Chron. 3:24). **[4]** Father of a priest in Solomon's time (1 Chron. 6:9–10). **[5], [6]** Two valiant men who joined David at Ziklag (1 Chron. 12:4, 12). **[7]** One who opposed making slaves of Judean captives in Ahaz's time (2 Chron. 28:12). **[8]** A returned exile (Ezra 8:12). **[9]** A priest who beckoned the exiles to Jerusalem (Ezra 10:6). **[10]** A son of Tobiah the Ammonite (Neh. 6:18). **[11]** A priest in the days of Joiakim (Neh. 12:22–23).

John (a contraction of Jehohanan, "gift of God"). **[1]** The son of Zacharias and Elisabeth who came to prepare the way for the Messiah. He was called John the Baptist and was beheaded by Herod (Matt. 3; 11:7–18; 14:1–10; Luke 1:13–17). **[2]** A relative of the high priest Annas, who sat in judgment on Peter (Acts 4:6). **[3]** A missionary better known by his surname, Mark (also see). *See also* Jehohanan; Johanan.

[4] When Jesus hung on the cross, dying, He looked down at His mother standing beside one of the first and dearest of His twelve disciples: an unidentified man that most scholars agree was John. "She is now your mother," Jesus said, entrusting Mary to John's care (John 20:27).

John and his brother James were fishermen whom Jesus nicknamed "Thunderbolts,"

John the Baptist prepared the way for the coming of Jesus, the Messiah (Matt. 3:1-6).

perhaps because of their fiery personalities. Once they asked permission to punish some inhospitable Samaritans with fire from heaven— a request Jesus denied. Yet along with Peter, they were the closest friends of Jesus—the inner circle of disciples. They alone saw Jesus transfigured into His celestial form (Matt. 17:1-2) and witnessed His agonizing prayer just before His arrest (Mark 14:33).

Early Christian writers say that John

J

outlived the other disciples and settled in Ephesus (western Turkey), where he wrote five New Testament books: the Gospel of John, 1, 2, and 3 John, and Revelation.

Joiada ("Jehovah knows"), an ancestor of the priest Jeshua (Neh. 12:10–11, 22; 13:28). *See* Jehoiada.

Joiakim ("Jehovah sets up"), the son of Jeshua who returned from the Babylonian Captivity (Neh. 12:10, 12, 26). Not to be confused with Jehoiakim.

Joiarib ("Jehovah knows"). [1] One whom Ezra sent to persuade ministers to return to the land of Israel (Ezra 8:16). [2] An ancestor of a family living in Jerusalem (Neh. 11:5). [3] A priest who returned from captivity (Neh. 11:10; 12:6, 19). He is called Jehoiarib in 1 Chronicles 9:10.

Jokim ("Jehovah sets up"), a descendant of Judah (1 Chron. 4:22).

Jokshan ("fowler"), a son of Abraham by Keturah (Gen. 25:2–3; 1 Chron. 1:32).

Joktan, a son of Eber of Shem's line (Gen. 10:25–26; 1 Chron. 1:19–20, 23). Perhaps the reference is to an Arabian tribe from whom many other Arabian groups sprang.

Jonah learned the hard way that he could not escape God's will (Jonah 1:1—2:10).

Jona [Jonah; Jonas] ("a dove"). **[1]** The father of Simon Peter (John 1:42; 21:15–17). **[2]** A Hebrew prophet sent to preach to Nineveh in the days of Jeroboam II. He was the first Hebrew prophet sent to a heathen nation (2 Kings 14:25; Jon. 1:1, 3, 5, 17; 2:10; Matt. 12:39–41).

Jonadab. *See* Jehonadab.

Jonah. *See* Jona.

Jonan ("grace"), an ancestor of Christ (Luke 3:30).

J

Jonathan ("Jehovah is given"). [1] A priest of an idol shrine in the territory of Ephraim (Judg. 18:30). [2] A son of Abiathar the high priest (2 Sam. 15:27, 36; 17:17; 1 Kings 1:42). [3] A son of Shimea, David's brother (2 Sam. 21:21; 1 Chron. 20:7). [4] One of David's mighty men (2 Sam. 23:32; 1 Chron. 11:34). [5] A grandson of Onam (1 Chron. 2:32-33). [6] An uncle of David (1 Chron. 27:32). [7] Father of one who returned with Ezra (Ezra 8:6). [8] One involved with the foreign wife controversy (Ezra 10:15). [9] A descendant of Jeshua the high priest (Neh. 12:11). [10] A priest (Neh. 12:14). [11] A scribe in whose house Jeremiah was kept prisoner (Jer. 37:15, 20; 38:26). [12] One who joined Gedaliah after the fall of Jerusalem (Jer. 40:8). [13] A son of Saul and close friend of David (1 Sam. 14; 18:1-4; 31:2). [14] *See* Jehonathan [3].

Jorah ("harvest-born"). *See* Hariph [2].

Jorai ("taught of God"), a chief of the tribe of Gad (1 Chron. 5:13).

Joram (shortened form of Jehoram). [1] A descendant of Moses (1 Chron. 26:25). [2] *See* Hadoram [2]. [3] *See* Jehoram [1], [2].

Jorim (a shortened form of Jehoram), an ancestor of Christ (Luke 3:29).

Jorkoam ("spreading the people"), a son of Raham, or a city he founded (1 Chron. 2:44).

Josabad. *See* Jozabad.

Josaphat, Greek form of Jehoshaphat (also see).

Jose, an ancestor of Christ (Luke 3:29). Not to be confused with Joses.

Josedech ("Jehovah is righteous"), a priest and father of Jeshua the high priest (Hag. 1:1, 12, 14; Zech. 6:11). He is also called Jozadak (Ezra 3:2, 8; 5:2; 10:18; Neh. 12:26) and Jehozadak (1 Chron. 6:14–15).

Joseph ("increaser"). **[1]** The son of Jacob and Rachel. He was sold into slavery but became the prime minister of Egypt (Gen. 37; 39—50). **[2]** Father of one of the spies sent into Canaan (Num. 13:7). **[3]** A son of Asaph (1 Chron. 25:2, 9). **[4]** One who married a foreign wife during the Exile (Ezra 10:42). **[5]** A priest of the family of Shebaniah (Neh. 12:14). **[6]** The husband of Mary, mother of Jesus (Matt. 1:16–24; 2:13; Luke 1:27; 2:4). **[7]** A converted Jew of Arimathea in whose tomb Jesus was laid (Matt. 27:57, 59; Luke 15:43). **[8]** An ancestor of Christ (Luke 3:24). **[9]** Another ancestor of Christ (Luke 3:26). **[10]** Yet another ancestor of Christ (Luke 3:30). **[11]** A disciple considered to take the place of Judas Iscariot (Acts

A famine made Joseph a ruler in Egypt and led to a reunion with his brothers (Gen. 41:1—46:7).

1:23). He was also known as Barsabas and Justus.

Joses ("helped"). **[1]** One of the brothers of Christ (Matt. 13:55; Mark 6:3). **[2]** The son of Mary, the wife of Cleophas (Matt. 27:56; Mark 15:40, 47). Not to be confused with Jose.

Joshah ("Jehovah is a gift"), a descendant of Simeon (1 Chron. 4:34).

Joshaphat ("Jehovah judges"), one of David's valiant men (1 Chron. 11:43). Not to be confused with Jehoshaphat.

Joshaviah ("Jehovah is equality"), one of David's valiant men (1 Chron. 11:46).

Joshbekashah ("seated in hardness"), a son of Heman, David's song leader (1 Chron. 25:4, 24).

Joshua [Jehoshua; Jeshua] ("Jehovah is salvation"). **[1]** The successor of Moses; the general who led the conquest of the Promised Land (Exod. 17:9–14; 24:13; Deut. 31:1–23; 34:9). Moses changed his name from Hoshea ("Jehovah is help") to Joshua. Oshea is another form of Hoshea (Num. 13:8, 16; Deut. 32:44).

Joshua's first major victory was at the town of Jericho (Josh. 6:1–27).

J

Joshua and Jehoshua are forms of the same name. He is also called Jeshua (Neh. 8:17). [2] A native of Beth-shem in the days of Eli (1 Sam. 6:14, 18). [3] The governor of Jerusalem under Josiah (2 Kings 23:8). [4] High priest at the rebuilding of the temple (Hag. 1:1, 12, 14; 2:2, 4; Zech. 3:1, 3, 6).

Josiah [Josias] ("Jehovah supports"). [1] Godly king of Judah during whose reign the Book of the Law was found (1 Kings 13:2; 2 Kings 22:1–23:30). He was an ancestor of Christ (Matt. 1:10–11). [2] A son of Zephaniah living in Jerusalem (Zech. 6:10). *See also* Hen.

Josias, Greek form of Josiah (also see).

Josibiah ("Jehovah causes to dwell"), a descendant of Simeon (1 Chron. 4:35).

Josiphiah ("Jehovah abides"), father of one who returned from the Exile (Ezra 8:10).

Jotham [Joatham] ("Jehovah is perfect"). [1] The son of Gideon who managed to escape from Abimelech (Judg. 9:5, 7, 21, 57). [2] A son of Jahdai (1 Chron. 2:47). [3] The twelfth king of Judah and an ancestor of Christ (2 Kings 15:5–38; Isa. 1:1; 7:1; Matt. 1:9).

Jozabad [Josabad] ("Jehovah endows"). [1] One who joined David at Ziklag (1 Chron. 12:4). [2], [3] Two descendants of Manasseh who joined David at Ziklag (1 Chron. 12:20). **[4]** An overseer of the dedicated things of the temple under Hezekiah (2 Chron. 31:13). **[5]** A chief of the Levites in Josiah's time (2 Chron. 35:9). **[6]** One who helped weigh the sanctuary vessels (Ezra 8:33). **[7], [8]** Two who had married foreign wives (Ezra 10:22–23). **[9]** One who interpreted the Law (Neh. 8:7). **[10]** A chief Levite after the Exile (Neh. 11:16). Not to be confused with Jehozabad.

Jozachar ("Jehovah remembers"), the servant and murderer of King Joash of Judah (2 Kings 12:21). He is called Zabad in 2 Chronicles 24:26.

Jozadak. *See* Josedech.

Jubal ("playing; nomad"), son of Lamech; he was skilled with musical instruments (Gen. 4:21).

Jucal. *See* Jehucal.

Juda [Judah; Judas; Jude] ("praise"). **[1]** A son of Jacob by Leah and an ancestor of Christ. He acquired the birthright Reuben lost. His descendants became one of the twelve tribes of Israel (Gen. 29:35; 37:26–28; 43:3–10; Matt. 1:2–3; Luke 3:33). **[2]** An ancestor of one who helped to rebuild the temple (Ezra 3:9). **[3]** One who married a foreign wife during

J

the Exile (Ezra 10:23). [4] Second in authority over Jerusalem after the Exile (Neh. 11:9). [5] One who came up to Jerusalem with Zerubbabel (Neh. 12:8). [6] A prince of Judah (Neh. 12:34). [7] A priest and musician (Neh. 12:36). [8] One of the twelve apostles. He betrayed his Lord and hanged himself (Matt. 10:4; 26:14, 25, 47; 27:3; Luke 6:16; 22:3, 47–48). He was called Iscariot, apparently meaning "a man of Kerioth," a town 19 km. (12 mi.) from Hebron. [9] One of the brothers of Jesus (Matt. 13:55; Mark 6:3). He wrote the epistle bearing his name (Jude 1). [10] A Galilean who caused a rebellion against Rome (Acts 5:37). [11] One with whom Paul stayed at Damascus (Acts 9:11). [12] A prophet sent to Antioch with Silas (Acts 15:22, 27); he was surnamed Barsabas. [13] *See* Thaddeus. [14], [15] Two ancestors of Christ (Luke 3:26, 30).

Judith ("Jewess"), a wife of Esau (Gen. 26:34). *See* Esau's Wives.

Julia ("soft-haired"), a Christian woman to whom Paul sent greetings (Rom. 16:15).

Julius ("soft-haired"), a centurion who delivered Paul to Rome (Acts 27:1, 3).

Junia ("youth"), a man or woman (probably a man) to whom Paul sent greetings (Rom. 16:7).

Jushab-hesed ("kindness is returned"), a son of Zerubbabel (1 Chron. 3:20).

Justus ("just"). **[1]** A believer in Corinth with whom Paul lodged (Acts 18:7). **[2]** *See* Jesus [2]. **[3]** *See* Joseph [11].

K

Kadmiel ("God the primeval; before God"). **[1]** One whose descendants returned from the Exile (Ezra 2:40; Neh. 7:43). **[2]** One who helped rebuild the temple (Ezra 3:9). **[3]** Levite who led the devotions of the people (Neh. 9:4, 5; 10:9).

Kallai ("Jehovah is light; swift"), a priest who returned with Zerubbabel (Neh. 12:20).

Kareah [Careah] ("bald head"), the father of Johanan and Jonathan (Jer. 40:8). The KJV spells the name Careah in 2 Kings 25:23.

Kedar ("powerful; dark"), second son of Ishmael (Gen. 25:13; 1 Chron. 1:29).

Kedemah ("eastward"), a son of Ishmael, head of a clan (Gen. 25:13; 1 Chron. 1:31).

Keilah ("fortress"), a descendant of Caleb (1 Chron. 4:19).

Kelaiah ("Jehovah is light; swift for Jehovah"), one of the priests who married a foreign wife during the Exile (Ezra 10:23). Possibly the same as Kelita (also see).

Kelita ("littleness"). [1] A priest who explained the Law when it was read by Ezra (Neh. 8:7). [2] One of those who sealed the covenant (Neh. 10:10); possibly the same as [1]. One or both of these may be identical with each other and/or Kelaiah (also see).

Kemuel ("God stands; God's mound"). [1] A son of Nahor and a nephew of Abraham (Gen. 22:21). [2] A prince of Ephraim (Num. 34:24). [3] A Levite (1 Chron. 27:17).

Kenan. *See* Cainan.

Kenaz [Kenez] ("side; hunting"). [1] A duke of Edom (Gen. 36:42; 1 Chron. 1:53). [2] The fourth son of Eliphaz (Gen. 36:11, 15; 1 Chron. 1:36); perhaps the same as [1]. [3] Father of Othniel the judge (Josh. 15:17; Judg. 1:13). [4] A grandson of Caleb (1 Chron. 4:15).

Keren-Happuch ("horn of antimony"), the third daughter of Job to be born after his restoration to health (Job 42:14).

Keros ("fortress; crooked"), ancestor of a clan who returned from the Exile to the land of Israel (Ezra 2:44; Neh. 7:47).

Keturah ("incense"), a wife of Abraham (Gen. 25:1, 4; 1 Chron. 1:32).

Keziah ("cassia"), the second daughter of Job to be born after his restoration from affliction (Job 42:14).

Kish [Cis] ("bow; power"). **[1]** A son of Gibeon (1 Chron. 8:30; 9:36). **[2]** A Levite in David's time (1 Chron. 23:21; 24:29). **[3]** A descendant of Levi who assisted in the cleansing of the temple under Hezekiah (2 Chron. 29:12). **[4]** Great-grandfather of Mordecai (Esther 2:5). **[5]** The father of King Saul (1 Sam. 9:1, 3; 14:51; Acts 13:21).

Kishi ("snarer; fowler"), father of Ethan, also known as Kushaiah (1 Chron. 6:44; 15:17).

Kittim ("knotty"), a son of Javan (Gen. 10:4; 1 Chron. 1:7). Possibly the name refers to the inhabitants of Cyprus and the islands nearby.

Koa ("male camel"), a prince or people dwelling between Egypt and Syria; named as enemy of Jerusalem (Ezek. 23:23).

Kohath ("assembly"), the second son of Levi and beginning of a priestly clan (Gen. 46:11; Exod. 6:16, 18).

Kolaiah ("voice of Jehovah"). **[1]** A descendant of Benjamin (Neh. 11:7). **[2]** Father of the false prophet Ahab (Jer. 29:21).

K

Korah [Core] ("baldness"). **[1]** A son of Esau by Aholibamah (Gen. 36:5, 14, 18; 1 Chron. 1:35). **[2]** A son of Eliphaz (Gen. 36:16). **[3]** A son of Hebron (1 Chron. 2:43). **[4]** Grandson of Kohath and ancestor of some sacred musicians (1 Chron. 6:22; Ps. 42; 45—46 titles). He was one of the leaders of the rebellion against Moses and Aaron; the earth swallowed them up (Num. 16:1–35).

Kore ("one who proclaims; quail"). **[1]** A Levite in charge of the freewill offerings in Hezekiah's time (2 Chron. 31:14). **[2]** A son of Asaph whose descendants were gatekeepers at the tabernacle (1 Chron. 9:19; 26:1, 19).

Koz ("thorn"). **[1]** The ancestor of a priestly family returning from captivity (Ezra 2:61; Neh. 7:63). In the Hebrew text, the name appears as *Hakkoz;* the KJV considers the *Ha-* of the name to be the prefixed Hebrew definite article—here denoting a *certain* family. Others take all the word as a name (i.e., *Hakkoz*). If this be the case, the Hakkoz of 1 Chronicles 24:10 probably also refers to this person. **[2]** An ancestor of one who helped to repair the walls of Jerusalem (Neh. 3:4, 21).

Kushaiah ("bow of Jehovah"). *See* Kishi.

Laadah ("order; festival"), a descendant of Judah (1 Chron. 4:21).

Laadan ("festive-born; ordered"). [1] A descendant of Ephraim (1 Chron. 7:26). [2] A Levite from the family of Gershon (1 Chron. 23:7–9; 26:21). Also known as Libni (Exod. 6:17; Num. 3:18).

Laban ("white; glorious"), the brother of Rebekah and father of Rachel and Leah. Jacob served him for seven years in order to marry Rachel, but Laban tricked him by substituting Leah at the wedding festivals (Gen. 24—31).

Lael ("belonging to God"), a descendant of Gershon (Num. 3:24).

Lahad ("oppression; dark colored"), a descendant of Judah (1 Chron. 4:2).

Lahmi ("warrior"), brother of Goliath, the giant (1 Chron. 20:5).

Laish ("lion"), father of Phalti, who became the husband of Michal (1 Sam. 25:44; 2 Sam. 3:15).

Lamech ("strong youth; overthrower"). [1] Father of Noah and ancestor of Christ (Gen. 5:25–31; Luke 3:36). [2] Father of Jabal and Jubal; he is the first recorded polygamist (Gen. 4:18–26).

Lapidoth ("flames; torches"), the husband of Deborah, the prophetess (Judg. 4:4).

Lazarus was still wrapped in burial cloth when Jesus called him out of his tomb (John 11:1–44);

Lazarus (abridged form of Eleazar, "God has helped"). **[1]** The brother of Mary and Martha whom Jesus raised from the dead (John 11:1–12:17). **[2]** A believing beggar who was carried to Abraham's bosom (Luke 16:19–31).

Leah ("weary"), Jacob's wife through the deception of her father, Laban (Gen. 29–31).

Lebana [Lebanah] ("white"), chief of a family of returning exiles (Ezra 2:45; Neh. 7:48).

Lebanah. *See* Lebana.

Lebbaeus. *See* Thaddeus.

Lecah ("walking; addition"), a descendant of Judah (1 Chron. 4:21).

Lehabim ("flame, red"), a descendant of Mizraim (Gen. 10:13; 1 Chron. 1:11). Possibly a reference to a tribe of Egyptians.

Lemuel ("Godward; dedicated"), an unknown king often supposed to be Solomon or Hezekiah, whose words are recorded in Proverbs 31:1–9.

Letushim ("hammered"), a son of Dedan (Gen. 25:3).

Leummim ("nations"), a son of Dedan (Gen. 25:3).

Levi ("joined"). **[1]** The third son of Jacob who avenged Dinah's wrong (Gen. 34:25–31), and went to Egypt with his father (Gen. 39:34; Exod. 6:16). His descendants became the priests of Israel. **[2]** An ancestor of Christ (Luke 3:24). **[3]** An ancestor of Christ (Luke 3:29). **[4]** Another name of Matthew (also see).

Libni ("whiteness; distinguished"). **[1]** A son of Merari (1 Chron. 6:29). **[2]** *See* Laadan.

Likhi ("learned"), a descendant of Benjamin (1 Chron. 7:19).

Linus ("net"), a Roman friend of Paul (2 Tim. 4:21).

Lo-ammi ("not my people"), symbolic name of Hosea's son (Hos. 1:9).

Lois ("pleasing; better"), the pious grandmother of Timothy (2 Tim. 1:5).

Lo-ruhamah ("receiving no compassion"), a figurative name of Hosea's daughter, indicating God's rejection of Israel (Hos. 1:6).

Lot ("veiled"), Abraham's nephew that escaped from wicked Sodom (Gen. 13:1–14; Gen. 19).

Lotan ("hidden"), an Edomite duke (Gen. 36:20–29).

Lucas. *See* Luke.

Lucifer (Latin, "light-bearer"), an epithet for the king of Babylon (Isa. 14:12). Lucifer translates a Hebrew word meaning "light-bearer." The title came to be applied to Satan.

Lucius ("morning born; of light"). [1] A prophet or teacher from Cyrene ministering at Antioch (Acts 13:1). [2] A Jewish Christian who saluted the community at Rome (Rom. 16:21). Perhaps the same as [1].

Lud, a son of Shem (Gen. 10:22). Possibly the Lydians are intended.

Ludim, a son of Mizraim (Gen. 10:13). Possibly a reference to the inhabitants of an unknown country connected with the Egyptians.

Luke [Lucas] ("light-giving"), evangelist, physician, and author of the third Gospel and Acts (Col. 4:14; 2 Tim. 4:11; Philem. 24).

Lydia ("native of Lydia"), a woman convert of Thyatira (Acts 16:14–15).

Lysanias ("that drives away sorrow"), the tetrarch of Abilene (Luke 3:1).

Lysias. *See* Claudius Lysias.

M

Maachah [Maacah] ("oppression"). **[1]** The son of Nahor, Abraham's brother (Gen. 22:24). **[2]** One of David's wives and mother of Absalom (2 Sam. 3:3; 1 Chron. 3:2). **[3]** A king of Maachah (2 Sam. 10:6). Some translate "the king of Maacah." **[4]** Father of Achish, king of Gath (1 Kings 2:39). He is called Maoch in 1 Samuel 27:2. **[5]** The mother of Asa, king of Judah (1 Kings 15:10, 13; 2 Chron. 15:16). She is called Michaiah (2 Chron. 13:2). **[6]** Concubine of Caleb (1 Chron. 2:48). **[7]** Wife of Machir, son of Manasseh (1 Chron. 7:15–16). **[8]** Wife of Jehiel (1 Chron. 8:29; 9:35). **[9]** Father of one of David's warriors (1 Chron. 11:43). **[10]** Father of Shephatiah, ruler of Simeon (1 Chron. 27:16).

Maadai ("Jehovah is ornament"), one who married a foreign wife (Ezra 10:34; Neh. 12:5).

Maadiah ("Jehovah is ornament"), a priest who returned from the Babylonian Captivity (Neh. 12:5). He is called Moadiah in Nehemiah 12:17.

Maai ("Jehovah is compassionate"), a priest who helped to purify the people who returned from the Exile (Neh. 12:36).

Maaseiah ("Jehovah is a refuge"). [1] A Levite of the praise service (1 Chron. 15:18, 20). [2] A captain who helped to make Joash king (2 Chron. 23:1). [3] Officer of King Uzziah (2 Chron. 26:11). [4] A son of Ahaz, king of Judah (2 Chron. 28:7). [5] Governor of Jerusalem under Josiah's reign (2 Chron. 34:8). [6], [7], [8], [9] Four men who took foreign wives during the Exile (Ezra 10:18, 21–22, 30). [10] Father of Azariah, who repaired part of the wall of Jerusalem (Neh. 3:23). [11] A priest who stood with Ezra while he read the Law (Neh. 8:4). [12] A priest who explained the Law (Neh. 8:7); possibly the same as [11]. [13] One who sealed the new covenant with God after the Exile (Neh. 10:25). [14] A descendant of Pharez living in Jerusalem (Neh. 11:5). [15] One whose descendants lived in Jerusalem (Neh. 11:7). [16], [17] Two priests who took part in the purification of the wall of Jerusalem (Neh. 12:41–42). [18] A priest whose son was sent by King Zedekiah to inquire of the Lord (Jer. 21:1; 29:25). **[19]** Father of a false prophet (Jer. 29:21). **[20]** An officer of the temple (Jer. 35:4). **[21]** Grandfather of Baruch, Jeremiah's scribe (Jer. 32:12).

Maasiai ("work of Jehovah"), a descendant of Aaron (1 Chron. 9:12).

Maath ("small"), an ancestor of Christ (Luke 3:26).

Maaz ("counselor"), a son of Ram (1 Chron. 2:27).

Maaziah ("strength of Jehovah"). **[1]** Priest to whom certain sanctuary duties were charged (1 Chron. 24:18). **[2]** A priest who sealed the new covenant with God after the Exile (Neh. 10:8).

Machbanai ("thick"), warrior who joined David at Ziklag (1 Chron. 12:13).

Machbenah ("knob, lump"). **[1]** A descendant of Caleb (1 Chron. 2:49). **[2]** Possibly a place identical with Cabbon (also see).

Machi ("decrease"), father of one of the spies sent into Canaan (Num. 13:15).

Machir ("salesman; sold"). **[1]** A son of Manasseh (Gen. 50:23; Num. 26:29; Josh. 13:31). **[2]** A descendant of Manasseh living near Mahanaim (2 Sam. 9:4–5; 17:27).

Machnadebai ("liberal; gift of the noble one"), one who had married a foreign wife (Ezra 10:40).

Madai, son of Japheth (Gen. 10:2; 1 Chron. 1:5). The name possibly refers to the inhabitants of Media.

Magdiel ("God is renowned"), a duke of Edom (Gen. 36:43; 1 Chron. 1:54).

Magog ("covering; roof"), the second son of Japheth (Gen. 10:2; 1 Chron. 1:5). Possibly a people inhabiting the north land. The name may denote the Scythians or be a comprehensive term for northern barbarians.

Magor-missabib ("terror is about"), symbolic name given to Pashur by Jeremiah (Jer. 20:1–3).

Magpiash ("collector of a cluster of stars; moth-killer"), one who sealed the new covenant with God after the Exile (Neh. 10:20).

Mahalah ("tenderness"), descendant of Manasseh (1 Chron. 7:18). *See* Mahlah.

Mahalaleel [Maleleel] ("God is splendor"). **[1]** Son of Cainan and an ancestor of Christ (Gen. 5:12–13, 15; Luke 3:37). **[2]** One whose descendants lived at Jerusalem (Neh. 11:4).

Mahalath ("mild"). **[1]** One of Esau's wives (Gen. 28:9). *See* Esau's Wives. **[2]** Wife of Rehoboam (2 Chron. 11:18).

M

Mahali. *See* Mahli.

Maharai ("hasty"), one of David's warriors (2 Sam. 23:28; 1 Chron. 11:30; 27:13).

Mahath ("dissolution; snatching"). **[1]** A descendant of Kohath who helped to purify the sanctuary (1 Chron. 6:35; 2 Chron. 29:12). **[2]** A Levite overseer of dedicated things during Hezekiah's reign (2 Chron. 31:13).

Mahazioth ("visions"), one set over the song service of the temple (1 Chron. 25:4, 30).

Maher-shalal-hash-baz ("the spoil hastens, the prey speeds"), symbolic name of Isaiah's son (Isa. 8:1–4).

Mahlah ("mildness; sick"), eldest daughter of Zelophehad allowed a share of the land because her father had no sons (Num. 26:33; 27:1; Josh. 17:3). *See* Mahalah.

Mahli [Mahali] ("mild; sickly"). **[1]** A son of Merari (Exod. 6:19; Num. 3:20; 1 Chron. 6:19, 29; Ezra 8:18). **[2]** A descendant of Levi (1 Chron. 6:47; 23:23; 24:30).

Mahlon ("mild; sickly"), the first husband of Ruth who died in Moab (Ruth 1:2–5).

Mahol ("dancer"), father of renowned wise men (1 Kings 4:31).

Malachi ("messenger of Jehovah; my messenger"), the last of the prophets recorded in the

Old Testament; he was contemporary with Nehemiah (Mal. 1:1).

Malcham ("their king"), a descendant of Benjamin (1 Chron. 8:9).

Malchiah [Malchijah; Melchiah] ("Jehovah is king"). [1] A leader of singing under David's reign (1 Chron. 6:40). [2] An Aaronite whose descendants dwelled in Jerusalem after the Captivity (1 Chron. 9:12; Neh. 11:12). [3] Head of a priestly family (1 Chron. 24:9). [4], [5], [6] Three who married foreign wives during the Exile (Ezra 10:25, 31). [7], [8], Three who helped to rebuild the wall of Jerusalem (Neh. 3:11, 14, 31). [10] A prince or Levite who stood beside Ezra as he read the Law (Neh. 8:4). [11] A priest who helped to purify the wall of Jerusalem (Neh. 10:3; 12:42). [12] Father of Pashur (Jer. 21:1; 38:1).

Malchiel ("God is a King"), a descendant of Asher (Gen. 46:17; Num. 26:45; 1 Chron. 7:31).

Malchijah. *See* Malchiah.

Malchiram ("my king is exalted"), a descendant of King Jehoiakim (1 Chron. 3:18).

Malchi-shua. *See* Melchi-shua.

Malchus ("counselor; ruler"), a servant of the high priest whose ear Peter cut off (John 18:10).

Maleleel, Greek form of Mahalaleel (also see).

Mallothi ("Jehovah is speaking"), one who was set over the song service of the temple (1 Chron. 25:4, 26).

Malluch ("counselor; ruling"). [1] A descendant of Levi (1 Chron. 6:44). [2], [3] Two who took foreign wives during the Exile (Ezra 10:29, 32). [4] A priest who sealed the covenant (Neh. 10:4). [5] A leader who sealed the new covenant with God after the Exile (Neh. 10:27). [6] One of the priests who returned with Zerubbabel (Neh. 12:2); he is called Melicu in verse 14.

Mamre ("firmness; vigor"), an Amorite chief who allied with Abraham (Gen. 14:13, 24).

Manaen ("comforter"), a teacher or prophet at Antioch (Acts 13:1).

Manahath ("resting place; rest"), a descendant of Seir (Gen. 36:23; 1 Chron. 1:40).

Manasseh [Manasses] ("causing forgetfulness"). [1] The first son of Joseph (Gen. 41:51). His descendants became one of the twelve tribes of Israel and occupied both sides of the Jordan (Josh. 16:4–9; 17). [2] The idolatrous successor of Hezekiah to the throne of Judah. He was an ancestor of Christ (2 Kings 21:1–18; Matt. 1:10). [3] One whose descendants set up graven images at Laish (Judg. 18:30). Most scholars suggest that we should read Moses here instead. Perhaps a scribe felt an idolatrous descendant would cast reproach on the great lawgiver. A few manuscripts of the Septuagint, Old Latin, and the Vulgate read Moses here. [4], [5] Two who had taken foreign wives (Ezra 10:30, 33).

Manasses, Greek form of Manasseh (also see).

Manoah ("rest"), the father of Samson the judge (Judg. 13:1–23).

Maoch ("poor"). See Maachah [4].

Maon ("abode"), a son of Shammai or a city he founded (1 Chron. 2:45).

Mara ("bitter"), name assumed by Naomi after the death of her husband (Ruth 1:20).

Marcus. See Mark.

Mareshah ("possession"). [1] Father of Hebron (1 Chron. 2:42). [2] Son of Laadah (1 Chron. 4:21).

Mark [Marcus] ("polite; shining"), a Christian convert and missionary companion of Paul (Acts 12:12, 25; 15:37, 39; Col. 4:10). Mark is his Latin name, John his Hebrew name. He wrote the Gospel bearing his name.

Marsena ("worthy"), a prince of Persia (Esther 1:14).

Martha ("lady"), sister of Mary and Lazarus in Bethany (Luke 10:38, 40–41; John 11:1–39).

Mary (Greek form of Miriam, "strong"). **[1]** The mother of Jesus Christ; her song of faith (Luke 1:46–55) reveals her deep faith (Matt. 1:16–20; see John 2:1–11). **[2]** Mary the sister of Martha. She anointed the Lord with ointment and received His approval (Luke 10:39, 42; John 11:1–45). **[3]** A woman of Magdala in Galilee. She had been converted after having "seven devils" cast out of her (Matt. 27:56, 61; 28:1; Luke 8:2; John 19:25). **[4]** The mother of John Mark (Acts 12:12). **[5]** A Roman Christian to whom Paul sent greetings (Rom. 16:6). **[6]** Mary, the mother of Joses (Mark 15:47) and James (Luke 24:10), the "other Mary" (Matt. 28:1), and the Mary, wife of Cleophas (John 19:25), are possibly to be identified as the same person (Mark 15:40).

Mash ("drawn out"), son or grandson of Shem (Gen. 10:23). In 1 Chronicles 1:18 he is called Meshech. Possibly an Aramean people dwelling near Mount Masius in northern Mesopotamia is meant.

Massa ("burden; oracle"), a son of Ishmael (Gen. 25:14; 1 Chron. 1:30).

Mathusala, Greek form of Methuselah (also see).

Matred ("God is pursuer; expulsion"), mother of Mehetabel, wife of Hadar (Gen. 36:39; 1 Chron. 1:50).

Matri ("Jehovah is watching; rainy"), ancestor of a tribe of Benjamin to which Saul belonged (1 Sam. 10:21).

Mattan ("gift"). [1] A priest of Baal slain by the Jews (2 Kings 11:18; 2 Chron. 23:17). [2] Father of a prince of Judah (Jer. 38:1).

Mattaniah ("gift of Jehovah"). [1] The original name of King Zedekiah (2 Kings 24:17). [2] A descendant of Asaph whose family dwelt at Jerusalem (1 Chron. 9:15; 2 Chron. 20:14; Neh. 11:17, 22; 13:13). [3] A son of Heman the singer (1 Chron. 25:4, 16). [4] One who helped to cleanse the temple (2 Chron. 29:13). [5] [6], [7], [8] Four who married foreign wives during the Exile (Ezra 10:26–27, 30, 37). [9] One of the gatekeepers (Neh. 12:25).

Mattatha ("gift"), ancestor of Jesus (Luke 3:31). Not to be confused with Mattathah.

Mattathah ("gift"), one who married a foreign wife (Ezra 10:33). Not to be confused with Mattatha.

Mattathias ("God's gift"). [1] An ancestor of Jesus (Luke 3:25). [2] Another ancestor of Christ (Luke 3:26).

Mattenai ("gift of Jehovah"). [1], [2] Two who married foreign wives during the Exile (Ezra 10:33, 37). [3] A priest who returned from the Exile (Neh. 12:19).

Matthan ("gift"), an ancestor of Jesus (Matt. 1:15).

Matthat ("gift"). [1] Grandfather of Joseph and ancestor of Jesus (Luke 3:24). [2] Another ancestor of Jesus (Luke 3:29).

Matthew ("gift of God"), one of the twelve apostles; he was a tax collector before his call. He was also known as Levi (Matt. 9:9; 10:3; Mark 2:14). He wrote the third Gospel.

Matthias ("God's gift"), a Christian chosen to become an apostle to fill the place of Judas (Acts 1:23, 26). He was surnamed Justus.

Mattithiah ("gift of Jehovah"). [1] A Levite in charge of "things made in pans" (1 Chron. 9:31). [2] A Levite singer and gatekeeper (1 Chron. 15:18, 21; 16:5). [3] A son of Jeduthun (1 Chron. 25:3, 21). [4] One who took a foreign wife during the Exile (Ezra 10:43). [5] One who stood with Ezra when he read the Law (Neh. 8:4).

Mebunnai ("built up"). *See* Sibbecai.

Medad ("love"), one of the elders of the Hebrews on whom the spirit fell (Num. 11:26–27).

Medan ("judgment"), a son of Abraham by Keturah (Gen. 25:2; 1 Chron. 1:32).

Mehetabel [Mehetabeel] ("God is doing good"). [1] Wife of King Hadar of Edom (Gen. 36:39; 1 Chron. 1:50). [2] Father of Delaiah who defied Nehemiah (Neh. 6:10).

Mehida ("famous"), an ancestor of returned captives (Ezra 2:52; Neh. 7:54).

Mehir ("dexterity"), a descendant of Caleb of Hur (1 Chron. 4:11).

Mehujael ("God is combating"), a descendant of Cain (Gen. 4:18).

Mehuman ("true"), one of the chamberlains of Ahasuerus (Esther 1:10).

Melatiah ("Jehovah delivers"), an assistant wall-builder (Neh. 3:7).

Melchi ("my King"). [1] An ancestor of Jesus (Luke 3:24). [2] Another ancestor of Jesus (Luke 3:28).

Melchiah. *See* Malchiah.

Melchisedec, Greek form of Melchizedek (also see).

Melchi-shua [Malchi-shua] ("the king, i.e., [God] is salvation"), the third son of King Saul (1 Sam. 14:49; 31:2; 1 Chron. 8:33).

Melchizedek [Melchisedec] ("king of righteousness"), king and high priest of Salem. He was a prophetic symbol or "type" of Christ (Gen. 14:18–20; Psa. 110:4; Heb. 5–7).

Melea ("full"), ancestor of Christ (Luke 3:31).

Melech ("king"), great-grandson of Saul (1 Chron. 8:35; 9:41).

Melicu. *See* Malluch [4].

Melzar ("the overseer"), one to whom Daniel and his companions were entrusted (Dan. 1:11, 16); this is possibly a title, rather than a proper name.

Memucan, a Persian prince (Esther 1:14–21).

Menahem ("comforter"), the idolatrous and cruel usurper of the throne of Israel who killed Shallum (2 Kings 15:14–23).

Menan, an ancestor of Christ (Luke 3:31).

Meonothai ("Jehovah is dwelling; my dwelling"), a descendant of Judah (1 Chron. 4:14).

Mephibosheth ("idol breaker"). [1] Son of Saul by his concubine Rizpah (2 Sam. 21:8). [2] A grandson of Saul. He was loyal to David, even though Ziba told David he was a traitor (2 Sam. 4:4; 9:6–13). He was also called Merib-baal ("Baal contends") (1 Chron. 8:34; 9:40).

Merab ("increase"), daughter of Saul promised to David but given to Adriel (1 Sam. 14:49; 18:17, 19). Apparently she was a sister of Michal.

Meraiah ("revelation of Jehovah"), a priest of Jerusalem in the days of Joiakim (Neh. 12:12).

Meraioth ("revelations"). [1] A descendant of Aaron and ancestor of Azariah (1 Chron. 6:6–7, 52; Ezra 7:3). [2] Another priest of the same line (1 Chron. 9:11; Neh. 11:11). [3] Another priest at the end of the Exile (Neh. 12:15); possibly the same as Meremoth [1] or [3].

Merari ("bitter; excited"), the third son of Levi and founder of a priestly clan (Gen. 46:11; Exod. 6:16, 19; Num. 3; 4:29–45).

Mered ("rebellious"), son of Ezra, descendant of Judah (1 Chron. 4:17–18).

Meremoth ("strong; firm"). [1] A priest who weighed the gold and silver vessels of the temple (Ezra 8:33; Neh. 3:4, 21). [2] One who took a foreign wife during the Exile (Ezra 10:36). [3] One who sealed the new covenant with God after the Exile (Neh. 10:5; 12:3).

Meres ("worthy"), one of the seven princes of Persia (Esther 1:14).

Merib-baal. *See* Mephibosheth.

Merodach-baladan (Babylonian, *Marduk-baladan*—"[the god] Marduk has given a son"), a king of Babylon in the days of Hezekiah (Jer. 50:2). Also called Berodach-baladan (2 Kings 20:12).

Mesha ("freedom"). [1] A king of Moab who rebelled against Ahaziah (2 Kings 3:4). [2] Eldest son of Caleb (1 Chron. 2:42). [3] A descendant of Benjamin (1 Chron. 8:9).

Meshach ("the shadow of the prince; who is this?"), the name given to Mishael after he went into Babylonian captivity. He was delivered from the fiery furnace (Dan. 1:7; 3:12–30).

Meshech [Mesech] ("long; tall"). [1] A son of Japheth (Gen. 10:2; 1 Chron. 1:5). Possibly a people inhabiting the land in the mountains north of Assyria; it was called Musku. [2] *See* Mash.

Meshelemiah ("Jehovah recompenses"), a descendant of Levi (1 Chron. 9:21; 26:1–2, 9). He is also called Shelemiah (1 Chron. 26:14).

Meshezabeel ("God is deliverer"). [1] A priest who helped rebuild the wall (Neh. 3:4). [2] One who signed the covenant (Neh. 10:21). [3] A descendant of Judah (Neh. 11:24).

Meshillemith ("retribution"), a priest whose descendants lived in Jerusalem (1 Chron. 9:12).

He is called Meshillemoth in Nehemiah 11:13.

Meshillemoth ("recompense"). [1] A descendant of Ephraim (2 Chron. 28:12). [2] *See* Meshillemith.

Meshobab, a prince of Simeon (1 Chron. 4:34).

Meshullam ("associate; friend"). [1] Grandfather of Shaphan, a scribe (2 Kings 22:3). [2] A descendant of King Jehoiakim (1 Chron. 3:19). [3] Head of a family of Gad (1 Chron. 5:13). [4] A descendant of Benjamin (1 Chron. 8:17). [5] One whose son lived in Jerusalem (1 Chron. 9:7). [6] One who lived in Jerusalem (1 Chron. 9:8). [7] A descendant of Aaron and an ancestor of Ezra (Neh. 11:11; 1 Chron. 9:11). He is also called Shallum (Ezra 7:2; 1 Chron. 6:12–13). [8] A priest (1 Chron. 9:12). [9] An overseer of the temple work (2 Chron. 34:12). [10] A chief man who returned with Ezra to Jerusalem (Ezra 8:16). [11] One who had assisted in taking account of those who had foreign wives after the Exile (Ezra 10:15). [12] One who took a foreign wife during the Exile (Ezra 10:29). [13], [14] Two who rebuilt part of the wall of Jerusalem (Neh. 3:4, 6, 30; 6:18). [15] A prince or priest who stood with Ezra while he read the Law (Neh. 8:4). [16] A priest who sealed the new covenant with God after the Exile (Neh. 10:7). **[17]** One who sealed the new covenant with God after the Exile (Neh. 10:20). **[18]** One whose descendants lived in Jerusalem (Neh. 11:7). **[19]** A priest who assisted in the dedication of the wall of Jerusalem (Neh. 12:13, 33). **[20]** A descendant of Ginnethon (Neh. 12:16). **[21]** A Levite and gatekeeper after the Exile (Neh. 12:25).

Meshullemeth ("friend"), wife of Manasseh and mother of Amon (2 Kings 21:19).

Methusael ("man of God"), the father of Lamech (Gen. 4:18).

Methuselah [Mathusala] ("man of the dart"), the longest-living human recorded in the Bible, the grandfather of Noah and an ancestor of Christ (Gen. 5:21–27; Luke 3:37).

Mezahab ("offspring of the shining one"), grandfather of Mehetabel, wife of Hadar, the eighth king of Edom (Gen. 36:39; 1 Chron. 1:50).

Miamin ("fortunate"). **[1]** One who took a foreign wife during the Exile (Ezra 10:25). **[2]** A priest who returned from the Exile (Neh. 12:5).

Mibhar ("choice; youth"), one of David's mighty men (1 Chron. 11:38).

Mibsam ("sweet odor"). **[1]** A son of Ishmael (Gen. 25:13; 1 Chron. 1:29). **[2]** A son of Simeon (1 Chron. 4:25).

Mibzar ("fortified"), chief of Edom (Gen. 36:42; 1 Chron. 1:53).

Mica [Micah, Micha, Michah—all probably contractions of **Micaiah**]. **[1]** Owner of a small private sanctuary (Judg. 17:1–5). **[2]** A descendant of Reuben (1 Chron. 5:5). **[3]** A son of Merib-baal, Mephibosheth in 2 Samuel 4:4 (1 Chron. 8:34). **[4]** A descendant of Kohath, son of Levi (1 Chron. 23:20; 24:24). **[5]** The father of Abdon (2 Chron. 34:20). He is called Michaiah in 2 Kings 22:12. **[6]** A prophet (Jer. 26:18; Mic. 1:1). **[7]** The son of Zichri (1 Chron. 9:15; Neh. 11:17). **[8]** One who signed the covenant (Neh. 10:11).

Michael ("who is like God?") **[1]** One sent to spy out the land of Canaan (Num. 13:13). **[2]** A descendant of Gad (1 Chron. 5:13). **[3]** Another descendant of Gad (1 Chron. 5:14). **[4]** An ancestor of Asaph (1 Chron. 6:40). **[5]** A chief of the tribe of Issachar (1 Chron. 7:3). **[6]** One residing in Jerusalem (1 Chron. 8:16). **[7]** A warrior who joined David at Ziklag (1 Chron. 12:20). **[8]** Father of Omri, a prince of Issachar (1 Chron. 27:18). **[9]** A son of Jehoshaphat (2 Chron. 21:2). **[10]** An ancestor of one who returned from the Exile (Ezra 8:8).

Michah. *See* Mica.

M

Michaiah [Micaiah] ("who is like Jehovah?"). [1] Wife of Rehoboam (2 Chron. 13:2). She is also called Maachah (1 Kings 15:2; 2 Chron. 11:20). *See* Maachah [5]. [2] *See* Mica [5]. [3] A prince of Judah (2 Chron. 17:7). [4] The son of Zaccur (Neh. 12:35). [5] One present at the dedication of the wall (Neh. 12:41). [6] A prophet who predicted Ahab's downfall (1 Kings 22:8—28; 2 Chron. 18:7—27).

Michal ("who is like God?"), a daughter of Saul whom David married (1 Sam. 14:49). Michal "had no child unto the day of her death" (2 Sam. 6:23). Yet 2 Samuel 21:8 states she had five sons. The KJV rendering, "whom she brought up for Adriel," is not a permissible translation—the Hebrew text states she bore them. A few Hebrew, Greek, and Syriac manuscripts read: "the five sons of Merab" instead of Michal, which seems a plausible solution to the problem. See 1 Samuel 18:19.

Michri ("Jehovah possesses"), an ancestor of a clan of Benjamin in Jerusalem (1 Chron. 9:8).

Midian ("contention"), a son of Abraham by Keturah and founder of the Midianites (Gen. 25:2, 4; 36:35; 1 Chron. 1:32).

Mijamin ("fortunate"). [1] A priest in the time of David (1 Chron. 24:9). *See also* Miniamin [2]. [2] One who sealed the new covenant (Neh.

10:7). **[3]** One who married a foreign wife (Ezra 10:25).

Mikloth ("twigs; sticks"). **[1]** A descendant of Benjamin living in Jerusalem (1 Chron. 8:32; 9:37–38). **[2]** A chief military officer under David (1 Chron. 27:4).

Mikneiah ("Jehovah is zealous"), a Levite musician (1 Chron. 15:18, 21).

Milalai ("Jehovah is elevated"), a priest who aided in the purification of the wall (Neh. 12:36).

Milcah ("counsel"). **[1]** A daughter of Haran, Abraham's brother, and wife of Nahor (Gen. 11:29; 22:20, 23). **[2]** A daughter of Zelophehad (Num. 26:33; 27:1).

Miniamin ("fortunate"). **[1]** A Levite who apportioned the tithes (2 Chron. 31:15). **[2]** A priest in the days of Joiakim (Neh. 12:17). He is possibly the same as Mijamin in 1 Chronicles 24:9. *See* Mijamin [1]. **[3]** A priest who helped dedicate the wall (Neh. 12:41).

Miriam ("fat; thick; strong"). **[1]** The sister of Moses and Aaron. She rebelled against Moses with Aaron at Hazeroth (Exod. 2:4–10; Num. 12:1–15; 20:1). **[2]** A woman descendant of Judah (1 Chron. 4:17).

Mirma ("height"), descendant of Benjamin (1 Chron. 8:10).

Mishael ("who is what God is?"). **[1]** One who carried away the dead Nadab and Abihu (Exod. 6:22; Lev. 10:4). **[2]** One who stood with Ezra at the reading of the Law (Neh. 8:4). **[3]** One of the companions of Daniel in Babylon (Dan. 1:6–7, 11, 19). *See* Meshach.

Misham ("impetuous; fame"), a descendant of Benjamin (1 Chron. 8:12).

Mishma ("fame"). **[1]** A son of Ishmael (Gen. 25:14; 1 Chron. 1:30). **[2]** A descendant of Simeon (1 Chron. 4:25).

Mishmannah ("strength; vigor"), one who joined David at Ziklag (1 Chron. 12:10).

Mispar. *See* Mispereth.

Mispereth ("writing"), one who returned from captivity (Neh. 7:7). He is called Mispar in Ezra 2:2.

Mithredath ("given by [the god] Mithra"). **[1]** The treasurer of Cyrus through whom he restored the temple vessels (Ezra 1:8). **[2]** One who wrote to the king of Persia protesting the restoration of Jerusalem (Ezra 4:7).

Mizraim, the second son of Ham (Gen. 10:6, 13; 1 Chron. 1:8, 11). Possibly the Egyptian people are intended.

Mizzah ("terror; joy"), a duke of Edom (Gen. 36:13, 17; 1 Chron. 1:37).

Mnason ("remembering"), a Cyprian convert who accompanied Paul from Caesarea on Paul's last visit to Jerusalem (Acts 21:16).

Moab ("from my father"), the son of Lot by his daughter and an ancestor of the Moabites (Gen. 19:34–37).

Moadiah. *See* Maadiah.

Molid ("begetter"), a descendant of Judah (1 Chron. 2:29).

Mordecai ("dedicated to Mars"). [1] A Jewish exile who became a vizier of Persia. He helped save the Jews from destruction (Esther 2—10). [2] A leader who returned from the Babylonian Captivity (Ezra 2:2; Neh. 7:7).

Moses ("drawer-out; child; one-born"). No one in the Old Testament is more heroic and influential than the shy and humble Moses. He freed the Israelites from Egyptian slavery, organized them into a nation, gave them the Ten Commandments and other laws that still guide Jews and Christians, and is credited with writing the first five books of the Bible.

Moses was born in Egypt to an Israelite slave, some four hundred years after Jacob's

God used Moses to lead His people out of bondage in Egypt, including crossing the Red Sea (Exod. 14:1–31).

family emigrated to Egypt to escape a famine. As an infant, he was set adrift on the Nile in a waterproof basket to escape the king's order to kill all newborn Hebrew boys. The king's daughter found and raised him. But at age forty, Moses fled the country after killing an Egyptian he saw beating an Israelite. He settled east of Egypt, married, and became a shepherd. While he was grazing his flock one day, God spoke to him from a burning bush and asked him to go back to Egypt and

After forty years in the wilderness, Moses saw the promised land from a mountaintop (Deut. 34:1–4).

demand the release of the Israelites. Reluctantly, Moses did as God asked.

Israel's deliverance, characterized by many spectacular miracles—ten plagues in Egypt, parting the waters of the Red Sea, manna from heaven, water from rocks—is the Exodus, the most celebrated event in Jewish history, still commemorated in religious holidays each year.

Moza ("origin; offspring"). **[1]** A son of Caleb (1 Chron. 2:46). **[2]** A descendant of Saul (1 Chron. 8:36–37; 9:42–43).

Muppim ("obscurities"), a son of Benjamin (Gen. 46:21). He is also called Shuppim (1 Chron. 7:12, 15; 26:16), Shupham (Num. 26:39), Shephuphan (1 Chron. 8:5). These last three names mean "serpent." While this individual may have borne many names, probably copyists' errors account for some of the diversity.

Mushi ("drawn out; deserted"), a son of Merari, son of Levi (Exod. 6:19; Num. 3:20; 1 Chron. 6:19, 47).

N

Naam ("pleasantness"), a son of Caleb (1 Chron. 4:15).

Naamah ("pleasant"). [1] Daughter of Lamech and Zillah (Gen. 4:22). [2] A wife of Solomon and mother of Rehoboam (1 Kings 14:21; 2 Chron. 12:13).

Naaman ("pleasantness"). [1] A Syrian general who was healed of leprosy by bathing in the Jordan (2 Kings 5; Luke 4:27). [2] Grandson of Benjamin (Gen. 26:38, 40). [3] A son of Benjamin and founder of a tribal family (Gen. 46:21).

Naarah ("a girl; posterity"), a wife of Ashur (1 Chron. 4:5–6).

Naaman was healed of leprosy when he followed Elisha's instructions (2 Kings 5:1–19, see page 211).

Naarai ("youthful"), one of David's valiant men (1 Chron. 11:37). Probably the same as Paarai (2 Sam. 23:35).

Naashon. *See* Nahson.

Naasson, Greek form of Nahshon (also see).

Nabal ("foolish; wicked"), a wealthy Carmelite who refused David and his men food (1 Sam. 25).

Naboth ("a sprout"), the owner whom Jezebel had killed in order to obtain his vineyard (1 Kings 21:1–18).

Nachon ("stroke"). Scripture refers to the threshing floor of Nachon/Chidon (1 Sam. 6:6;

1 Chron. 13:9). This is either the combined name of two individuals, of two place names, or a combination of both. *Chidon* possibly means "destruction or a javelin."

Nachor, Greek form of Nahor (also see).

Nadab ("liberal"). **[1]** Firstborn son of Aaron, struck dead for offering "strange fire" to God (Exod. 6:23; Lev. 10:1–3). **[2]** A descendant of Jerahmeel (1 Chron. 2:28, 30). **[3]** A brother of Gibeon (1 Chron. 8:30). **[4]** Son of Jeroboam I; he ruled Israel for two years (1 Kings 15:25–31).

Nagge ("splendor"), ancestor of Jesus (Luke 3:25). *See also* Neariah.

Naham ("comfort"), a descendant of Judah, a chieftain (1 Chron. 4:19).

Nahamani ("compassionate"), one who returned with Zerubbabel (Neh. 7:7).

Naharai [Nahari] ("snorting one"), Joab's armorbearer (1 Chron. 11:39; 2 Sam. 23:37).

Nahari. *See* Naharai.

Nahash ("oracle; serpent"). **[1]** The father of Abigail and Zeruiah (2 Sam. 17:25). **[2]** An Ammonite king that was defeated by Saul (1 Sam. 11:1–2; 12:12). **[3]** Another king of Ammon (2 Sam. 10:2; 17:27; 1 Chron. 19:1–2). Not to be confused with Ir-nahash.

Nahath ("lowness"). [1] A descendant of Esau (Gen. 36:13; 1 Chron. 1:37). [2] An overseer of the offerings at the temple (2 Chron. 31:13). [3] *See* Toah.

Nahbi ("Jehovah is protection"), the spy of Naphtali whom Moses sent out to explore Canaan (Num. 13:14).

Nahor [Nachor] ("piercer"). [1] Grandfather of Abraham and ancestor of Christ (Gen. 11:22-25; Luke 3:34). [2] A brother of Abraham (Gen. 11:26-27, 29; 22:20, 23; Josh. 24:2).

Nahshon [Naashon; Naasson] ("oracle"), a descendant of Judah and ancestor of Christ. Perhaps Aaron's brother-in-law (Exod. 6:23; Num. 1:7; Matt. 1:4).

Nahum ("comforter"), one of the later prophets; he prophesied against Nineveh (Nah. 1:1). Not to be confused with Naum.

Naomi ("pleasantness; my joy"), mother-in-law to Ruth (Ruth 1:2—4:17).

Naphish ("numerous"), son of Ishmael (Gen. 25:15; 1 Chron. 1:31).

Naphtali ("wrestling"), the sixth son of Jacob (Gen. 30:7-8). His descendants became one of the twelve tribes.

Naphtuhim, a son of Mizraim (Gen. 10:13; 1 Chron. 1:11). Many think this refers to a district in Egypt, possibly a designation for the people of the Egyptian Delta.

Narcissus (meaning unknown), a Roman Christian (Rom. 16:11).

Nathan ("gift"). [1] Prophet and royal advisor to David (2 Sam. 7:2–17; 12:1–25). [2] A son of King David and ancestor of Christ (2 Sam. 5:14; 1 Chron. 3:5; Luke 3:31). [3] Father of Igal (2 Sam. 23:36). [4] A descendant of Jerahmeel (1 Chron. 2:36). [5] A companion of Ezra (Ezra 8:16). [6] One of those who had married a foreign wife (Ezra 10:39). [7] Brother of Joel, one of David's valiant men (1 Chron. 11:38). [8] Father of Solomon's chief officer (1 Kings 4:5). [9] A chief man of Israel (Zech. 10:10). *See* Nathan-melech.

Nathanael ("God has given"), a Galilean called by Christ to be a disciple. He is probably to be identified with Bartholomew (John 1:45–49; 21:2; Acts 1:13). *See also* Bartholomew.

Nathan-Melech ("King's gift"), an official under Josiah (2 Kings 23:11).

Naum ("comforter"), an ancestor of Christ (Luke 3:25). Not to be confused with Nahum.

Neariah ("Jehovah drives away"). [1] A descendant of David (1 Chron. 3:22). [2] A descendant of Simeon who smote the Amalekites in Mount Seir (1 Chron. 4:42).

Nebai ("projecting"), a co-covenanter with Ezra (Neh. 10:19).

Nebaioth [Nebajoth] ("husbandry"), oldest son of Ishmael (Gen. 25:13; 28:9; 36:3; 1 Chron. 1:29).

Nebajoth. *See* Nebaioth.

Nebat ("cultivation"), father of Jeroboam I (1 Kings 11:26).

Nebo ("height"), an ancestor of Jews who had taken foreign wives during the Exile (Ezra 10:43). This reference quite possibly refers to a city.

Nebuchadnezzar [Nebuchadrezzar] (Babylonian, *Nabur-kudurri-utsur*—"may [the god] Nabu guard my boundary stones"), great king of the Babylonian Empire; he captured Jerusalem three times and carried Judah into captivity (2 Kings 24:1, 10–11; 25:1, 8, 22; Dan. 1–4).

Nebushasban ("Nabu delivers me"), a Babylonian prince (Jer. 39:13).

Nebuzaradan (Babylonian, "[the god] Nabu has given seed"), a Babylonian captain of the guard at the siege of Jerusalem (2 Kings 25:8, 11, 20).

Necho, pharaoh of Egypt who fought Josiah at Megiddo (2 Chron. 35:20).

Nedabiah ("Jehovah is willing"), a descendant of Jehoiakim king of Judah (1 Chron. 3:18).

Nehemiah ("Jehovah is consolation"). [1] Governor of Jerusalem; he helped rebuild the fallen city (Neh. 1:1; 8:9; 12:47). [2] A chief man who returned from the Exile (Ezra 2:2; Neh. 7:7). [3] One who repaired the wall of Jerusalem (Neh. 3:16).

Nehum. *See* Rehum.

Nehushta ("basis; ground"), wife of Jehoiakim; mother of Jehoiachin (2 Kings 24:8).

Nekoda ("herdsman"). [1] Head of a family of Nethinim (Ezra 2:48; Neh. 7:50). [2] The head of a family without genealogy after the Exile (Ezra 2:60; Neh. 7:62).

Nemuel ("God is speaking"). [1] A descendant of Reuben (Num. 26:9). [2] A son of Simeon (Num. 26:12; 1 Chron. 4:24). In Genesis 46:10 and Exodus 6:15, he is called Jemuel.

Nepheg ("sprout; shoot"). [1] A brother of Korah (Exod. 6:21). [2] A son of David (2 Sam. 5:15; 1 Chron. 3:7; 14:6).

Nephishesim [Nephusim] ("expansions"), ancestor of returned captives (Neh. 7:52). He is called Nephusim in Ezra 2:50. This man is possibly identical with Naphish.

Nephusim. *See* Nephishesim.

Ner ("light"). **[1]** An uncle (?) of Saul, father of Abner (1 Sam. 14:50). **[2]** Grandfather of Saul (1 Chron. 8:33; 9:39). These relationships are unclear. Abner may have been Saul's uncle. If so, Ner [1] and [2] are the same. He is also called Abiel (1 Sam. 9:1). It is also possible that Ner [2] (Abiel) had sons named Ner [1] and Kish, the father of Saul.

Nereus ("lamp"), a Roman Christian (Rom. 16:15).

Nergal-sharezer ("may the god Nergal defend the prince"), a Babylonian officer who released Jeremiah (Jer. 39:3, 13–14).

Neri ("whose lamp is Jehovah"), ancestor of Christ (Luke 3:27).

Neriah ("whose lamp is Jehovah"), father of Baruch (Jer. 32:12, 16; 36:4, 8, 32).

Nethaneel ("God gives"). **[1]** Chief of Issachar whom Moses sent to spy out the land of Canaan (Num. 1:8; 2:5; 7:18, 23; 10:15). **[2]** Fourth son of Jesse (1 Chron. 2:14). **[3]** One of the trumpet blowers when the ark of the covenant was brought up (1 Chron. 15:24). **[4]** A Levite (1 Chron. 24:6). **[5]** A son of Obededom and gatekeeper of the tabernacle (1 Chron. 26:4). [6] A prince commissioned by Jehoshaphat to teach the people (2 Chron. 17:7). [7] A Levite in the days of Josiah (2 Chron. 35:9). [8] A priest who married a foreign wife (Ezra 10:22). [9] A priest in the days of Joiakim (Neh. 12:21). [10] Levite musician at the purification ceremony (Neh. 12:36).

Nethaniah ("Jehovah gives"). [1] A musician in David's worship services (1 Chron. 25:2, 12). [2] A Levite whom Jehoshaphat sent to teach in Judah's cities (2 Chron. 17:8). [3] Father of Jehudi (Jer. 36:14). [4] Father of Ishmael, the murderer of Gedaliah (Jer. 40:8, 14–15; 41:11).

Neziah ("preeminent"), head of a Nethinim family that returned to Jerusalem with Zerubbabel (Ezra 2:54; Neh. 7:56).

Nicanor ("conqueror"), one of the seven chosen in the ministry to the poor (Acts 6:5).

Nicodemus ("innocent blood"), a Pharisee and ruler of the Jews who assisted in Christ's burial (John 3:1–15; 7:50–52; 19:39–42).

Nicolaus ("conqueror of the people"), one of the seven chosen to aid in the ministration to the poor (Acts 6:5).

Niger, surname of Simeon (also see).

Nimrod ("valiant; strong"), a son of Cush (Gen. 10:8–9; 1 Chron. 1:10). His kingdom included Babel, Erech, Accad, and Calneh, cities in Shinar, but also included Assyria.

Nimshi ("Jehovah reveals"), an ancestor of Jehu (1 Kings 19:16; 2 Kings 9:2, 14).

Noadiah ("Jehovah assembles"). [1] Son of Binnui to whom Ezra entrusted the sacred vessels of the temple (Ezra 8:33). [2] A prophetess opposed to Nehemiah (Neh. 6:14).

Noah [Noe] ("rest"), son of Lamech; the patriarch chosen to build the ark. Only his family survived the flood (Gen. 5:28–32; 6:8–22; 7–10). He was an ancestor of Christ (Luke 3:36).

Noah ("flattery; movement"), a daughter of Zelophehad (Num. 26:33; Josh. 17:3).

Nobah ("prominent"), a descendant of Manasseh who conquered Kenath (Num. 32:42).

Noe, Greek form of Noah (also see).

Nogah ("splendor"), a son of David (1 Chron. 3:7; 14:6).

Nohah ("rest"), a son of Benjamin (1 Chron. 8:2).

Non. *See* Nun.

Nun [Non] ("continuation; fish"). [1] A descendant of Ephraim (1 Chron. 7:27); possibly the same as [2]. **[2]** The father of Joshua (Exod. 33:11; 1 Kings 16:34).

Nymphas ("bridegroom"), a Christian of Laodicea to whom Paul sends greetings (Col. 4:15). Some manuscripts read Nympha, which would make this individual a woman.

--- **O** ---

Obadiah ("servant of Jehovah"). **[1]** The governor or prime minister of Ahab who tried to protect the prophets against Jezebel (1 Kings 18:3–16). **[2]** A descendant of David (1 Chron. 3:21). **[3]** A chief of the tribe of Issachar (1 Chron. 7:3). **[4]** A descendant of King Saul (1 Chron. 8:38; 9:44). **[5]** A man of the tribe of Zebulun (1 Chron. 27:19). **[6]** A chief of the Gadites who joined David at Ziklag (1 Chron. 12:9). **[7]** One of the princes whom Jehoshaphat commissioned to teach the Law (2 Chron. 17:7–9). **[8]** A Levite overseer in work done on the temple (2 Chron. 34:12). **[9]** The chief of a family that returned to Jerusalem (Ezra 8:9). **[10]** One who sealed the covenant with Nehemiah (Neh. 10:5). **[11]** A gatekeeper for the sanctuary of the temple (Neh. 12:25). **[12]** The fourth of the "minor prophets." His message was directed against Edom (Obad. 1). **[13]** *See* Abda [2].

Obal. *See* Ebal.

Obed ("servant"). **[1]** A son of Boaz and Ruth, father of Jesse, and ancestor of Christ (Ruth 4:17; Matt. 1:5; Luke 3:32). **[2]** A descendant of Judah (1 Chron. 2:37–38). **[3]** One of David's warriors (1 Chron. 11:47). **[4]** A Levite gatekeeper in David's time (1 Chron. 26:7). **[5]** Father of Azariah, who helped make Joash king of Judah (2 Chron. 23:1).

Obed-edom ("servant of [the god] Edom"). **[1]** A man who housed the ark for three months (2 Sam. 6:10–12; 1 Chron. 13:13–14). **[2]** One of the chief Levitical singers and doorkeepers (1 Chron. 15:18, 21, 24; 16:5, 38; 26:4, 8, 15). **[3]** A temple treasurer or official, or perhaps the tribe that sprang from [2] (2 Chron. 25:24).

Obil ("camel-keeper; leader"), a descendant of Ishmael who attended to David's camels (1 Chron. 27:30).

Ocran ("troubler"), a descendant of Asher (Num. 1:13; 2:27).

Oded ("aiding; restorer"). **[1]** Father of Azariah the prophet (2 Chron. 15:1). **[2]** A prophet of Samaria who persuaded the northern army to free their Judean slaves (2 Chron. 28:9–15).

Og ("giant"), the giant king of Bashan, defeated at Edrei (Num. 21:33–35; Deut. 3:1–13).

Ohad ("strength"), a son of Simeon (Gen. 46:10; Exod. 6:15).

Ohel ("tent"), a son of Zerubbabel (1 Chron. 3:20).

Olympas (meaning unknown), a Roman Christian (Rom. 16:15).

Omar ("speaker; mountaineer"), a grandson of Esau and a duke of Edom (Gen. 36:15).

Omri ("Jehovah apportions; pupil"). [1] The sixth king of Israel and founder of the third dynasty. He founded Samaria and made it Israel's capital (1 Kings 16:15–28). [2] A descendant of Benjamin, the son of Becher (1 Chron. 7:8). [3] A descendant of Perez living at Jerusalem (1 Chron. 9:4). [4] A prince of Issachar in the days of David (1 Chron. 27:18).

On ("sun; strength"), a Reubenite who rebelled against Moses and Aaron (Num. 16:1).

Onam ("vigorous"). [1] A grandson of Seir (Gen. 36:23; 1 Chron. 1:40). [2] A son of Jerahmeel of Judah (1 Chron. 2:26, 28).

Onan ("vigorous"), the second son of Judah. He was slain by God for disobedience (Gen. 38:4–10; Num. 26:19).

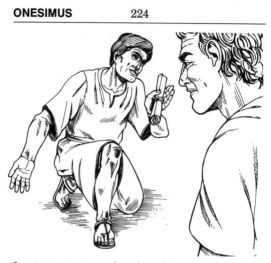

Onesimus, a runaway slave, brought a message from Paul to his master, Philemon (Philem. 1–25).

Onesimus ("useful"), a slave on whose behalf Paul wrote an epistle to his master, Philemon (Col. 4:9; Philem. 10, 15).

Onesiphorus ("profit-bringer"), a loyal friend of Paul's who often refreshed him in prison (2 Tim. 1:16; 4:19).

Ophir ("fruitful; rich"), a son of Joktan (Gen. 10:29; 1 Chron. 1:23). The name may possibly refer to a tribe who inhabited modern Somaliland.

Ophrah ("fawn; hamlet"), a descendant of Judah (1 Chron. 4:14).

Oreb ("raven"), a Midianite chieftain defeated by Gibeon and beheaded by the Ephraimites (Judg. 7:25).

Oren ("pine; strength"), a son of Jerahmeel of Judah (1 Chron. 2:25).

Ornan ("active"), a Jebusite from whom David bought a piece of land, on which Solomon's temple was erected (1 Chron. 21:15–25). He is called Araunah in 2 Samuel 24:16.

Orpah ("fawn; youthful freshness"), daughter-in-law of Naomi (Ruth 1:4–14).

Osee, Greek form of Hosea (also see).

Oshea. *See* Joshua.

Othni ("Jehovah is power"), a Levite, son of Shemaiah and tabernacle gatekeeper in David's time (1 Chron. 26:7).

Othniel ("God is power"), Caleb's younger brother who liberated Israel from foreign rule (Judg. 1:13; 3:8–11; 1 Chron. 27:15).

Ozem ("strength"). **[1]** A brother of David (1 Chron. 2:15). **[2]** A son of Jerahmeel of Judah (1 Chron. 2:25).

Ozias, Greek form of Uzziah (also see).

Ozni. *See* Ezbon [1].

P

Paarai ("revelation of Jehovah" or "devotee of Peor"), one of David's mighty men (2 Sam. 23:35); probably the same as Naarai (1 Chron. 11:37).

Padon ("redemption"), one who returned with Zerubbabel (Ezra 2:44; Neh. 7:47).

Pagiel ("God's intervention"), a chief of Asher (Num. 1:13; 2:27).

Pahath-Moab ("ruler of Moab"), a Jewish family named after an ancestor of the above name or title (Ezra 2:6; Neh. 3:11). The one who sealed the covenant bearing this name is either another Jew or else the above family is intended (Neh. 10:1, 14).

Palal ("judge"), one who helped rebuild the wall (Neh. 3:25).

Pallu [Phallu] ("distinguished"), a son of Reuben (Gen. 46:9; Exod. 6:14; 1 Chron. 5:3).

Palti ("Jehovah delivers"). [1] The man selected from Benjamin to spy out the land (Num. 13:9). [2] *See* Paltiel-[2].

Paltiel [Phaltiel] ("God delivers"). [1] A prince of the tribe of Issachar (Num. 34:26). [2] The man who married David's wife (2 Sam. 3:15). He is called Phalti in 1 Samuel 25:44.

Parmashta ("stronger"), a son of Haman (Esther 9:9).

Parmenas ("steadfast"), one of the seven deacons (Acts 6:5).

Parnach ("gifted"), a descendant of Zebulun (Num. 34:25).

Parosh [Pharosh] ("fleeing; fugitive"). [1] One whose descendants returned from the Exile (Ezra 2:3; Neh. 7:8). [2] Another whose family returned from the Exile (Ezra 8:3). [3] One whose descendants had taken foreign wives during the Exile (Ezra 10:25). [4] One who sealed the covenant (Neh. 10:14). [5] The father of one who helped repair the wall of Jerusalem (Neh. 3:25). All of these are possibly the same.

Parshandatha ("given by prayer"), a son of Haman slain by the Jews (Esther 9:7).

Paruah ("blooming"), father of Jehoshaphat (1 Kings 4:17).

Pasach ("limping"), a descendant of Asher (1 Chron. 7:33).

Paseah [Phaseah] ("limping"). [1] A descendant of Judah through Caleb (1 Chron. 4:12). [2] One whose family returned (Ezra 2:49; Neh. 7:51). [3] Father of Jehoiada, who helped repair the wall (Neh. 3:6).

Pashur ("splitter; cleaver"). [1] Head of a priestly family (Ezra 2:38; 10:22; Neh. 7:41).

[2] A priest who sealed the covenant with God after the Exile (Neh. 10:1, 3). Possibly identical with [1]. [3] A priest, the "chief governor in the house of the Lord," who persecuted Jeremiah (Jer. 20:1-6). [4] Son of Melchiah, whose family returned to Jerusalem (1 Chron. 9:12; Neh. 11:12; Jer. 21:1; 38:1).

Pathrusim, a descendant of Mizraim (Gen. 10:14; 1 Chron. 1:12). Possibly the inhabitants of Pathros.

Patrobas ("paternal"), a Roman Christian (Rom. 16:14).

Paul (Latin, *Paulus*—"little"). Next to Jesus, the person most responsible for Christianity was this fiery Jew who took the story of Jesus on the road for ten thousand miles and wrote over one-fourth of the New Testament. The Book of Acts tells of his journeys.

More than any human being, it was Paul who turned a religion full of Jews into a religion made up mostly of non-Jews. In the earliest days of the church, if you wanted to be a Christian you had to be a Jew. If you hadn't been born Jewish, you had to convert and agree to keep all the Old Testament laws, including a painful one for grown men: circumcision. Paul convinced church leaders that non-Jews should be granted full membership

Paul became an effective spokesman for the gospel, especially defending the right of non-Jews to join the church (Acts 15:1–21).

without having to obey Jewish laws. Old Testament laws, Paul argued, were part of God's old agreement with humanity. Jesus' death and resurrection marked the beginning of God's new covenant, prophesied by Jeremiah: "I will write my laws on their hearts and minds" (Jer. 31:33).

Paul was often assaulted and arrested. His final arrest, in Rome, led to his execution. As

Much of the New Testament consists of letters Paul wrote to churches or individuals (see Phil. 1:1–29).

a Roman citizen, Paul had the right to a swift death and was probably beheaded.

Pedahel ("whom God redeems"), a prince of Naphtali (Num. 34:28).

Pedahzur ("the rock delivers"), father of Gamaliel (Num. 1:10; 2:20).

Pedaiah ("Jehovah delivers"). **[1]** Father of Joel (1 Chron. 27:20). **[2]** Grandfather of King Josiah (2 Kings 23:36). **[3]** Son or grandson of

Jeconiah (1 Chron. 3:18–19). **[4]** One who helped to rebuild the wall of Jerusalem (Neh. 3:25). **[5]** One who stood with Ezra when he read the Law (Neh. 8:4; 13:13). **[6]** A descendant of Benjamin (Neh. 11:7).

Pekah ("opening"), a usurper of the throne of Israel; he ruled for twenty years (2 Kings 15:25–31).

Pekahiah ("Jehovah watches"), son and successor of Menahem on the throne of Israel. He was murdered by Pekah (2 Kings 15:22–26).

Pelaiah ("Jehovah is distinguished"). **[1]** A son of Elioenai (1 Chron. 3:24). **[2]** A Levite who explained the Law when Ezra read it (Neh. 8:7). **[3]** A Levite who sealed the covenant (Neh. 10:10); he may be the same as [2].

Pelaliah ("Jehovah judges"), a priest whose grandson dwelled in Jerusalem after the Exile (Neh. 11:12).

Pelatiah ("Jehovah delivers"). **[1]** One who sealed the new covenant with God after the Exile (Neh. 10:22). **[2]** A descendant of David (1 Chron. 3:21). **[3]** A captain of Simeon (1 Chron. 4:42–43). **[4]** A wicked prince seen in Ezekiel's vision (Ezek. 11:1, 13).

Peleg [Phalec] ("division"), son of Eber and ancestor of Christ (Gen. 10:25; 11:16; Luke 3:35).

Pelet ("deliverance"). **[1]** A son of Jahdai of the family of Caleb (1 Chron. 2:47). **[2]** One who joined David at Ziklag (1 Chron. 12:3).

Peleth ("flight; haste"). **[1]** Father of On (Num. 16:1). **[2]** A son of Jonathan and a descendant of Pharez (1 Chron. 2:33).

Peninnah ("coral; pearl"), second wife of Elkanah, father of Samuel (1 Sam. 1:2, 4).

Penuel ("face of God"). **[1]** A descendant of Benjamin (1 Chron. 8:25). **[2]** A chief or father of Gedar (1 Chron. 4:4).

Peresh ("separate"), son of Machir, son of Manasseh (1 Chron. 7:16).

Perez [Phares; Pharez] ("bursting through"), eldest son of Judah and an ancestor of Christ (1 Chron. 27:3; Neh. 11:4). He is also called Pharez (Gen. 38:29; 46:12; Luke 3:33).

Perida [Peruda] ("separation"), one whose descendants returned from the Exile (Neh. 7:57; Ezra 2:55).

Persis ("Persian"), a Christian woman at Rome (Rom. 16:12).

Peruda. *See* Perida.

Peter ("stones; rock"). Lead disciple of Jesus, Peter is famous for trying to walk on water—and sinking. Ironically, his name was Simon until Jesus renamed him Peter, which means "rock." Jesus wasn't making a joke; the name change came later to emphasize Peter's rock-solid devotion to the Lord. Peter graphically demonstrated this allegiance when officials arrested Jesus: Peter cut off one man's ear.

Peter and his brother Andrew were fishermen when Jesus invited them to become His disciples. Bold and strong-minded, Peter established himself as the leader, often speaking to Jesus on behalf of the others, and vowing to defend Jesus to the death. Unfortunately,

P

Peter's sermon on Pentecost marked the beginning of the church's outreach (Acts 2:14–47).

Peter is best known for his cowardice. While Jesus stood trial, Peter waited outside and three times denied knowing the Lord.

After the resurrected Jesus ascended to heaven, a re-energized Peter directed the emerging Christian church. He preached the first sermon, which produced three thousand converts. And he defended Christians before the same Jewish leaders who tried Jesus.

Two New Testament letters bear Peter's name as author, and early Christian writers say that his sermons provided the source for Mark's Gospel. These writers add that Peter was crucified upside down on what is now Vatican Hill in Rome, when Nero persecuted Christians.

Pethahiah ("Jehovah opens up"). [1] A chief Levite in the time of David (1 Chron. 24:16). [2] A Levite having a foreign wife (Ezra 10:23). [3] A descendant of Judah (Neh. 11:24). [4] A Levite who regulated the devotions of the people after Ezra had finished reading the Law (Neh. 9:5).

Pethuel ("God's opening"), father of Joel the prophet (Joel 1:1).

Peullethai ("Jehovah's seed"), a son of Obed-edom and gatekeeper in the time of David (1 Chron. 26:5).

Phalec, Greek form of Peleg (also see).

Phallu. *See* Pallu.

Phalti. *See* Paltiel [2].

Phaltiel. *See* Paltiel.

Phanuel ("vision of God"), father of Anna (Luke 2:36).

Pharaoh ("inhabitant of the palace"), royal title of Egyptian kings, equivalent to our word *king* (Gen. 12:15; 37:36; Exod. 2:15; 1 Kings 3:1; Isa. 19:11).

Phares, Greek form of Perez (also see).

Pharez. *See* Perez.

Pharosh. *See* Parosh.

Phaseah. *See* Paseah.

Phebe ("shining"), a servant of the church at Corinth or Cenchrea who helped Paul (Rom. 16:1).

Phichol ("dark water"), a captain or captains of the army of Abimelech, king of the Philistines (Gen. 21:22; 26:26). Some scholars think this is not a proper name (nor Abimelech), but a Philistine military title. Abraham and Isaac journeyed to Gerar many years apart yet both encountered an Abimelech and Phichol residing there. If these names are titles, that would help explain this puzzling situation; *See* Abimelech.

Philemon ("friendship"), a convert at Colossae to whom Paul wrote an epistle on behalf of his runaway servant, Onesimus (Philem. 1, 5–7).

Philetus ("amiable"), a convert who was condemned by Paul because of his stand on the Resurrection (2 Tim. 2:17).

Philip ("lover of horses"). [1] One of the twelve apostles of Christ (Matt. 10:3; John 1:44–48; 6:5–9). [2] An evangelist mentioned several times in Acts (Acts 6:5; 8:5–13). [3] *See* Herod [3], [4].

Philistim. The reference to Philistim in Genesis 10:14 is to the Philistines.

Philologus ("a lover of learning"), a Roman Christian to whom Paul sent greetings (Rom. 16:15).

Phinehas ("mouth of brass"). [1] Grandson of Aaron and high priest (Exod. 6:25; Num. 25:6–18; 1 Chron. 6:4; 9:20). [2] Younger son of Eli; he was a priest who abused his office (1 Sam. 1:3; 2:22–24, 34). [3] Father of Eleazar (Ezra 8:33).

Phlegon ("burning"), a Roman Christian (Rom. 16:14).

Phurah ("beauty"), a servant of Gideon (Judg. 7:10–11).

Phut [Put] ("bow"), the third son of Ham (Gen. 10:6; 1 Chron. 1:8). Possibly a reference to a people related to the Egyptians. Many consider the reference to be to a people related to the Libyans.

Phuvah [Pua; Puah] ("utterance"). [1] Second son of Issachar (Gen. 46:13; Num. 26:23; 1 Chron. 7:1). [2] Father of Tola the judge (Judg. 10:1).

P

Phygellus ("fugitive"), one who deserted Paul in Asia (2 Tim. 1:15).

Pilate. *See* Pontius Pilate.

Pildash ("flame of fire"), a son of Nahor, Abraham's brother (Gen. 22:22).

Pileha ("worship"), one who sealed the covenant (Neh. 10:24).

Piltai ("Jehovah causes to escape"), a priest in Jerusalem in the days of Joiakim (Neh. 12:17).

Pinon ("darkness"), a chief of Edom (Gen. 36:41; 1 Chron. 1:52).

Piram ("indomitable; wild"), an Amorite king slain by Joshua (Josh. 10:3).

Pispah ("expansion"), a descendant of Asher (1 Chron. 7:38).

Pithon ("harmless"), a son of Micah and great-grandson of Saul (1 Chron. 8:35).

Pochereth ("binding"), one whose children returned (Ezra 2:57; Neh. 7:59).

Pontius Pilate (Latin, *Pontius Pilatus*—"marine dart-carrier"), a Roman procurator of Judea. When Christ was brought before him for judgment, Pilate, fearing the Jews, turned Him over to the people even though he found Him not guilty (Matt. 27:2–24; John 18:28–40).

Poratha ("favored"), a son of Haman slain by the Jews (Esther 9:8).

Porcius Festus. *See* Festus.

Potiphar ("belonging to the sun-god"), Egyptian captain of the guard who became the master of Joseph (Gen. 37:36; 39).

Poti-pherah ("given of the sun-god"), a priest of On; father-in-law of Joseph (Gen. 41:45, 50).

Prisca, shortened form of Priscilla (also see).

Priscilla [Prisca] ("ancient one"), the wife of Aquila; a Jewish Christian deeply loyal to her faith (Acts 18:2, 18, 26; Rom. 16:3).

Prochorus ("choir leader"), one of the seven deacons (Acts 6:5).

Pua. *See* Phuvah.

Puah. *See* Phuvah.

Publius ("common; first"), governor of Malta who courteously received Paul and his company when they were shipwrecked (Acts 28:1–10).

Pudens ("shame faced"), a Roman Christian (2 Tim. 4:21).

Pul. *See* Tiglath-pileser.

Put. *See* Phut.

Putiel ("God enlightens"), father-in-law of Eleazer, son of Aaron (Exod. 6:25).

------------------- **Q** -------------------

Quartus ("fourth"), a Corinthian Christian who sent greetings to the church in Rome (Rom. 16:23).

------------------- **R** -------------------

Raamah ("trembling"), a son of Cush (Gen. 10:7; 1 Chron. 1:9). Possibly a reference to the inhabitants of a place in southwest Arabia.

Raamiah ("Jehovah causes trembling"), a chief who returned to the land (Neh. 7:7). In Ezra 2:2, he is called Reelaiah ("Jehovah causes trembling").

Rabmag ("chief magician; priest"), not a proper name, but an official position of some sort. It is unclear whether it is a high religious or governmental position (Jer. 39:3, 13). Nergal-sharezer of Babylonia bore this title.

Rabsaris. Not a proper name, but an official position in the Babylonian and Assyrian governments. Its precise nature is unknown (Jer. 39:3, 13; 1 Kings 18:17).

Rabshakeh, the title of an office in the Assyrian government. Its precise function is unknown, but suggestions include that of a field marshal or governor of the Assyrian provinces east of Haran (2 Kings 18:17–28; 19:4, 8).

Rachab, Greek form of Rahab (also see).

Rachel [Rahel] ("ewe"), daughter of Laban, wife of Jacob, and mother of Joseph and Benjamin (Gen. 29–35).

Raddai ("Jehovah subdues; beating down"), brother of David (1 Chron. 2:14).

Ragau, Greek form of Reu (also see).

Raguel. *See* Jethro.

Rahab [Rachab] ("broad"), the harlot of Jericho who helped the Hebrew spies and who became an ancestor of Christ (Josh. 2:1–21; 6:17–25; Matt. 1:5).

Raham ("pity; love"), a descendant of Caleb (1 Chron. 2:44).

Rahel. *See* Rachel.

Rakem ("friendship"), a descendant of Manasseh (1 Chron. 7:16).

Ram [Aram] ("exalted"). [1] An ancestor of David and of Christ (Ruth 4:19; Matt. 1:3–4; Luke 3:33). [2] Son of Jerahmeel of Judah (1 Chron. 2:27). [3] Head of the family of Elihu (Job 32:2).

Ramiah ("Jehovah is high"), one who married a foreign wife during the Exile (Ezra 10:25).

Ramoth ("heights"), one who had taken a foreign wife (Ezra 10:29).

Rapha ("fearful"). [1] The fifth son of Benjamin (1 Chron. 8:2). He is called Rephaiah in 1 Chronicles 9:43. [2] A descendant of King Saul (1 Chron. 8:37).

Raphu ("feared; one healed"), father of a spy sent into Canaan (Num. 13:9).

Reaia [Reaiah] ("Jehovah sees"). [1] A descendant of Reuben (1 Chron. 5:5). [2] One whose descendants returned from the Exile (Ezra 2:47; Neh. 7:50). [3] A descendant of Judah (1 Chron. 4:2); perhaps the same as Haroeh (1 Chron. 2:52).

Reba ("fourth part; sprout; offspring"), one of the Midianite chieftains slain by the Israelites under Moses (Num. 31:8; Josh. 13:21).

Rebecca, Greek form of Rebekah (also see).

Rebekah [Rebecca] ("flattering"), wife of Isaac and mother of Jacob and Esau (Gen. 22:23; 24—28).

Rechab ("companionship"). [1] A descendant of Benjamin who murdered Ishbosheth (2 Sam. 4:2, 5–9). [2] Founder of a tribe called Rechabites (2 Kings 10:15; Jer. 35). [3] A descendant of Hemath (1 Chron. 2:55). [4] One who helped to build the wall of Jerusalem (Neh. 3:14).

Reelaiah. *See* Raamiah.

Regem ("friendship"), a descendant of Caleb (2 Chron. 2:47). *See* Regem-melech.

Regem-melech ("royal friend"), a messenger sent out by some Jews. Some authorities do not take this as a proper name but read: ". . . Sherezer, the friend of the king" (Zech. 7:2).

Rehabiah ("Jehovah is a widener"), eldest son of Eliezer, son of Moses (1 Chron. 23:17; 24:21).

Rehob ("width; breadth"). [1] Father of Hadadezer, king of Zobah (2 Sam. 8:3, 12). [2] A Levite who sealed the covenant (Neh. 10:11).

Rehoboam [Roboam] ("freer of the people"), the son of Solomon; when he was king, ten tribes revolted from him and he set up the southern kingdom of Judah (1 Kings 11:43; 12; 14). He was an ancestor of Christ (Matt. 1:7).

Rehum ("pity"). [1] A chief man that returned from the Exile with Zerubbabel (Ezra 2:2). He is called Nehum ("comfort") in Nehemiah 7:7. [2] A chancellor of Artaxerxes (Ezra 4:8, 17). [3] A Levite who helped to repair the wall of Jerusalem (Neh. 3:17). [4] One who sealed the covenant (Neh. 10:25). [5] One who went up with Zerubbabel (Neh. 12:3).

Rei ("friendly"), a friend of David (1 Kings 1:8).

Rekem ("friendship"). [1] A Midianite king slain by the Israelites (Num. 31:8; Josh. 13:21). [2] A son of Hebron (1 Chron. 2:43–44).

Remaliah ("Jehovah increases; whom Jehovah has adorned"), father of Pekah (2 Kings 15:25–37). This is perhaps not a proper name, but a slur on Pekah's impoverished background.

Rephael ("God has healed"), firstborn son of Obed-edom and tabernacle gatekeeper (1 Chron. 26:7).

Rephah ("healing; support"), a descendant of Ephraim (1 Chron. 7:25).

Rephaiah ("Jehovah is healing"). [1] Head of a family of the house of David (1 Chron. 3:21).

[2] A captain of Simeon (1 Chron. 4:42). [3] A son of Tola (1 Chron. 7:2). [4] One who helped to rebuild the wall of Jerusalem (Neh. 3:9). [5] *See* Rapha [1].

Resheph (the name of a Canaanite deity; meaning unknown), a descendant of Ephraim (1 Chron. 7:25).

Reu [Ragau] ("friendship"), son of Peleg and ancestor of Christ (Gen. 11:18–21; Luke 3:35).

Reuben ("behold, a son"), eldest son of Jacob and Leah; he lost his birthright through sin against his father (Gen. 29:32; 35:22; 37:29). His descendants became one of the twelve tribes of Israel.

Reuel ("God is his friend"). [1] A son of Esau by Bashemath (Gen. 36:4; 1 Chron. 1:35, 37). [2] Descendant of Benjamin (1 Chron. 9:8). [3] *See* Jethro. [4] *See* Deuel.

Reumah ("pearl; coral"), Nahor's concubine (Gen. 22:24).

Rezia ("Jehovah is pleasing"), a descendant of Asher (1 Chron. 7:39).

Rezin ("dominion"). [1] The last king of Syria who, along with Pekah, fought Judah (2 Kings 15:37; 16:5–10). [2] One whose descendants returned from the Babylonian Captivity (Ezra 2:48; Neh. 7:50).

Rezon ("prince; noble"), a Syrian rebel who set up his own government in Damascus (1 Kings 11:23). Many scholars think Rezon simply is a title denoting a prince and identify him with Hezion (also see).

Rhesa ("head"), an ancestor of Christ (Luke 3:27).

Rhoda ("rose"), a maid in the house of Mary (Acts 12:12–15).

Ribai ("Jehovah contends"), father of Ittai, one of David's valiant men (2 Sam. 23:29; 1 Chron. 11:31).

Rimmon ("pomegranate"), father of Ish-bosheth's murderers (2 Sam. 4:2–9).

Rinnah ("praise to God; strength"), a descendant of Judah (1 Chron. 4:20).

Riphath ("spoken"), a son of Gomer (Gen. 10:3). A copyist's mistake makes him Diphath in 1 Chronicles 1:6. Possibly a reference to the Paphlagonians on the Black Sea.

Rizpah ("variegated; hot stone"), a concubine of Saul (2 Sam. 3:7; 21:8–11).

Roboam, Greek form of Rehoboam.

Rodanim. *See* Dodanim.

Rohgah ("outcry; alarm"), a chief of Asher (1 Chron. 7:34).

Romamti-ezer ("highest help"), son of Heman appointed over the service of song (1 Chron. 25:4, 31).

Rosh ("head"), a descendant of Benjamin (Gen. 46:21).

Rufus ("red"). **[1]** A son of Simon of Cyrene (Mark 15:21). He was probably well-known to those to whom Mark wrote his Gospel. **[2]** A Roman Christian (Rom. 16:13); some identify him with [1].

Ruth ("friendship; companion"), Moabite wife of Mahlon and Boaz; she was the great-

Ruth's faithful help to her mother-in-law Naomi caught the attention of Boaz (Ruth 2:1–23).

grandmother of David and an ancestor of Christ (Ruth 1:4–5, 14–16; 4:10; Matt. 1:5).

S

Sabta [Sabtah] ("striking"), the third son of Cush (Gen. 10:7; 1 Chron. 1:9). Possibly a people of southern Arabia is intended.

Sabtecha [Sabtechah] ("striking"), the fifth son of Cush (Gen. 10:7; 1 Chron. 1:9). Possibly a reference to a people of south Arabia.

Sacar ("hired"). [1] The father of one of David's mighty men (1 Chron. 11:35). He is called Sharar ("strong") in 2 Samuel 23:33. [2] A Levite tabernacle gatekeeper in the days of David (1 Chron. 26:4).

Sadoc (Greek form of Zadok—"righteous"), an ancestor of Christ (Matt. 1:14).

Sala [Salah] ("petition; sprout"), a son of Arphaxad and ancestor of Christ (Gen. 10:24; 11:12; Luke 3:35). He is called Shelah in 1 Chronicles 1:18, 24.

Salathiel, Greek form of Shealtiel (also see).

Sallai ("rejecter"). [1] A chief man of the tribe of Benjamin (Neh. 11:8). [2] A priest who returned with Zerubbabel from the Exile (Neh. 12:20). He is called Sallu in Nehemiah 12:7.

Sallu ("weighed; dear"). **[1]** A descendant of Benjamin dwelling in Jerusalem (1 Chron. 9:7; Neh. 11:7). **[2]** *See* Sallai [2].

Salma [Salmon] ("strength; clothing"). **[1]** A son of Caleb, son of Hur (1 Chron. 2:51, 54). **[2]** Father of Boaz and ancestor of Christ (Ruth 4:20–21; Matt. 1:4–5; Luke 3:32). Not to be confused with Zalmon.

Salome ("clothing; strength"). **[1]** One of the women who saw the Crucifixion (Mark 15:40; 16:1). Matthew 27:56 mentions that the mother of the sons of Zebedee was present; she is probably to be identified with Salome. John 19:25 lists the sister of Jesus' mother among those near the cross; some scholars identify her with Salome, but others deny this. **[2]** The daughter of Herodias who danced before Herod (Matt. 14:6; Mark 6:22).

Salu ("miserable; unfortunate"), father of Zimri, who was slain (Num. 25:14).

Samgar-nebo, a Babylonian officer who sat with other officials in the middle gate of Jerusalem (Jer. 39:3). Some take this as a proper name (perhaps meaning "be gracious, Nebo"). Others view it as a title of Nergal-sharezer.

Samlah ("garment"), king of Edom (Gen. 36:36; 1 Chron. 1:47–48).

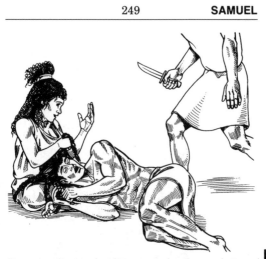

Strongman Samson lost his power when he was betrayed by Delilah (Judg. 16:4–31).

S

Samson ("distinguished; strong"), judge of Israel for twenty years. His great strength and moral weakness have made him famous (Judg. 13:24; 14—16).

Samuel ("asked of God; heard of God"). Once settled in their new land, the Israelites lived in a loose federation led by judges. Perhaps the most important of these judges was Samuel. Though Samuel had a family, from early childhood he lived with the priest in Israel's worship center to fulfill a vow his mother made. Infertile, Hannah had promised that if God gave her a son, she would return this child to the Lord's service.

Samuel grew into a wise and righteous man who served God in many capacities. While he was still a boy, he received messages from God and delivered them to the people, as a prophet. He offered sacrifices, as a priest. And he trav-

Samuel's mother Hannah promised him to God before he was born (1 Sam. 1:1–28).

eled the countryside settling disputes, as a judge. In fact, Samuel was the last of the judges in the era before Israel crowned a king.

When Samuel grew old, the Israelites asked him to select their first king. Samuel believed that the people should continue thinking of God as their king. But God granted Israel's request, though he considered it a rejection of His kingship. Samuel chose Saul.

Samuel annointed Saul as the first king of Israel (1 Sam 9:1—10:24).

Later, when Saul sinned and became an unworthy leader, Samuel secretly anointed David as the future king. When Samuel died of old age, the nation gathered to mourn him.

Sanballat ("strong"), a leading opponent of the Jews at the time they were rebuilding the walls of Jerusalem (Neh. 2:10; 4:1, 7; 6:1–14).

Saph ("preserver"), a descendant of Rapha the giant (2 Sam. 21:18). He is called Sippai ("Jehovah is preserver") in 1 Chronicles 20:4.

Sapphira ("beautiful; sapphire"), the dishonest wife of Ananias, who was struck dead by God (Acts 5:1–10).

Sara, Greek form of Sarah (also see).

Sarah [Sara; Sarai] ("princess"), the wife of Abraham and mother of Isaac (Gen. 17–18; 20–21; Heb. 11:11; 1 Pet. 3:6). Her name was changed from Sarai ("Jehovah is prince") to Sarah ("princess") because she would be the progenitor of a great nation (Gen. 17:15). *See* Serah.

Sarai. *See* Sarah.

Saraph ("burning"), a descendant of Judah (1 Chron. 4:22).

Sargon ("[the god] has established the king [ship]"), an important king of Assyria who finished the siege of Samaria and carried away Israel. He is called by name only once in Scripture (Isa. 20:1).

Sarsechim ("chief of the eunuchs"), a prince of Babylon who sat at the gate (Jer. 39:3).

Saruch, Greek form of Serug (also see).

Saul [Shaul] ("asked"). [1] The first king of Israel; God eventually gave him up. He tried several times to slay David, but was killed himself at Gilboa (1 Sam. 9—31). [2] The original name of Paul (also see). [3] *See* Shaul [1].

Sceva ("fitted"), a Jewish priest at Ephesus whose sons attempted to cast out a demon, but were wounded by it instead (Acts 19:14–16).

Seba ("drunkard"), eldest son of Cush (Gen. 10:7; 1 Chron. 1:9). Not to be confused with Sheba. Possibly the name refers to a people of southern Arabia.

Secundus ("second"), a Thessalonian Christian and friend of Paul (Acts 20:4).

Segub ("might; protection"). [1] Younger son of Hiel who rebuilt Jericho in the days of Ahab (1 Kings 16:34). [2] A grandson of Judah (1 Chron. 2:21–22).

Seled ("exultation"), a descendant of Judah (1 Chron. 2:30).

Sem, Greek form of Shem (also see).

Semachiah ("Jehovah supports"), a gatekeeper of the tabernacle in David's day (1 Chron. 26:7).

Semei (Greek form of Shimei), an ancestor of Christ (Luke 3:26).

Senaah. *See* Hassenaah.

Sennacherib (Babylonian, *Sin-ahi-eriba*—"[the god] Sin has substituted for my brother"), an Assyrian king who killed his brother to usurp the throne. He unsuccessfully invaded Judah. The amazing story of the destruction of his army is told in 2 Kings 19 (2 Kings 18:13; Isa. 36:1; 37:17, 21, 37).

Senuah ("the violated"), a descendant of Benjamin (Neh. 11:9). Possibly the same as Hasenuah (also see).

Seorim ("fear; distress"), a priest in the days of David (1 Chron. 24:8).

Serah ("extension"), a daughter of Asher (Gen. 46:17; 1 Chron. 7:30). Numbers 26:46 should read Serah, not Sarah.

Seraiah ("Jehovah is prince; Jehovah has prevailed"). **[1]** A scribe of David (2 Sam. 8:17). In 2 Samuel 20:25, he is called Sheva and Shavsha in 1 Chronicles 18:16. He is also called Shisha in 1 Kings 4:3. **[2]** Chief priest of Jerusalem (2 Kings 25:18; 1 Chron. 6:14;

Ezra 7:1). **[3]** One whom Gedaliah advised to submit to Chaldea (2 Kings 25:23; Jer. 40:8). **[4]** The brother of Othniel (1 Chron. 4:13–14). **[5]** A descendant of Simeon (1 Chron. 4:35). **[6]** A priest that returned to Jerusalem with Zerubbabel (Ezra 2:2). **[7]** A leader sent to capture Jeremiah (Jer. 36:26). **[8]** A prince of Judah who went to Babylon (Jer. 51:59, 61). **[9]** A son of Hilkiah dwelling in Jerusalem after the Exile (Neh. 11:11). **[10]** A chief of the priests who returned from Babylon (Neh. 12:1, 7).

Sered ("escape; deliverance"), eldest son of Zebulun (Gen. 46:14; Num. 26:26).

Sergius Paulus, the Roman deputy of Cyprus who was converted because Elymas was struck blind (Acts 13:7).

S

Serug [Saruch] ("strength; firmness"), father of Nahor and ancestor of Christ (Gen. 11:20, 21; Luke 3:35).

Seth [Sheth] ("compensation; sprout"), son of Adam and Eve, and an ancestor of Christ (Gen. 4:25–26; 1 Chron. 1:1; Luke 3:38).

Sethur ("secreted; hidden"), one sent to spy out the land (Num. 13:13).

Shaaph ("union; friendship"). **[1]** A descendant of Judah (1 Chron. 2:47). **[2]** A son of Caleb (1 Chron. 2:49).

Shaashgaz ("lover of beauty; one anxious to learn"), a chamberlain of Ahasuerus (Esther 2:14).

Shabbethai ("sabbath-born"). [1] An assistant to Ezra (Ezra 10:15). [2] One who explained the Law to the people (Neh. 8:7). [3] A chief Levite in Jerusalem (Neh. 11:16). All three may be identical.

Shachia ("fame of Jehovah"), a descendant of Benjamin (1 Chron. 8:10).

Shadrach ("servant of [the god] Sin"), the name given to Hananiah at Babylon. He was cast into a fiery furnace and rescued (Dan. 1:7; 3).

Shage ("erring; wandering"), father of one of David's mighty men (1 Chron. 11:34). Possibly another name of Shammah (also see).

Shaharaim ("double dawn"), a descendant of Benjamin who went to Moab (1 Chron. 8:8).

Shallum [Shallun] ("recompenser"). [1] The youngest son of Naphtali (1 Chron. 7:13). He is also called Shillem (Gen. 46:24; Num. 26:49). [2] A descendant of Simeon (1 Chron. 4:25). [3] A descendant of Judah (1 Chron. 2:40–41). [4] One who usurped the throne of Israel and reigned for one month (2 Kings 15:10–15). [5] Husband of Huldah the prophetess

(2 Kings 22:14; 2 Chron. 34:22). **[6]** *See* Jehoahaz [2]. **[7]** *See* Meshullam [7]. **[8]** A gatekeeper of the tabernacle (1 Chron. 9:17–19, 31; Ezra 2:42; Neh. 7:45). **[9]** Father of Jehizkiah (2 Chron. 28:12). **[10]**, **[11]** Two who married foreign wives during the Exile (Ezra 10:24, 42). **[12]** One who helped to repair the wall of Jerusalem (Neh. 3:12). **[13]** One who helped to repair the gate of Jerusalem (Neh. 3:15). **[14]** An uncle of Jeremiah (Jer. 32:7).

Shadrach, Meshach, and Abed-nego walked through the king's fiery furnace, joined by a fourth man who was "like the Son of God" (Dan. 3:19–25).

[15] Father of one who was a temple officer in the days of Jehoiakim (Jer. 35:4).

Shalmai ("Jehovah is recompenser"), ancestor of returned exiles (Ezra 2:46; Neh. 7:48).

Shalman, the king who sacked Beth-arbel (Hos. 10:14). Perhaps he was either Shalmaneser V of Assyria or Shalman king of Moab.

Shalmaneser (Babylonian, *Shulmaner-asharidu*—"[the god] Shulman is chief"), the king of Assyria to whom Hoshea became subject was Shalmaneser V (2 Kings 17:3). Either Shalmaneser or Sargon, his successor, was the king to whom Samaria fell after a long siege (2 Kings 17:6; 18:9).

Shama ("hearer"), one of David's heroes (1 Chron. 11:44).

Shamariah. *See* Shemariah.

Shamed ("destroyer"), a son of Elpaal (1 Chron. 8:12).

Shamer ("preserver"). **[1]** A descendant of Merari (1 Chron. 6:46). **[2]** A descendant of Asher (1 Chron. 7:34). He is called Shomer in 1 Chronicles 7:32.

Shamgar ("cupbearer; fleer"), judge of Israel who rescued his people from the Philistines (Judg. 3:31; 5:6).

Shamhuth ("fame; renown"), a captain of David's army (1 Chron. 27:8).

Shamir ("thorn hedge; approved"), a son of Micah, a Levite (1 Chron. 24:24).

Shamma ("fame; renown"), a descendant of Asher (1 Chron. 7:37). *See* Shammah.

Shammah ("fame; renown"). **[1]** A grandson of Esau (Gen. 36:13, 17; 1 Chron. 1:37). **[2]** A son of Jesse (1 Sam. 16:9; 17:13). He is also called Shimeah or Shimea (2 Sam. 13:3; 21:21; 1 Chron. 20:7), and Shimma (1 Chron. 2:13). **[3]** One of David's mighty men or the father of one of David's mighty men (2 Sam. 23:11). **[4]** Another of David's mighty men (2 Sam. 23:33), called Shammoth in 1 Chronicles 11:27. **[5]** Yet another of David's mighty men (2 Sam. 23:25).

Shammai ("celebrated"). **[1]** A descendant of Judah (1 Chron. 2:28, 32). **[2]** A descendant of Caleb, son of Hezron (1 Chron. 2:44–45). **[3]** A son or grandson of Ezra (1 Chron. 4:17).

Shammoth. *See* Shammah [4].

Shammua [Shammuah] ("famous"). **[1]** One sent to spy out the land of Canaan (Num. 13:4). **[2]** One of David's sons (2 Sam. 5:14; 1 Chron. 14:4). In 1 Chronicles 3:5, he is called Shimea. **[3]** A Levite who led the temple worship after the Exile (Neh. 11:17). He is also called Shemaiah (1 Chron. 9:16). **[4]** The head of a priestly family in Nehemiah's day (Neh. 12:18).

Shamsherai ("heroic"), a descendant of Benjamin (1 Chron. 8:26).

Shapham ("youthful; vigorous"), a chief of Gad (1 Chron. 5:12).

Shaphan ("prudent; sly"). **[1]** A scribe of Josiah who read him the Law (2 Kings 22:3; 2 Chron. 34:8–21). **[2]** Father of a chief officer under Josiah (2 Kings 22:12; 2 Chron. 34:20). **[3]** Father of Elasah (Jer. 29:3). **[4]** Father of Jaazaniah whom Ezekiel saw in a vision (Ezek. 8:11). Many scholars consider all of the above to be identical.

Shaphat ("judge"). **[1]** One sent to spy out the land of Canaan (Num. 13:5). **[2]** Father of Elisha the prophet (1 Kings 19:16, 19; 2 Kings 3:11; 6:31). **[3]** One of the family of David (1 Chron. 3:22). **[4]** A chief of Gad (1 Chron. 5:12). **[5]** One over David's herds in the valley (1 Chron. 27:29).

Sharai ("Jehovah is deliverer"), one who took a foreign wife (Ezra 10:40).

Sharar. *See* Sacar [1].

Sharezer [Sherezer] (Babylonian, *Shar-utsur*—"he has protected the king"). **[1]** A son of the Assyrian king Sennacherib who, with his brother, killed their father (2 Kings 19:37; Isa. 37:38). **[2]** One sent to consult the priests and prophets (Zech. 7:2).

Shashai ("noble; free"), one who married a foreign wife during the Exile (Ezra 10:40).

Shashak ("assaulter; runner"), a descendant of Benjamin (1 Chron. 8:14, 25).

Shaul [Saul] (variant form of Saul). **[1]** The sixth king of Edom (Gen. 36:37–38; 1 Chron. 1:48–49). **[2]** A descendant of Levi (1 Chron. 6:24). **[3]** A son of Simeon found in several lists (Gen. 46:10; Exod. 6:15; 1 Chron. 4:24).

Shavsha. *See* Seraiah [1].

Sheal ("request"), one who took a foreign wife (Ezra 10:29).

Shealtiel [Salathiel] ("lent by God"), father of Zerubbabel and an ancestor of Christ (Ezra 3:2, 8; 5:2; Hag. 1:1, 12; Matt. 1:12).

Sheariah ("Jehovah is decider"), a descendant of Saul (1 Chron. 8:38; 9:44).

Shear-jashub ("a remnant returns"), symbolic name given a son of Isaiah (Isa. 7:3).

Sheba ("oath; covenant"). **[1]** A chief of Gad (1 Chron. 5:13). **[2]** One who rebelled against

S

David and was beheaded for it (2 Sam. 20). [3] A grandson of Abraham (Gen. 25:3; 1 Chron. 1:32). [4] A descendant of Shem (Gen. 10:28; 1 Chron. 1:22). Some scholars identify [5] with [4]. They believe Sheba is a tribe or people and stress that close genealogical ties account for the occurrence of the name in both Ham's and Shem's genealogy. [5] A descendant of Ham (Gen. 10:7; 1 Chron. 1:9).

Shebaniah ("Jehovah is powerful"). [1] A priest who aided in bringing the ark of the covenant to the temple (1 Chron. 15:24). [2] A Levite who guided the devotions of the people (Neh. 9:4–5; 10:10). [3], [4] Two priests who sealed the covenant (Neh. 10:4, 12, 14).

Sheber ("breach"), a descendant of Jephunneh (1 Chron. 2:48).

Shebna ("youthfulness"), the scribe or secretary of Hezekiah replaced by Eliakim (2 Kings 18:18; Isa. 22:15–25; 36:3–22).

Shebuel ("God is renown"). [1] A son of Gershom (1 Chron. 23:16; 26:24). [2] A son of Haman, chief singer in the sanctuary (1 Chron. 24:4). He is called Shubael in verse 20.

Shechaniah [Shecaniah] ("Jehovah is a neighbor"). [1] Head of a family of the house of David (1 Chron. 3:21–22). [2], [3] Two whose descendants returned from the Babylonian Captivity (Ezra 8:3, 5). **[4]** One who took a foreign wife during the Exile (Ezra 10:2). **[5]** Father of one who repaired the wall of Jerusalem (Neh. 3:29). **[6]** Father-in-law to one who opposed Nehemiah (Neh. 6:18). **[7]** A priest who returned from the Exile (Neh. 12:3). **[8]** A priest in the time of David (1 Chron. 24:11). **[9]** A priest in Hezekiah's day (2 Chron. 31:15).

Shechem [Sychem] ("shoulder"). **[1]** Son of Hamor who defiled Dinah; he and his family were soon destroyed for that act (Gen. 33:19; 34). **[2]** A descendant of Manasseh (Num. 26:31; Josh. 17:2). **[3]** Another descendant of Manasseh (1 Chron. 7:19).

Shedeur ("shedder of light"), one who helped number the people (Num. 1:5; 2:10; 7:30, 35).

Shehariah ("Jehovah is the dawn"), a descendant of Benjamin (1 Chron. 8:26).

Shelah ("peace"). **[1]** The youngest son of Judah (Gen. 38:5–26; 1 Chron. 2:3; 4:21). **[2]** *See* Sala.

Shelemiah ("Jehovah is recompense"). **[1]** *See* Meshelemiah. **[2]**, **[3]** Two who married foreign wives during the Exile (Ezra 10:39, 41). **[4]** Father of Hananiah (Neh. 3:30). **[5]** A priest over the treasury (Neh. 13:13). **[6]** An ancestor of one who was sent by the princes to get Baruch (Jer. 36:14). **[7]** One ordered to capture Baruch and Jeremiah (Jer. 36:26). **[8]** Father of one sent to Jeremiah to ask for prayers (Jer. 37:3; 38:1). **[9]** Father of the guard who apprehended Jeremiah (Jer. 37:13).

Sheleph ("drawn out"), a son of Joktan (Gen. 10:26; 1 Chron. 1:20). A Semitic people dwelling in Arabia is possibly intended.

Shelesh ("might"), a descendant of Asher (1 Chron. 7:35).

Shelomi ("Jehovah is peace"), father of a prince of Asher (Num. 34:27).

Shelomith ("peacefulness"). **[1]** Mother of one stoned for blasphemy in the wilderness (Lev. 24:11). **[2]** Daughter of Zerubbabel (1 Chron. 3:19). **[3]** A descendant of Gershon (1 Chron. 23:9). **[4]** A descendant of Levi and Kohath (1 Chron. 23:18). **[5]** One over the treasures in the days of David (1 Chron. 26:25–28). **[6]** Child of Rehoboam (2 Chron. 11:20). **[7]** An ancestor of a family that returned from the Exile (Ezra 8:10). Not to be confused with Shelomoth.

Shelomoth ("peacefulness"), a descendant of Izhar (1 Chron. 24:22). Many identify him with Shelomith [4].

Shelumiel ("God is peace"), a chief of Simeon appointed to assist Moses (Num. 1:6; 2:12; 7:36).

Shem [Sem] ("name; renown"), son of Noah and ancestor of Christ (Gen. 5:32; 6:10; 10:1; Luke 3:36).

Shema ("fame; repute"). **[1]** A son of Hebron (1 Chron. 2:43–44). **[2]** A descendant of Reuben (1 Chron. 5:8). **[3]** A chief of the tribe of Benjamin (1 Chron. 8:13). **[4]** One who stood with Ezra when he read the Law (Neh. 8:4).

Shemaah ("the fame"), father of two valiant men who joined David (1 Chron. 12:3).

Shemaiah ("Jehovah is fame" or "Jehovah hears"). **[1]** A prophet who warned Rehoboam against war (1 Kings 12:22; 2 Chron. 11:2). **[2]** A descendant of David (1 Chron. 3:22). **[3]** Head of a family of Simeon (1 Chron. 4:37). **[4]** Son of Joel (1 Chron. 5:4). **[5]** A descendant of Merari (1 Chron. 9:14; Neh. 11:15). **[6]** One who helped to bring the ark of the covenant to the temple (1 Chron. 15:8, 11). **[7]** A Levite who recorded the allotment in David's day (1 Chron. 24:6). **[8]** A gatekeeper for the tabernacle (1 Chron. 26:4, 6–7). **[9]** A Levite whom Jehoshaphat sent to teach the people (2 Chron. 17:8). **[10]** One who helped to cleanse the temple (2 Chron. 29:14). **[11]** A

S

Levite in Hezekiah's day (2 Chron. 31:15). [12] A chief Levite in Josiah's day (2 Chron. 35:9). [13] One who returned with Ezra (Ezra 8:13). [14] A person sent to Iddo to enlist ministers (Ezra 8:16). [15], [16] Two who married foreign wives during the Exile (Ezra 10:21, 31). [17] One who helped to repair the wall of Jerusalem (Neh. 3:29). [18] One who tried to intimidate Nehemiah (Neh. 6:10). [19] One who sealed the new covenant with God after the Exile (Neh. 10:8). [20] One who helped to purify the wall of Jerusalem (Neh. 12:36). [21] One at the dedication of the wall of Jerusalem (Neh. 12:42). [22] Father of the prophet Urijah (Jer. 26:20). [23] One who wanted the priests to reprimand Jeremiah (Jer. 29:24, 31). [24] Father of a prince of the Jews (Jer. 36:12). [25] *See* Shammua [3]. [26] A prince of Judah who took part in the dedication of the wall (Neh. 12:34). [27] A Levite of the line of Asaph (Neh. 12:35). [28] A chief of the priests who returned with Zerubbabel (Neh. 12:6–7).

Shemariah [Shamariah] ("whom Jehovah guards"). [1] One who joined David at Ziklag (1 Chron. 12:5). [2] A son of King Rehoboam (2 Chron. 11:19). [3], [4] Two who married foreign wives during the Exile (Ezra 10:32, 41).

Shemeber ("splendor of heroism"), the king of Zeboim in the days of Abraham (Gen. 14:2).

Shemer ("watch"), owner of the hill which Omri bought and on which he built Samaria (1 Kings 16:24).

Shemida [Shemidah] ("fame of knowing"), a grandson of Manasseh (Num. 26:32; Josh. 17:2; 1 Chron. 7:19).

Shemidah. *See* Shemida.

Shemiramoth ("fame of the highest"). **[1]** A Levite in the choral service (1 Chron. 15:18, 20; 16:5). **[2]** One sent by Jehoshaphat to teach the Law (2 Chron. 17:8).

Shemuel (variant form of Samuel—"asked of God"). **[1]** One appointed to divide the land of Canaan (Num. 34:20). **[2]** Head of a family of Issachar (1 Chron. 7:2). **[3]** *See* Samuel.

Shenazar ("ivory keeper; Sin [the god] protect"), son or grandson of Jeconiah (1 Chron. 3:18).

S

Shephathiah [Shephatiah] ("Jehovah is judge"). **[1]** A son of David by Abital (2 Sam. 3:4; 1 Chron. 3:3). **[2]** Father of Meshullam who dwelled in Jerusalem (1 Chron. 9:8). **[3]** A valiant man who joined David at Ziklag (1 Chron. 12:5). **[4]** A prince of Simeon (1 Chron. 27:16). **[5]** A son of Jehoshaphat (2 Chron. 21:2). **[6]** An ancestor of returned captives (Ezra 2:4; Neh. 7:9). **[7]** One of Solomon's servants whose descendants returned from the Babylonian

Captivity (Ezra 2:57; Neh. 7:59). [8] An ancestor of returned captives (Ezra 8:8). He is possibly identical with [6]. [9] A descendant of Pharez whose descendants dwelled in Jerusalem (Neh. 11:4). [10] A prince of Judah in Zedekiah's time (Jer. 38:1).

Shephi [Shepho] ("unconcern"), a descendant of Seir the Horite (1 Chron. 1:40). He is called Shepho in Genesis 36:23.

Shepho. *See* Shephi.

Shephuphan. *See* Muppim.

Sherah ("blood-relationship"), a woman descendant of Ephraim (1 Chron. 7:24). She was either his daughter or granddaughter; the text is unclear.

Sherebiah ("Jehovah is originator"). [1] A priest who returned from the Exile (Ezra 8:18, 24; Neh. 8:7; 9:4–5). [2] A Levite who sealed the new covenant with God after the Exile (Neh. 10:12; 12:8, 24).

Sheresh ("union"), a descendant of Manasseh (1 Chron. 7:16).

Sherezer. *See* Sharezer.

Sheshai ("free; noble"), a son of Anak slain by Caleb (Num. 13:22; Josh. 15:14).

Sheshan ("free; noble"), a descendant of Judah through Jerahmeel (1 Chron. 2:31, 34, 35).

Sheshbazzar ("O Shamash [the god], protect the father"), the prince of Judah into whose hands Cyrus placed the temple vessels. Many believe he is the same as Zerubbabel, but others deny this. They claim Sheshbazzar was governor under Cyrus and Zerubbabel under Darius (Ezra 1:8, 11; 5:14–16).

Sheth ("compassion"), a chief of the Moabites (Num. 24:17). Not to be confused with Seth.

Sheth ("tumult"), a descriptive name given to Moabites (Num. 24:17). Possibly an ancient tribal name of the Moabites.

Shethar ("star; commander"), one of the seven princes of Persia and Media (Esther 1:14). Not to be confused with Shethar-boznai.

Shethar-boznai ("starry splendor"), an official of the king of Persia (Ezra 5:3, 6; 6:6, 13).

Sheva ("self-satisfying"). **[1]** A son of Caleb (1 Chron. 2:49). **[2]** See Seraiah [1].

Shilhi ("a warrior; one with darts"), grandfather of King Jehoshaphat (1 Kings 22:42; 2 Chron. 20:31).

Shillem ("retribution"). See Shallum [1].

Shiloni ("weapon; armor"), father of Zechariah (Neh. 11:5).

Shilshah ("might; heroism"), a son of Zophath (1 Chron. 7:37).

Shimea [Shimeah] ("'[God] has heard [a prayer]"). **[1]** A descendant of Merari (1 Chron. 6:30). **[2]** Father of Berachiah (1 Chron. 6:39). **[3]** *See* Shammah [2]. **[4]** *See* Shammua [2]. **[5]** One of the family of King Saul whose descendants dwelled in Jerusalem (1 Chron. 8:32; 9:38). In the latter passage he is called Shimeam.

Shimeam ("fame; rumor"). *See* Shimeah [2].

Shimeath ("fame"), mother of one who aided in killing King Jehoash (2 Kings 12:21; 2 Chron. 24:26).

Shimei [Shimhi; Shimi] ("Jehovah is fame; Jehovah hear me"). **[1]** A son of Gershon and a grandson of Gershon (Exod. 6:17; Num. 3:18, 21; Zech. 12:13). **[2]** A descendant of Benjamin who cursed David when he was fleeing from Absalom (2 Sam. 16:5–13; 19:16–23). **[3]** A loyal officer of David (1 Kings 1:8). **[4]** An officer of Solomon (1 Kings 4:18). **[5]** Grandson of King Jeconiah (1 Chron. 3:19). **[6]** A man who had sixteen sons and six daughters (1 Chron. 4:26–27). **[7]** A descendant of Reuben (1 Chron. 5:4). **[8]** A son of Libni (1 Chron. 6:29). **[9]** Father of a chief of Judah (1 Chron. 8:21). **[10]** A Levite (1 Chron. 23:9). **[11]** A Levite in the temple song service in the days of David (1 Chron. 25:17). **[12]** One in charge of many vineyards (1 Chron. 27:27). **[13]** One who helped to cleanse the temple (2 Chron. 29:14). **[14]** A Levite in charge of the temple offerings under Hezekiah (2 Chron. 31:12–13). **[15]**, **[16]**, **[15]**, **[16]**, **[17]** Three men who took foreign wives during the Exile (Ezra 10:23, 33, 38). **[18]** Grandfather of Mordecai (Esther 2:5).

Shimeon ("hearing"), one who married a foreign wife (Ezra 10:31). Not to be confused with Simeon.

Shimhi. *See* Shimei.

Shimi. *See* Shimei.

Shimma. *See* Shammah [2].

Shimon ("trier; valuer"), a descendant of Caleb (1 Chron. 4:20).

Shimrath ("watch"), a descendant of Benjamin (1 Chron. 8:21).

Shimri [Simri] ("Jehovah is watching"). **[1]** Head of a family of Simeon (1 Chron. 4:37). **[2]** Father of one of David's mighty men (1 Chron. 11:45). **[3]** Gatekeeper of the tabernacle in David's day (1 Chron. 26:10). **[4]** One who helped to cleanse the temple (2 Chron. 29:13).

Shimrith ("watch"), a woman of Moab, mother of Jehozabad who killed Joash (2 Chron. 24:26). She is called Shomer in 2 Kings 12:21.

S

Shimrom [Shimron] ("watch"), the fourth son of Issachar (Gen. 46:13; Num. 26:24; 1 Chron. 7:1).

Shimshai ("Jehovah is splendor"), a scribe who, with Rehum, wrote to the king of Persia opposing the rebuilding of the wall of Jerusalem (Ezra 4:8–9, 17, 23).

Shinab, the king of Admah attacked by Chedorlaomer and his allies (Gen. 14:2).

Shiphi ("Jehovah is fulness"), father of a chief of Simeon (1 Chron. 4:37).

Shiphrah ("beauty"), one of the Hebrew midwives at the time of the birth of Moses (Exod. 1:15).

Shiphtan ("judge"), father of Kemuel, a chief of Ephraim (Num. 34:24).

Shisha ("distinction; nobility"), father of two of Solomon's scribes (1 Kings 4:3). Possibly the same as Seraiah [1].

Shishak, another name for Shishak I, king of Egypt. He sheltered Jeroboam against Solomon and in later years invaded Judah (1 Kings 11:40; 14:25; 2 Chron. 12).

Shitrai ("Jehovah is deciding"), a man in charge of David's herds in Sharon (1 Chron. 27:29).

Shiza ("splendor"), father of one of David's valiant men (1 Chron. 11:42).

Shobab ("returning"). [1] A son of David (2 Sam. 5:14; 1 Chron. 3:5). [2] A son of Caleb (1 Chron. 2:18).

Shobach ("expansion"), captain of the army of Hadarezer of Zobah (2 Sam. 10:16, 18); he is also called Shophach (1 Chron. 19:16).

Shobai ("Jehovah is glorious"), a tabernacle gatekeeper whose descendants returned from the Babylonian Captivity (Ezra 2:42; Neh. 7:45).

Shobal ("wandering"). [1] A son of Seir (Gen. 36:20, 23; 1 Chron. 1:38, 40). [2] A son of Caleb, son of Hur (1 Chron. 2:50, 52). [3] A son of Judah (1 Chron. 4:1–2).

Shobek ("free"), one who sealed the covenant with Nehemiah (Neh. 10:24).

Shobi ("Jehovah is glorious"), a man who helped David when he fled from Absalom (2 Sam. 17:27).

Shoham ("leek-green beryl"), a descendant of Merari (1 Chron. 24:27).

Shomer ("keeper"). [1] *See* Shamer [2]. [2] *See* Shimrith.

Shophach. *See* Shobach.

Shua [Shuah] ("prosperity"). [1] A daughter of Heber (1 Chron. 7:32). [2] A Canaanite whose daughter Judah married (Gen. 38:2, 12; 1 Chron. 2:3).

Shuah ("depression"). [1] A son of Abraham by Keturah (Gen. 25:2; 1 Chron. 1:32). [2] A brother of Chelub; descendant of Caleb (1 Chron. 4:11).

Shual ("jackal"), the third son of Zophah (1 Chron. 7:36).

Shubael ("God's captive"). [1] A son or descendant of Amram, a descendant of Levi (1 Chron. 24:20). [2] *See* Shebuel [2].

Shuham ("depression"). *See* Hushim [1].

Shuni ("fortunate"), a son of Gad (Gen. 46:16; Num. 26:15).

Shupham. *See* Muppim.

Shuppim ("serpent"). [1] A gatekeeper in the days of David (1 Chron. 26:16). [2] *See* Muppim.

Shuthelah ("setting of Telah"). [1] A son of Ephraim (Num. 26:35–36; 1 Chron. 7:20). [2] Another descendant of Ephraim (1 Chron. 7:21).

Siaha [Sia] ("congregation"), ancestor of returned captives (Ezra 2:44; Neh. 7:47).

Sibbechai ("Jehovah is intervening"), a mighty man who killed a Philistine giant (2 Sam.

21:18; 1 Chron. 11:29; 20:4). He is called Mebunnai in 2 Samuel 23:27.

Sidon [Zidon] ("fortress"), eldest son of Canaan, son of Ham (Gen. 10:15). He is called Zidon in 1 Chronicles 1:13. Possibly a reference to the inhabitants of the ancient city of Sidon.

Sihon ("great; bold"), an Amorite king that was defeated by Israel (Num. 21:21–31; Deut. 1:4; 2:24–32; Josh. 13:15–28).

Silas [Silvanus] ("forest; woody; third; asked"), an eminent member of the early church who traveled with Paul through Asia Minor and Greece and was imprisoned with him at Philippi (Acts 15:22, 32–34; 2 Cor. 1:19; 1 Thess. 1:1).

Silvanus. *See* Silas.

Simeon [Simon] ("hearing"). **[1]** The second son of Jacob by Leah (Gen. 29:33; 34:25; 48:5; 49:5). His descendants became one of the twelve tribes of Israel. **[2]** A devout Jew who blessed the Christ child in the temple (Luke 2:25–34). **[3]** An ancestor of Jesus (Luke 3:30). **[4]** A disciple and prophet at Antioch (Acts 13:1); he was surnamed Niger ("black"). **[5]** Original name of Peter (also see). Simon is but another form of Simeon. Not to be confused with Shimeon.

Simon ("hearing"). [1] Original name of the apostle Peter (Matt. 4:18; 16:16–17; Luke 4:38; Acts 10:18). [2] Another of the twelve apostles, called Simon the Canaanite, indicating his fierce loyalty either to Israel or to his faith (Matt. 10:4; Mark 3:18; Luke 6:15; Acts 1:13). [3] One of Christ's brothers (Matt. 13:55; Mark 6:3). [4] A leper of Bethany in whose house Christ was anointed (Matt. 26:6; Mark 14:3). [5] A Cyrenian who was forced to bear the cross of Christ (Matt. 27:32; Mark 15:21). [6] A Pharisee in whose house the feet of Christ were anointed (Luke 7:40, 43, 44). [7] The father of Judas Iscariot (John 6:71; 12:4; 13:2). [8] A sorcerer who tried to buy the gifts of the Holy Spirit (Acts 8:9, 13, 18, 24). [9] A tanner of Joppa with whom Peter lodged (Acts 9:43; 10:6, 17, 32).

Simri. *See* Shimri.

Sippai. *See* Saph.

Sisamai ("Jehovah is distinguished"), a descendant of Jerahmeel, son of Pharez (1 Chron. 2:40).

Sisera ("mediation; array"). [1] Captain of the army of Jabin who was murdered by Jael (Judg. 4:1–22; 5:26, 28). [2] One whose descendants returned (Ezra 2:53; Neh. 7:55).

So ("vizier"), a king of Egypt, either Osorkon IV or Tefnakht. Others believe this name is a reference to a city (2 Kings 17:3–7).

Socho ("brambly"), a son of Heber (1 Chron. 4:18).

Sodi ("Jehovah determines"), father of one of the spies sent into Canaan (Num. 13:10).

Solomon ("peace"), son of David by Bath-sheba and king of a united, strong Israel for forty years. His wisdom and carnal sin stand out in his multi-faceted character (1 Kings 1:11;

The queen of Sheba came to see Solomon's wealth and wisdom for herself (1 Kings 10:1–13).

2:11). He was an ancestor of Christ (Matt. 1:6-7).

Sopater ("one who defends the father"), a man of Berea who accompanied Paul to Asia (Acts 20:4). Perhaps the same as Sosipater (also see).

Sophereth ("learning"), servant of Solomon whose ancestors returned from exile (Ezra 2:55; Neh. 7:57).

Sosipater ("one who defends the father"), one who sent greetings to the Roman Christians (Rom. 16:21). He was Jewish (a "kinsman" of Paul) and is possibly the same as Sopater (also see).

Sosthenes ("strong; powerful"). **[1]** Chief ruler of the synagogue at Corinth, beaten by the Greeks (Acts 18:17). **[2]** A believer who united with Paul in addressing the Corinthian church (1 Cor. 1:1). Some believe he was [1] after conversion.

Sotai, head of a family of servants (Ezra 2:55; Neh. 7:57).

Stachys ("ear of corn"), a believer of Rome to whom Paul sent greetings (Rom. 16:9).

Stephanas ("crown"), one of the first believers of Achaia (1 Cor. 1:16; 16:15-17).

Stephen became the first Christian martyr after proclaiming Jesus to the Sanhedrin (Acts 7:1-60).

Stephen ("crown"), one of the seven deacons. He became the first martyr of the church after Christ (Acts 6:5-9; 7:59; 8:2).

Suah ("riches; distinction"), a son of Zophah, a descendant of Asher (1 Chron. 7:36).

Susanna ("lily"), one of the women who ministered to Christ and was His follower (Luke 8:3).

Susi ("Jehovah is swift or rejoicing"), father of one of the spies (Num. 13:11).

Syntyche ("fortunate"), a woman of the church at Philippi (Phil. 4:2).

T

Tabbaoth ("spots; rings"), one whose descendants returned with Zerubbabel (Ezra 2:43; Neh. 7:46).

Tabeal [Tabeel] ("God is good"). [1] Father of a man the kings of Israel and Damascus planned to make king of Judah (Isa. 7:6). [2] A Persian official who tried to hinder the rebuilding of the wall of Jerusalem (Ezra 4:7).

Tabeel. *See* Tabeal.

Tabitha ("gazelle"), the Christian woman of Joppa whom Peter raised from the dead (Acts 9:36–42). Dorcas is the Greek form of the name.

Tabrimon ("[the god] Rimmon is good"), father of Ben-hadad I, king of Syria (1 Kings 15:18).

Tahan ("graciousness"). [1] A descendant of Ephraim (Num. 26:35). [2] Another descendant of Ephraim (1 Chron. 7:25).

Tahath ("depression; humility"). [1] A descendant of Kohath (1 Chron. 6:24, 37). [2] A descendant of Ephraim (1 Chron. 7:20). [3] A grandson of the above (1 Chron. 7:20).

Tahpenes, an Egyptian queen, wife of the Pharaoh, who received the fleeing Hadad, an enemy of Solomon (1 Kings 11:18–20).

Tahrea [Tarea] ("flight"), son of Micah, descendant of Saul (1 Chron. 8:35; 9:41).

Talmai ("bold; spirited"). **[1]** A man or clan defeated by Caleb (Num. 13:22; Josh. 15:14; Judg. 1:10). **[2]** King of Geshur and father-in-law of David (2 Sam. 3:3; 13:27).

Talmon ("oppressor; violent"), a Levite in Ezra's day; a temple porter (1 Chron. 9:17; Ezra 2:42; Neh. 7:45).

Tamah [Thamah] ("combat"), one whose descendants returned from the Babylonian Captivity (Ezra 2:53; Neh. 7:55).

Tamar [Thamar] ("palm"). **[1]** The wife of Er, mother of Perez, and an ancestor of Christ (Gen. 38:6, 11, 13; Ruth 4:12; Matt. 1:3). **[2]** The daughter of David violated by Amnon (2 Sam. 13:1–32). **[3]** A daughter of Absalom (2 Sam. 14:27).

Tanhumeth ("comfort"), father of one of Gedaliah's captains (2 Kings 25:23; Jer. 40:8).

Taphath ("ornament"), a daughter of Solomon (1 Kings 4:11).

Tappuah ("apple; hill place"), a descendant of Judah (1 Chron. 2:43).

Tarea [Tharshish]. *See* Tahrea.

Tarshish ("hard"). **[1]** A son of Javan and grandson of Noah (Gen. 10:4; 1 Chron. 1:7). Possibly a people who inhabited a region in Spain (Tartessus), near Gibraltar. **[2]** One of the seven princes of Persia (Esther 1:14). **[3]** A descendant of Benjamin (1 Chron. 7:10).

Tartan (meaning unknown), the title of a high Assyrian officer. There is evidence that the office was second only to the king. There are two tartans mentioned in Scripture (2 Kings 18:17; Isa. 20:1).

Tatnai ("gift"), a Persian governor of Samaria in the days of Zerubbabel (Ezra 5:3; 6:6, 13).

Tebah ("thick; strong"), a son of Nahor, the brother of Abraham (Gen. 22:24).

Tebaliah ("Jehovah is protector; Jehovah has purified"), a Levite gatekeeper in the days of David (1 Chron. 26:11).

Tehinnah ("entreaty; supplication"), a descendant of Judah (1 Chron. 4:12).

Telah ("vigor"), a descendant of Ephraim (1 Chron. 7:25).

Telem ("a lamb"), one who married a foreign wife during the Exile (Ezra 10:24).

Tema ("south" or "sun burnt"), a son of Ishmael (Gen. 25:15; 1 Chron. 1:30).

Teman ("south; sun burnt"). **[1]** A grandson of Esau (Gen. 36:11, 15; 1 Chron. 1:36). **[2]** A duke of Edom (Gen. 36:42; Chron. 1:53).

Temeni ("fortunate"), a son of Ashur (1 Chron. 4:5–6).

Terah [Thara] ("turning; duration"), the father of Abraham and ancestor of Christ (Gen. 11:27–32; Luke 3:34).

Teresh ("strictness; reverence"), a chamberlain of the Persian court that plotted against the crown (Esther 2:21; 6:2).

Tertius ("third"), the scribe to whom the epistle to the Romans was dictated (Rom. 16:22). Some conjecture that he is Silas (also see).

Tertullus ("third"), an orator hired by the Jews to state skillfully their case against Paul before Felix (Acts 24:1–8).

Thaddeus (a name derived from an Aramaic word for the female breast), one of the twelve apostles (Matt. 10:3; Mark 3:18). He is the same as Judas, the brother of James (Luke 6:16; John 14:22; Acts 1:13). He was also named Lebbeus ("heart").

Thahash ("reddish"), a son of Nahor, Abraham's brother (Gen. 22:24).

Thamah. *See* Tamah.

Thamar, Greek form of Tamar (also see).

Thara, Greek form of Terah (also see).

Theophilus ("loved by God"), an unknown person, possibly a Roman official, to whom Luke addressed his Gospel and Acts (Luke 1:3; Acts 1:1).

Theudas ("the gift of God"), instigator of a rebellion against the Romans, which was crushed by them (Acts 5:36).

Thomas ("twin"), one of the twelve apostles of Jesus. When Christ rose from the dead, he was most skeptical (Matt. 10:3; Mark 3:18; John 20:24–29). His Aramaic name is Didymus in Greek.

Tiberius ("son of [the river] Tiber"), third emperor of the Roman Empire (Luke 3:1).

Tibni ("intelligent"), one who rivaled Omri for the throne of Israel (1 Kings 16:21–22).

Tidal ("splendor; renown"), king of Goyim who, with his allies, invaded the Cities of the Plain (Gen. 14:1, 9).

Tiglath-pileser (Babylonian, *Tukulti-apil-Esharra*—"my trust is in the son of Asharra"), a king of Assyria who invaded Naphtali during the time of Pekah of Israel. He conquered northern Palestine and deported many from Naphtali (2 Kings 15:29; 16:7, 10; 1 Chron. 5:6, 26). His native name was Pul (2 Kings 15:19).

Realizing he bore two names, we should translate 1 Chronicles 5:26, ". . . God . . . stirred . . . Pul king of Assyria *even* [not *and*] Tilgath-pileser king of Assyria."

Tikvah [Tikvath] ("hope"). [1] The father-in-law of Huldah the prophetess (2 Kings 22:14; 2 Chron. 34:22). [2] The father of Jahaziah (Ezra 10:15).

Tilon ("mockery; scorn"), a descendant of Judah (1 Chron. 4:20).

Timaeus ("honorable"), father of the blind Bartimaeus (Mark 10:46).

Timna [Timnah] ("allotted portion; restraining"). [1] A concubine of a son of Esau (Gen. 36:12). [2] A daughter of Seir the Horite (Gen. 36:22; 1 Chron. 1:39). [3] A chief of Edom (Gen. 36:40; 1 Chron. 1:51). [4] A son of Eliphaz (1 Chron. 1:36).

Timon ("honorable"), one of the seven deacons (Acts 6:1–6).

Timotheus [Timothy] ("honored of God"), a young friend and convert of Paul; he traveled extensively with the apostle. He was from Lystra and was the son of Eunice, a Jewess, and a Greek father (Acts 16:1; 17:14, 15; 1 Tim. 1:2, 18; 6:20).

Timothy. *See* Timotheus.

Tiras ("longing"), youngest son of Japheth (Gen. 10:2; 1 Chron. 1:5). Possibly the inhabitants of Thrace. Other scholars consider reference to be to the Tyrsenoi, a people who inhabited the islands and coastlands of the Aegean.

Tirhakah, a king of Ethiopia and Egypt who aided Hezekiah in his fight against Sennacherib (2 Kings 19:9; Isa. 37:9).

Tirhanah ("kindness"), a descendant of Hezron (1 Chron. 2:48).

Tiria ("foundation"), a descendant of Judah (1 Chron. 4:16).

Tirshatha ("reverend—i.e., his excellency"), a title of the governor of Judea under Persian rule (Ezra 2:63; Neh. 7:65, 70; 8:9; 10:1).

Tirzah ("delight"), youngest daughter of Zelophehad (Num. 26:33; 27:1; Josh. 17:3).

Titus ("pleasant"), a converted Greek entrusted with a mission to Crete (2 Cor. 2:13; Gal. 2:1; Titus 1:4).

Toah ("depression; humility"), an ancestor of Samuel the prophet (1 Chron. 6:34). He is called Nahath in verse 26 and Tohu in 1 Samuel 1:1.

Tob-adonijah ("the Lord Jehovah is good"), one sent by Jehoshaphat to teach the Law (1 Chron. 17:8).

Tobiah [Tobijah] ("Jehovah is good"). **[1]** A Levite sent by Jehoshaphat to teach the Law (2 Chron. 17:8). **[2]** An ancestor of returning captives who had lost their genealogy (Ezra 2:60; Neh. 7:62). **[3]** An Ammonite servant of Sanballat who opposed Nehemiah (Neh. 2:10–20). **[4]** A leader who returned from the Babylonian Captivity (Zech. 6:10, 14).

Tobijah. *See* Tobiah.

Togarmah, a son of Gomer (Gen. 10:3; 1 Chron. 1:6). Possibly a people of the far north who inhabited the mountains northwest of Mesopotamia, between the Anti-Taurus and the Euphrates, or possibly the area on the upper Euphrates between Samosata and Melita.

Tohu. *See* Toah.

Toi [Tou] ("error; wandering"), a king of Hamath who sent his son to congratulate David on his victory over Hadadezer (2 Sam. 8:9–10; 1 Chron. 18:9–10).

Tola ("warm; crimson"). **[1]** A son of Issachar (Gen. 46:13; 1 Chron. 7:1–2). **[2]** A judge of Israel (Judg. 10:1).

Tou. *See* Toi.

Trophimus ("a foster child"), a Christian convert and afterward a companion-in-travel with Paul (Acts 20:4; 21:29; 2 Tim. 4:20).

Tryphena ("dainty; shining"), a Christian woman of Rome to whom Paul sent greetings (Rom. 16:12).

Tryphosa ("delicate; shining"), a Christian woman at Rome sent greetings by Paul (Rom. 16:12).

Tubal, a son of Japheth (Gen. 10:2; 1 Chron. 1:5). Possibly a reference to a people in eastern Asia Minor; they are called Tabal in Assyrian inscriptions.

Tubal-cain, one of the sons of Lamech and expert metalsmith (Gen. 4:22).

Tychicus ("fortunate"), a disciple and messenger of Paul (Acts 20:4; Eph. 6:21; 2 Tim. 4:12).

Tyrannus ("tyrant"), a Greek rhetorician or Jewish rabbi in whose school Paul taught at Ephesus (Acts 19:9).

——————— **U** ———————

Ucal ("I can; to be consumed"). *See* Ithiel.

Uel ("will of God"), a son of Bani who had taken a foreign wife (Ezra 10:34).

Ulam ("solitary; preceding"). **[1]** A descendant of Manasseh, the son of Peresh (1 Chron. 7:16–17). **[2]** A descendant of Benjamin whose sons were "mighty men of valor" (1 Chron. 8:39–40).

Ulla ("elevation; burden"), a descendant of Asher (1 Chron. 7:39).

Unni ("answering is with Jehovah"). **[1]** One of the Levites chosen as singers (1 Chron. 15:10, 18, 20). **[2]** A Levite that returned to the land with Zerubbabel (Neh. 12:9).

Ur ("flame; light"), father of one of David's mighty men (1 Chron. 11:35).

Urbane [Urbanus] ("pleasant; witty"), a faithful Roman Christian whom Paul greeted (Rom. 16:9).

Uri ("enlightened; my light"; a contracted form of Uriah). **[1]** The son of Hur, and father of Bezaleel (Exod. 31:1–2; 1 Chron. 2:20). **[2]** The father of Geber (1 Kings 4:19). **[3]** A porter of Levi who had married a foreign wife (Ezra 10:24).

Uriah [Urias; Urijah] ("Jehovah is my light"). **[1]** A Hittite soldier in David's army. He was killed in a fierce battle, for David, desiring to marry his wife, Bath-sheba, had placed him on the front battle line (2 Sam. 11). **[2]** A priest under Ahaz who built a pagan altar on the king's command; then placed it in the temple (2 Kings 16:10–16). **[3]** A prophet whose message of judgment so offended Jehoiakim that he murdered him (Jer. 26:20–23). **[4]** A priest,

U

the father of Meremoth (Ezra 8:33; Neh. 3:4, 21). **[5]** A man who stood by Ezra when he read the Law (Neh. 8:4). Possibly the same as [4]. **[6]** A priest whom Isaiah took as a witness (Isa. 8:2).

Urias, Greek form of Uriah (also see).

Uriel ("God is my light"). **[1]** A chief of the sons of Kohath (1 Chron. 6:24; 15:5, 11). Possibly the same as Zephaniah [2]. **[2]** Father of Michaiah, one of Rehoboam's sons (2 Chron. 13:2).

Urijah. *See* Uriah.

Uthai ("my iniquity; Jehovah is help"). **[1]** A son of Bigvai who returned to the land of Israel with Ezra (Ezra 8:14). **[2]** A descendant of Judah (1 Chron. 9:4).

Uz [Hur] ("counsel; firmness"). **[1]** Eldest son of Aram (Gen. 10:23). Possibly the name refers to an Aramean tribe or people. **[2]** A son of Shem (1 Chron. 1:17). The Septuagint makes this Uz identical with [1] naming Aram as his father. It is also possible the Hebrew text was abbreviated here. **[3]** A son of Dishan, son of Seir (Gen. 36:28). **[4]** The son of Nahor by Milcah (Gen. 22:21).

Uzai ("hoped for"), the father of Palal (Neh. 3:25).

Uzal ("wandering"), a son of Joktan (Gen. 10:27; 1 Chron. 1:21). Possibly the name refers to an Arabian tribe.

Uzza [Uzzah] ("strength"). [1] A man who was struck dead by God when he touched the ark of the covenant (2 Sam. 6:2–7; 1 Chron. 13:6–10). [2] A descendant of Merari (1 Chron. 6:29). [3] A descendant of Ehud (1 Chron. 8:7). [4] An ancestor of a Nethinim family that returned from Babylon (Ezra 2:49; Neh. 7:51).

Uzzah. *See* Uzza.

Uzzi ("Jehovah is strong; my strength"). [1] A descendant of Issachar (1 Chron. 7:1–3). [2] Chief of a priestly family of Jedaiah (Neh. 12:19, 42). [3] Descendant of Benjamin (1 Chron. 7:7). [4] The overseer of the Levites at Jerusalem (Neh. 11:22). [5] The father of Elah, a descendant of Benjamin (1 Chron. 9:8). [6] A son of Bukki; even though in the line of high priests, he does not seem to have held this office (1 Chron. 6:5–6, 51; Ezra 7:4).

Uzzia ("Yahweh is strong"), one of David's valiant men (1 Chron. 11:44).

Uzziah [Ozias] ("Jehovah is strong" or "my strength is Jehovah"). [1] The eleventh king of Judah. When he attempted to offer incense unlawfully, God struck him with leprosy. He was also called Azariah (2 Kings 15:1–8; 2 Chron. 26). He was an ancestor of Christ (Matt. 1:8–9). **[2]** A Levite descended from Kohath and ancestor of Samuel (1 Chron. 6:24). **[3]** Father of Jehonathan (1 Chron. 27:25). **[4]** A priest who had married a foreign wife (Ezra 10:21). **[5]** A descendant of Judah (Neh. 11:4).

Uzziel ("God is my strength; God is strong"). **[1]** The ancestor of the Uzzielites; the son of Kohath (Exod. 6:18). **[2]** Captain of the sons of Simeon (1 Chron. 4:42). **[3]** A son of Bela and grandson to Benjamin (1 Chron. 7:7). **[4]** An assistant wall-builder (Neh. 3:8). **[5]** A Levite, son of Jeduthun, who helped to cleanse the temple (2 Chron. 29:14). **[6]** A musician set by David over the service of song in the temple (1 Chron. 25:4). Uzziel is the same as Azareel in verse 18.

––––––––––––– **V** –––––––––––––

Vajezatha ("born of Ized; given-of-the-Best-One"), one of the sons of Haman slain by the Jews (Esther 9:9).

Vaniah ("praise, or nourishment, of Jehovah"), a son of Bani who had sinned by marrying a foreign wife (Ezra 10:36).

Vashni ("the second"), according to 1 Chronicles 6:28, the firstborn son of Samuel, but 1 Samuel 8:2 states Joel was his firstborn. Because of this, some scholars follow the Septuagint and Syriac versions, where verse 28 reads thus: "And the sons of Samuel: the firstborn, Joel, and *the second* Abiah."

Vashti ("beautiful woman; best"), the queen of Persia who was divorced by King Ahasuerus because she refused to come to his great feast (Esther 1:10–22).

Vophsi ("fragrant; rich"), a descendant of Naphtali, the father of Nahbi the spy (Num. 13:14).

--------- **Z** ---------

Zaavan [Zavan] ("causing fear"), a descendant of Seir (Gen. 36:27). Also called Zavan (1 Chron. 1:42).

Zabad ("endower"). [1] A descendant of Jerahmeel of Judah (1 Chron. 2:36–37). [2] A man of Ephraim and son of Tahath (1 Chron. 7:21). [3] Son of Alai and one of David's mighty men (1 Chron. 11:41). [4], [5], [6] Three who married foreign wives during the Exile (Ezra 10:27, 33, 43). [7] See Jozachar.

Zabbai ("roving about; pure"). [1] One who took a foreign wife during the Exile (Ezra 10:28). [2] Father of Baruch (Neh. 3:20).

Z

Zabbud ("endowed"), one who returned from the Exile with Ezra (Ezra 8:14).

Zabdi ("Jehovah is endower"). **[1]** Father of Carmi (Josh. 7:1, 17–18); called Zimri in 1 Chronicles 2:6. **[2]** A descendant of Benjamin (1 Chron. 8:19). **[3]** One of David's storekeepers (1 Chron. 27:27). **[4]** An ancestor of Mattaniah (Neh. 11:17); also called Zichri (1 Chron. 9:15) and Zaccur (1 Chron. 25:2, 10; Neh. 12:35).

Zabdiel ("my gift is God"). **[1]** Father of Jashobeam, David's captain (1 Chron. 27:2). **[2]** An overseer of the priests (Neh. 11:14).

Zabud ("bestowed"), officer and friend of Solomon (1 Kings 4:5).

Zabulon. Greek form of Zebulun (also see).

Zaccai ("pure"), one whose descendants returned (Ezra 2:9; Neh. 7:14). Possibly the same as Zabbai [2].

Zaccheus ("pure"), a publican with whom Jesus lodged during His stay at Jericho (Luke 19:1–10).

Zaccur [Zacchur] ("well remembered"). **[1]** A descendant of Simeon (1 Chron. 4:26). **[2]** Father of Shammua, one of the spies (Num. 13:4). **[3]** Descendant of Merari (1 Chron. 24:27). **[4]** See Zabdi [4]. **[5]** A Levite who sealed the covenant (Neh. 10:12). **[6]** Father of Hanan (Neh. 13:13); possibly the same as [5]. **[7]** One who rebuilt part of the wall of Jerusalem (Neh. 3:2).

Zachariah [Zechariah] ("memory of the Lord"). **[1]** Son and successor of Jeroboam II. He reigned only six months (2 Kings 14:29; 15:8–11). **[2]** Father of Abi or Abijah, mother of Hezekiah (2 Kings 18:2); written *Zechariah* in 2 Chronicles 29:1.

Zacchaeus climbed a tree to see Jesus, but Jesus invited him down to talk (Luke 19:1–26).

Z

Zacharias (Greek form of Zechariah—"memory of the Lord"). **[1]** The prophet whom the Jews stoned (Matt. 23:35; Luke 11:51). Some believe this prophet to be identical with Zechariah **[11]** or **[16]**, though it is possible the reference is to an unknown prophet. **[2]** A priest, father of John the Baptist (Luke 1).

Zacher ("fame"), son of Jeiel (1 Chron. 8:31); called Zechariah in 1 Chronicles 9:37.

Zadok ("righteous"). **[1]** A high priest in the time of David (2 Sam. 8:17; 15:24–36; 1 Kings 1:8–45). **[2]** Father of Jerusha, wife of Uzziah and mother of Jotham, both kings of Israel (2 Kings 15:33; 2 Chron. 27:1). **[3]** Son of Ahitub and father of Shallum or Meshullam (1 Chron. 6:12, 13; Ezra 7:2). **[4]** A young man of valor (1 Chron. 12:28). **[5]**, **[6]** Two who repaired the wall of Jerusalem (Neh. 3:4, 29). **[7]** One who sealed the covenant with Nehemiah (Neh. 10:21). **[8]** A scribe under Nehemiah (Neh. 13:13).

Zaham ("fatness"), a son of Rehoboam (2 Chron. 11:19).

Zalaph ("purification"), the father of one who repaired the wall of Jerusalem (Neh. 3:30).

Zalmon ("terrace; accent"), the Ahohite who was one of David's guards (2 Sam. 23:28). He is called Ilai ("exalted") in 1 Chronicles 11:29. Not to be confused with Salmon.

Zalmunna ("withdrawn from protection"), a Midianite king slain by Gideon (Judg. 8:5–21).

Zanoah ("broken district"), one of the family of Caleb (1 Chron. 4:18).

Zaphnath-paaneah ("savior of the world; revealer of secrets"), name given to Joseph by Pharaoh (Gen. 41:45).

Zara, Greek form of Zara or Zerah (also see).

Zarah. *See* Zerah.

Zattu [Zatthu] ("lovely; pleasant"). [1] One whose descendants returned from the Exile (Ezra 2:8; 10:27; Neh. 7:13). [2] A co-sealer of the new covenant (Neh. 10:14).

Zavan. *See* Zaavan.

Zaza ("projection"), a son of Jonathan (1 Chron. 2:33).

Zealotes. *See* Simon [2].

Zebadiah ("Jehovah is endower"). [1] A descendant of Benjamin (1 Chron. 8:15). [2] A son of Elpaal (1 Chron. 8:17). [3] One who joined David (1 Chron. 12:7). [4] A descendant of Levi through Kohath (1 Chron. 26:2). [5] A son of Asahel (1 Chron. 27:7). [6] A Levite sent by Jehoshaphat to teach the Law (2 Chron. 17:8).

Z

[7] A son of Ishmael (2 Chron. 19:11). [8] Head of a family who returned from exile (Ezra 8:8). [9] A priest who had taken a foreign wife (Ezra 10:20).

Zebah ("victim"), Midianite king slain by Gideon (Judg. 8:5–21).

Zebedee ("the gift of Jehovah"), a fisherman of Galilee, husband of Salome, and father of the apostles James and John (Matt. 4:21; 27:56; Mark 1:19–20).

Zebina ("bought"), one who married a foreign wife during the Exile (Ezra 10:43).

Zebudah ("endowed"), wife of Josiah, king of Judah (2 Kings 23:36).

Zebul ("dwelling"), ruler of Shechem (Judg. 9:28–41).

Zebulun [Zabulon] ("dwelling"), tenth son of Jacob and ancestor of one of the twelve tribes (Gen. 30:20; 49:13; 1 Chron. 2:1).

Zechariah ("Jehovah my righteousness"). [1] A chief of the tribe of Reuben (1 Chron. 5:7). [2] A Levite gatekeeper in the days of David (1 Chron. 9:21; 26:2, 14). [3] A Levite set over the service of song in the days of David (1 Chron. 15:18, 20; 16:5). [4] A priest in the days of David (1 Chron. 15:24). [5] A descendant of Levi through Kohath (1 Chron. 24:25).

[6] A descendant of Levi through Me-rari (1 Chron. 26:11). [7] Father of Iddo (1 Chron. 27:21). [8] A prince of Jehoshaphat sent to teach the people (2 Chron. 17:7). [9] A Levite who encouraged Jehoshaphat against Moab (2 Chron. 20:14). [10] A son of Jehoshaphat (2 Chron. 21:2). [11] A son of Jehoiada who was stoned (2 Chron. 24:20). *See* Zacharias [1]. [12] Prophet in the days of Uzziah (2 Chron. 26:5). [13] A Levite who helped to cleanse the temple (2 Chron. 29:13). [14] A descendant of Levi (2 Chron. 34:12). [15] A prince of Judah in the days of Josiah (2 Chron. 35:8). [16] A prophet in the days of Ezra. His book still exists (Ezra 5:1; 6:14; Zech. 1:1, 7; 7:1, 8). [17] A chief man of Israel (Ezra 8:3). [18] One who returned from the Exile (Ezra 8:11). The chief man in Ezra 8:16 was probably [17] or [18]. [19] One who took a foreign wife during the Exile (Ezra 10:26). [20] A prince with Ezra (Neh. 8:4). [21] A descendant of Perez (Neh. 11:4). [22] One whose descendants dwelled in Jerusalem (Neh. 11:5). [23] A priest (Neh. 11:12). [24] A Levite trumpeter (Neh. 12:35–36). [25] A priest who took part in the dedication ceremony (Neh. 12:41). [26] One whom Isaiah took as a witness (Isa. 8:2). [27] *See* Zachariah [2]. [28] *See* Zacher.

Z

Zedekiah ("Jehovah my righteousness; Jehovah is might"). [1] A false prophet who encouraged Ahab to attack the Syrians at Ramoth-gilead (1 Kings 22:11, 24; 2 Chron. 18: 10, 23). [2] A false prophet (Jer. 29:21–23). [3] A prince of Judah in the days of Jehoiakim (Jer. 36:12). [4] The last king of Judah; his rebellion spelled the doom of Judah (2 Kings 24:18–25:7; 2 Chron. 36:11–21). He is probably referred to in 1 Chronicles 3:16 as a "son" or successor of Jeconiah. *See* Mattaniah [1].

Zeeb ("wolf"), a prince of Midian slain by Gideon (Judg. 7:25; 8:3).

Zelek ("split"), an Ammonite, a valiant man of David (2 Sam. 23:37; 1 Chron. 11:39).

Zelophehad ("firstborn"), grandson of Gilead (Num. 26:33; 27:1, 7; Josh. 17:3).

Zemira ("song"), a son of Becher, a descendant of Benjamin (1 Chron. 7:8).

Zenas ("living"), a Christian who had been a teacher of the Law (Titus 3:13).

Zephaniah ("Jehovah is darkness; Jehovah has treasured"). [1] A prophet in the days of Josiah (Zeph. 1:1). [2] A Levite or priest, ancestor of Samuel (1 Chron. 6:36). Possibly the same as Uriel [1]. [3] Son of Josiah the priest

(Zech. 6:10, 14). **[4]** A priest who opposed Babylonian rule (2 Kings 25:18; Jer. 21:1; 37:3).

Zephi [Zepho] ("watch"), a son of Eliphaz (Gen. 36:11, 15; 1 Chron. 1:36).

Zepho. *See* Zephi.

Zephon ("dark; wintry"), a son of Gad (Num. 26:15). Also called Ziphion in Genesis 46:16.

Zerah [Zara; Zarah] ("sprout"). **[1]** A son of Reuel (Gen. 36:13, 17; 1 Chron. 1:37). **[2]** Father of Jobab (Gen. 36:33; 1 Chron. 1:44). **[3]** A son of Judah (Gen. 38:30; 1 Chron. 2:4, 6). **[4]** A descendant of Gershon (1 Chron. 6:21). **[5]** A Levite (1 Chron. 6:41). **[6]** A king of Ethiopia who warred with Asa (2 Chron. 14:9). **[7]** *See* Zohar [2].

Zerahiah ("Jehovah has come forth"). **[1]** A priest of the line of Eleazar (1 Chron. 6:6, 51; Ezra 7:4). **[2]** Head of a family who returned from the Exile with Ezra (Ezra 8:4).

Zeresh ("gold"), wife of Haman (Esther 5:10, 14; 6:13).

Zereth ("brightness"), a descendant of Judah (1 Chron. 4:7).

Zeri ("balm"), a musician in the days of David (1 Chron. 25:3); perhaps the same as Izri (v. 11).

Z

Zeror ("bundle"), an ancestor of Kish (1 Sam. 9:1).

Zeruah ("full-breasted"), the mother of Jeroboam I (1 Kings 11:26).

Zerubbabel [Zorobabel] ("seed of Babylon"). **[1]** The leader of a group who returned from exile; he began the rebuilding of the temple (Ezra 3—5; Neh. 7:7; 12:1, 47). He was an ancestor of Christ (Matt. 1:12–13). **[2]** An ancestor of Christ (Luke 3:27); perhaps the same as [1].

Zeruiah ("balm"), a daughter of Jesse and David's sister (1 Sam. 26:6; 2 Sam. 2:13, 18).

Zetham ("shining"), son or grandson of Laadan (1 Chron. 23:8; 26:22).

Zethan ("olive tree"), a descendant of Benjamin (1 Chron. 7:10).

Zethar ("conqueror"), a eunuch of Ahasuerus (Esther 1:10).

Zia ("terrified"), a descendant of Gad (1 Chron. 5:13).

Ziba ("plantation"), a steward of Saul (2 Sam. 9:2–13; 16:1–4; 19:17–29).

Zibeon ("wild robber"). **[1]** A Hivite man (Gen. 36:2, 14). **[2]** A son of Seir (Gen. 36:20, 24; 1 Chron. 38, 40).

Zibia ("gazelle"), a descendant of Benjamin (1 Chron. 8:9).

Zibiah ("gazelle"), mother of King Joash of Judah (2 Kings 12:1; 2 Chron. 24:1).

Zichri ("renowned"). [1] A son of Izhar (Exod. 6:21). [2] A descendant of Benjamin (1 Chron. 8:19). [3] A descendant of Benjamin of Shishak (1 Chron. 8:23). [4] A descendant of Benjamin of Jeroham (1 Chron. 8:27). [5] A descendant of Eliezer in the days of Moses (1 Chron. 26:25). [6] Father of Eliezer, a descendant of Reuben (1 Chron. 27:16). [7] Father of Amaziah (1 Chron. 27:16). [8] Father of Elishaphat (2 Chron. 23:1). [9] A man of valor who slew the son of King Ahaz (2 Chron. 28:7). [10] Father of Joel (Neh. 11:9). [11] A priest of the sons of Abijah (Neh. 12:17). [12] *See* Zabdi [4].

Zidkijah ("Jehovah my righteousness"), a chief prince of the Jews (Neh. 10:1).

Zidon. *See* Sidon.

Ziha ("dried"). [1] One whose children returned from the Babylonian Captivity (Ezra 2:43; Neh. 7:46). [2] A ruler of the Nethinim (Ezra 2:43; Neh. 11:21).

Zillah ("protection; screen"), one of the wives of Lamech (Gen. 4:19, 22–23).

Zilpah ("myrrh dropping"), mother of Gad and Asher (Gen. 29:24; 30:9–13; 35:26).

Zilthai ("shadow"). [1] A descendant of Benjamin (1 Chron. 8:20). [2] A captain who joined David at Ziklag (1 Chron. 12:20).

Zimmah ("counsel"). [1] A Levite of the family of Gershon (1 Chron. 6:20). [2] A Levite in the fourth or fifth degree of temple service (1 Chron. 6:42). [3] A Levite who assisted in cleansing the temple (2 Chron. 29:12).

Zimran ("celebrated"), a son of Abraham by Keturah (Gen. 25:2; 1 Chron. 1:32).

Zimri ("celebrated"). [1] A disobedient Israelite slain by Phinehas (Num. 25:14). [2] A captain who slew Elah (1 Kings 16:9–20). [3] A son of Zerah of Judah (1 Chron. 2:6). [4] A descendant of Benjamin (1 Chron. 8:36; 9:42).

Zina ("fruitful"), second son of Shimei (1 Chron. 23:10). He is called Zizah in verse 11.

Ziph ("refining place"). [1] Grandson of Caleb (1 Chron. 2:42). [2] A son of Jehaleleel (1 Chron. 4:16).

Ziphah ("lent"), a son of Jehaleleel (1 Chron. 4:16).

Ziphion ("looking out; serpent; dark"). *See* Zephon.

Zippor ("bird"), father of Balak, king of Moab (Num. 22:2, 4, 10, 16).

Zipporah ("little bird"), the wife of Moses and daughter of Reuel (Exod. 2:21; 4:25; 18:2).

Zithri ("Jehovah is protection"), a descendant of Levi through Kohath (Exod. 6:22).

Ziza [Zizah] ("shining; brightness"). **[1]** A chief of Simeon (1 Chron. 4:37). **[2]** A son of King Rehoboam (2 Chron. 11:20). **[3]** *See* Zina.

Zobebah ("the affable"), a descendant of Judah (1 Chron. 4:8).

Zohar ("nobility; distinction"). **[1]** Father of Ephron, from whom Abraham bought a field (Gen. 23:8; 25:9). **[2]** A son of Simeon of Judah (Gen. 46:10; Exod. 6:15). He is also called Zerah (1 Chron. 4:24).

Zoheth ("strong"), a descendant of Judah (1 Chron. 4:20).

Zophah ("watch"), a descendant of Asher (1 Chron. 7:35–36).

Zophai ("watcher"), a brother of Samuel (1 Chron. 6:26). He is called Zuph in verse 35.

Zophar ("hairy; rough"), a Naamathite and "friend" of Job (Job 2:11; 11:1; 20:1).

Zorobabel, Greek form of Zerubbabel (also see).

Z

Zuar ("little"), father of Nethaneel and a chief of Issachar (Num. 1:8; 2:5).

Zuph. *See* Zophai.

Zur ("rock"). **[1]** A prince of Midian slain by Phinehas (Num. 25:15; 31:8). **[2]** A son of Jehiel (1 Chron. 8:30; 9:36).

Zuriel ("God is my rock"), a chief of the Levites, descendant from Merari (Num. 3:35).

Zurishaddai ("the Almighty is a rock"), father of Shelumiel (Num. 1:6; 2:12).